More Praise for
The Six Disciplines of Breakthrough Learning

"*Six Disciplines* is a timely book written by experienced authors to help learning and development professionals deliver results. With proven methods, presented in a logical style, this book is a must-read for anyone interested in improving the impact of training and development."

> —Jack J. Phillips, chairman, ROI Institute

"Nothing matters without results. *Six Disciplines* offers a straightforward but profound methodology for achieving extraordinary results, time after time."

> —Leo Burke, associate dean and director of executive education, Mendoza College of Business, University of Notre Dame

"The pundits all talk about breakthrough learning, but until now, no one has provided clear, concise coaching about how to attain it. This vital and must-read book should affect the way every thinking person looks at learning."

> —Richard J. Leider, founder, The Inventure Group, and author, *The Power of Purpose* and *Claiming Your Place at the Fire*

"Finally, a book that effectively links training and development to business results and shows us how to make strategy happen. A classic in the making."

> —Al Vicere, executive education professor of strategic leadership, Smeal College of Business, Penn State University, and president, Vicere Associates, Inc.

"*The Six Disciplines of Breakthrough Learning* is imperative for executives competing in today's fast moving knowledge economy which makes learning and adjustment so crucial. I'm eagerly applying their extraordinary insights regarding turning costs into investments and new knowledge into improved results."

> —Mickey Connolly, CEO, Conversant Solutions, and coauthor, *The Communications Catalyst*

About This Book

This book is for everyone who is a provider, purchaser, or consumer of corporate training and development. It describes a proven set of disciplines and tools to achieve a breakthrough in corporate education and thus significantly improve the return on the investment that companies make in learning and development.

Why is this topic important?

Competitiveness increasingly depends on know-how, human capital, and the ability to learn quickly at both the individual and organizational levels. Companies invest heavily in training and development—more than $50 billion annually in the United States alone—in an effort to improve the quality of their leadership, product development, quality, customer service, and so forth (Dolezalek, 2004). There is compelling evidence that these investments can and do pay dividends.

There is equally compelling evidence, however, that the business impact of learning and development can be much greater than most organizations currently achieve. Substantial value is being left on the table in the form of "learning scrap"—training and development that is never transferred to the work of the organization in a way that produces results.

What can you achieve with this book?

This book describes and illustrates six disciplines that together represent a breakthrough in training and development: (1) define outcomes in business terms, (2) design the complete experience, (3) deliver for results, (4) drive follow-through, (5) deploy active support, and (6) document results. By practicing these six disciplines, readers will be able to design, deliver, and document learning and development programs that produce greater business impact and higher returns on investment.

How is the book organized?

In the first chapter we provide a brief overview of the six disciplines. We then dedicate a full chapter to each discipline, exploring it in depth and providing recommendations and tools to maximize its contribution. Insights from exceptional business and learning leaders, as well as case studies, are used to illustrate key concepts. At the end of each chapter, we provide action items for both general managers and learning leaders, because maximizing return on investment from learning and development requires a true partnership between line management and learning leaders.

About Pfeiffer

Pfeiffer serves the professional development and hands-on resource needs of training and human resource practitioners and gives them products to do their jobs better. We deliver proven ideas and solutions from experts in HR development and HR management, and we offer effective and customizable tools to improve workplace performance. From novice to seasoned professional, Pfeiffer is the source you can trust to make yourself and your organization more successful.

Essential Knowledge Pfeiffer produces insightful, practical, and comprehensive materials on topics that matter the most to training and HR professionals. Our Essential Knowledge resources translate the expertise of seasoned professionals into practical, how-to guidance on critical workplace issues and problems. These resources are supported by case studies, worksheets, and job aids and are frequently supplemented with CD-ROMs, websites, and other means of making the content easier to read, understand, and use.

Essential Tools Pfeiffer's Essential Tools resources save time and expense by offering proven, ready-to-use materials—including exercises, activities, games, instruments, and assessments—for use during a training or team-learning event. These resources are frequently offered in looseleaf or CD-ROM format to facilitate copying and customization of the material.

Pfeiffer also recognizes the remarkable power of new technologies in expanding the reach and effectiveness of training. While e-hype has often created whizbang solutions in search of a problem, we are dedicated to bringing convenience and enhancements to proven training solutions. All our e-tools comply with rigorous functionality standards. The most appropriate technology wrapped around essential content yields the perfect solution for today's on-the-go trainers and human resource professionals.

Pfeiffer *Essential resources for training and HR professionals*
www.pfeiffer.com

THE SIX DISCIPLINES OF
BREAKTHROUGH LEARNING

THE SIX DISCIPLINES OF BREAKTHROUGH LEARNING

How to Turn Training and Development Into Business Results

Calhoun W. Wick, Roy V. H. Pollock,

Andrew McK. Jefferson, and Richard D. Flanagan

•

foreword by
Kevin D. Wilde

afterword by
Marshall Goldsmith

Pfeiffer

A Wiley Imprint
www.pfeiffer.com

Library of Congress Cataloging-in-Publication Data

The six disciplines of breakthrough learning: how to turn training and development into business results / Calhoun W. Wick . [et al.]; foreword by Kevin D. Wilde.
     p. cm.
  Includes bibliographical references and index.
  ISBN-13: 978-0-7879-8254-6 (cloth)
  ISBN-10: 0-7879-8254-7 (cloth)
  1. Organizational learning. I. Wick, Calhoun W.
  HD58.82.S59 2006
  658.3'124-dc22   2006006227

Acquiring Editor: Matthew Davis   Editor: Suzanne Copenhagen
Director of Development: Kathleen Dolan   Manufacturing Supervisor: Becky Carreño
  Davies   Editorial Assistant: Leota Higgins
Production Editor: Nina Kreiden   Illustrations: Lotus Art

Printed in the United States of America
Printing   10 9 8 7 6 5 4 3

To our clients, for allowing us to work with
them in their pursuit of excellence; to our
employees, for making it happen; and to our
families, for encouraging us to pursue our dreams.

10-16-08

CONTENTS

Foreword   xv
    Kevin D. Wilde

Introduction: The Six Disciplines   1

D1. Define Outcomes in Business Terms   13

D2. Design the Complete Experience   46

D3. Deliver for Application   72

D4. Drive Follow-Through   98

D5. Deploy Active Support   138

D6. Document Results   167

Coda   202

The Last Word   209
    Marshall Goldsmith

References   211

Index   219

About the Authors   233

FOREWORD

Good books are hard to put down. This is a great book you *will* want to put down.

When I first read *The Six Disciplines of Breakthrough Learning,* I found myself stopping repeatedly and putting it down so I could take notes on ideas I wanted to apply to my own work or an insight in the book that really hit me.

The first time I put the book down came after reading a compelling example. The first discipline, "Define Outcomes in Business Terms," seems simple enough. The example was about a new management development program. A talented and hard-working training team designed an air-tight course: activities planned to the minute, world-class external faculty and cutting-edge simulations . . . all grounded in specific learning objectives. But the team fell short by failing to first clearly identify how the company would benefit from having leaders attend the program. I've been there—so caught up in crafting the excellence of the learning event that we failed to ground everything in the real business case. When that happens, the results leave you heartbroken, far short of the learning breakthrough you intended.

The second time I put the book down was when it challenged me to reconsider what I thought was none of my business. The second discipline, "Design the Complete Experience," stresses the necessity for training and development professionals to start owning the whole process of learning—before, during, and after a development offering. This notion goes far beyond traditional pre-work to areas such as setting expectations upfront for application and learner accountability and actively employing the participant's manager in the process. After reflecting on the case examples and tools provided, I realized that actively and skillfully managing the "before" and "after" really are my core responsibilities.

The last time I put the book down, the whole picture became clear. When I finished the book, I realized that achieving the true potential of development happens with the consistent application of all six disciplines. Work any one area and you'll see improvement. Work all six areas consistently and you can achieve breakthrough learning.

The Six Disciplines of Breakthrough Learning integrates the latest thinking in the field of development from a number of diverse perspectives and fills in the gaps with original material and insight. All in all, this book will move you to action, and I am convinced it will move the learning and development field ahead.

Kevin D. Wilde
Vice President Chief Learning Officer
General Mills, Inc.

INTRODUCTION:
THE SIX DISCIPLINES

Execution is not just tactics; it is a discipline and a system.

—Larry Bossidy and Ram Charan

WE HAVE BEEN PART of corporate education programs that were truly transformational, that helped propel their companies to a higher level of performance and delivered results of significant value. We became interested in what differentiated programs that delivered breakthrough results from those that did not. We discovered that there is no one "magic bullet." Rather, breakthrough programs are the result of a disciplined and systematic approach to learning and development, executed with passion and excellence. Over the past six years, we have distilled the practices that characterize breakthrough learning and development initiatives into six disciplines (Figure I.1).

**Figure I.1. The Six Disciplines
That Turn Learning into Business Results.**

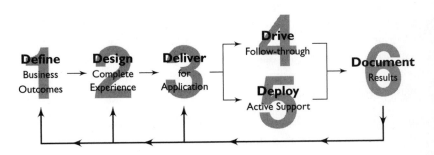

We began to teach and use these disciplines to help companies improve the outcomes of their learning and development initiatives. Although most of our work has been with classroom-based programs, the principles also apply to e-learning, action learning, and blended approaches. We discovered that starting each of the six disciplines with a *D* served as a valuable mnemonic for thinking about program design, execution, and evaluation. More important, we were able to show a connection between how well each discipline was practiced and the overall effectiveness of the learning intervention.

Here we provide a brief introduction to each of the six disciplines. In the remainder of the book, we dedicate a full chapter to each, exploring it in depth and providing examples and tools to maximize its contribution.

DI: DEFINE OUTCOMES IN BUSINESS TERMS

A central theme of our work is that learning and development programs are critical *investments* that companies make in their human capital for which they expect a *return* in terms of greater effectiveness, improved productivity, enhanced customer satisfaction, and so forth.

A reality of corporate life is that there are always more good ideas for investments—in research, training, marketing, sales, or manufacturing—than even the most affluent company can afford. Hence, one of management's most important tasks is to decide where to invest the company's human and financial assets in order to generate the greatest return for shareholders. To earn a share of the annual investment pool in this era of increased competition and pressure for economic performance, corporate learning and development must be able to show how its efforts contribute to better business results.

Therefore, the first, and most critical, discipline in developing a breakthrough program is to define its objectives in business terms. The phrase "in business terms" is key. Every program has learning objectives in educational terms, which might include, for example, "appreciate and accept their managerial role," "define the coaching process," or "describe the four developmental levels." From a line manager's perspective, however, it is not clear how achieving objectives stated in this way contributes to the way in which the company creates value. Business leaders want to know

- What benefit will this program return to the *business*?
- How will it translate into improved performance for the participants and for the organization as a whole?

- How will the change be measured?
- What will it be worth?

The program participants' ability to understand, describe, list, or appreciate may be important prerequisites to business application, but if they are all that the program achieves, then it will fall short of business leaders' expectations.

Learning needs to be an integral part of the business strategy. In Chapter D1 we underscore the importance of making sure that there is open, transparent, and readily apparent alignment between the goals of learning programs and the needs of the business. We share suggestions and case studies on how learning and line leaders can work together to achieve this vital articulation. We examine the real-life roadblocks to this endeavor and ways to overcome them. Finally, we underscore the benefits of understanding the value chain of learning, mapping the intended impact, picking the right problems to address, and managing management's expectations.

"[T]he good learning strategy seeks out the most important points of failure in an organization; it then replaces risk with competence and support so that people on those points find ways to succeed where they might otherwise fail" (Bordonaro, 2005, p. 142).

D2: DESIGN THE COMPLETE EXPERIENCE

A second theme throughout this book is that in business, learning creates value only when it is transferred to the participant's work and applied to good effect. Factors that influence the *transfer of learning*, therefore, influence the impact achieved, the return on investment, and whether or not the program is considered a success from the business's perspective.

Historically, corporate educational units have focused on instruction; little or no attention was paid to what happened after the instruction was completed. The second discipline—design the complete experience—recognizes that learning and development is now being judged by the business results it generates; therefore, learning initiatives should incorporate all the factors that help maximize results, including some outside the traditional scope of training and development.

Achieving a breakthrough requires treating learning as an ongoing process, rather than an isolated event. The second discipline of breakthrough learning demands a new paradigm: that program design must encompass the participant's *complete* experience—not just what happens in the classroom (or its virtual equivalent). High-impact programs appreciate that learning begins before, and continues after, the course itself.

Figure I.2. Training and Development Needs to
Design the Complete Experience, Not Just Hope
for a Miracle to Transform Learning into Results.

**"I think you should be more
explicit here in step two."**

Source: *Copyright © 2005 Sidney Harris from cartoonbank.com.*

They approach learning holistically and systemically, paying special attention to the impact of the participant's manager and work environment on learning transfer and application.

In Chapter D2, we examine the elements that constitute the "complete experience" and that support or impede learning transfer. We suggest methods and tools to optimize results, many of which are outside the traditional purview of the training organization, and which, we hope, challenge conventional thinking. Our goal is to change the paradigm about learning and development by redefining the finish line from the last day of instruction to documented delivery of business results. We show that Phase III of learning—the postinstructional transfer and application period—is a particularly rich opportunity for a breakthrough.

Designing for the complete experience—especially the way in which the work environment influences learning transfer—allows corporate education to realize its full promise of delivering value to the organization. Since future programs will be funded (or not funded) according to the results they deliver, we believe that it is in everyone's best interest to actively plan, support, and manage the learning transfer and application process—not leave it to chance.

D3: DELIVER FOR APPLICATION

The third discipline that characterizes breakthrough training programs is that they deliver for application. That is, irrespective of the specific delivery vehicle, they ensure that information, concepts, and skills are introduced in ways that facilitate their transfer and application on the job. Delivering for application helps participants bridge the learning-doing gap between the learning environment and their day-to-day work.

In Chapter D3, we look at innovative ways that progressive companies are narrowing the learning-doing gap by making the relevance of the material clear, showing how each element is connected to real business issues, illustrating how the material can be *applied* to business needs, motivating application by answering the "what's in it for me?" question, and helping participants actively plan for transfer and application.

Figure I.3. There Is Always a Gap Between Learning
in the Program and Doing the Work, Which Must
Be Traversed to Achieve Improved Results.

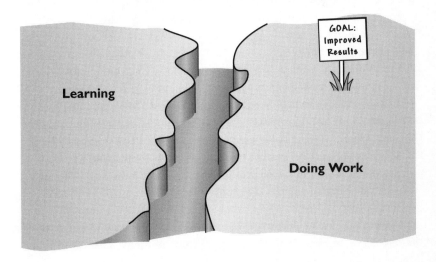

Figure I.4. Delivering for Results Helps Build a Bridge Between Learning and Doing That Accelerates the Passage from Current State to Improved Results.

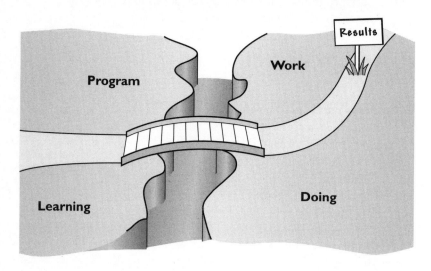

Delivering for application in a program that has clearly defined business outcomes, active support for transfer, and a system of follow-through hastens the learner's journey from current to improved performance.

D4: DRIVE FOLLOW-THROUGH

The objectives that people set to follow through on learning and development experiences are important *business* objectives. They should be treated as such. The fourth discipline of breakthrough learning is to drive follow-through—to actively manage the transfer and application process for optimum results.

Companies that derive the greatest payback from their educational investments are those that put in place mechanisms to ensure that participants set the right objectives, that they follow through on their commitments, and that their managers hold them accountable for doing so. Unfortunately, putting these mechanisms in place has proven difficult. "Talk to any group of layman or professionals about what's broken in the current learning and development process, and most will tell you it's the lack of serious post-training follow-through" (Zenger, Folkman, & Sherwin, 2005, p. 30).

In Chapter D4 we discuss the breakthrough in follow-through management made possible by recent developments in technology. We set out the requirements for effectively practicing the discipline of driving follow-through, address the current impediments to learning transfer and how to overcome them, point out the high cost of doing nothing, and provide case examples of how follow-through management enhances the value of already effective programs.

D5: DEPLOY ACTIVE SUPPORT

Companies that are serious about maximizing the return on their investment in learning and development recognize that the program isn't over until the learning is successfully applied and new skills mastered. To ensure that this occurs, they practice the fifth discipline: they provide various forms of ongoing support after the participant returns to his or her job. Learning and line leaders work together to develop a culture that recognizes that support for learning transfer is *everyone's* responsibility. They "put their money where their mouth is" by reallocating some of their resources from pure instruction to providing support for transfer and application.

In Chapter D5, we review the profound influence that the work environment—particularly the participant's manager—has on whether learning is applied or scrapped. We discuss the need to balance accountability and support and the new demands this places on the learning organization and line management and we present innovative methods and technologies to ensure that the environment is conducive to optimizing results.

D6: DOCUMENT RESULTS

The sixth discipline of breakthrough learning and development is to document results to justify continued investment and support continuous improvement. Requiring proof of results to justify continued investment in learning is no different from what is expected of other departments.

If marketers want money to redesign packaging because they believe it will improve sales, they have to present their rationale—the chain of evidence and assumptions—that supports their proposal. And if the package redesign is approved, they know that they will be called on the carpet at some future date to provide evidence that they achieved the promised results. Departments and leaders who consistently deliver on their objectives gain resources and influence; those who fail to deliver, or who are unable to offer evidence one way or the other, lose. In other words, it is much more difficult to cut the budget of a learning and development organization that has credible, documented evidence of business impact than one that has only measures of training *activity*.

The sixth discipline of documenting results is essential to supporting a cycle of continuous learning, adaptation, and improvement. The results documented in D6 become the raw material for the next cycle of defining outcomes, designing experiences, delivering, driving, deploying, and documenting. A never-ending cycle of reinvention and renewal ensures that corporate education keeps pace with the changing competitive environment, workforce, and business needs.

In Chapter D6, we discuss *why* learning and development must document results. We provide guidance on *what* to measure (what really matters to the sponsors), *how* to collect and analyze the information, and, especially important, how to *market* the results internally.

SUMMARY

Learning and development programs are investments by a company in its workforce. Management has a fiduciary and ethical responsibility

Figure I.5. The Six Disciplines That
Characterize Breakthrough Learning.

Define
Business Outcomes

- Link program objectives to business needs
- Agree on definition of success
- Define what participants will do differently and better

Design
Complete Experience

- Include what happens before and after the classroom
- Redefine the finish line from the end of class to the generation of results

Deliver
for Application

- Show how the content relates to current business issues
- Give participants time to reflect on how they will apply

Drive
Follow-Through

- Actively manage the process
- Involve managers
- Ensure accountability

Deploy
Active Support

- Provide ongoing support from facilitators, coaches, managers
- Provide practical "how-to" guides to facilitate transfer

Document
Results

- Collect credible data on the outcomes defined in D1
- Report results to management and use to market the program

to ensure that those investments produce a return: results that increase enterprise value.

We have identified six disciplines—the 6Ds™—that characterize breakthrough learning and development initiatives (Figure I.5).

When the six disciplines are practiced diligently by learning and development organizations, their programs make a greater contribution to business success and they gain the recognition and reward they deserve.

In the following chapters, we explore each of the six disciplines in depth and provide practical tools and advice for their implementation. Each discipline is illustrated with case examples and insights from corporate leaders.

Our experience in helping companies apply the six disciplines has renewed our optimism about people, learning, and organizations. We have been privileged to work with talented and creative learning and line professionals and to see breakthrough results; we believe that we are at the beginning of a true renaissance in corporate education.

We are confident that you will extend the principles articulated in this book to achieve even greater successes. We look forward to hearing your stories.

•

ACTION POINTS

For Learning Leaders

- Evaluate the extent to which you are practicing the six disciplines.
- Identify the one program for which you are responsible that is the most important (that is, that has the highest potential payback).
  - Check your understanding with the relevant business leaders.
- Score the selected program using the 6Ds scorecard (Exhibit I.1).
- With your team, decide which discipline, if strengthened, will produce the greatest improvement for the least effort (low-hanging fruit).
- Use the relevant chapters of this book and your own organizational knowledge to develop a plan.
- Present your findings, the target, your plan and rationale to the relevant management team.
  - Ask for the resources and cooperation needed to implement your recommendations.

Exhibit I.1. 6Ds™ Learning Transfer and Application Scorecard.

Use this tool to evaluate the readiness of a program to deliver results. For each of the items below, check the box that best describes the program according to the following key:

	2 = To a		4 = To a	5 = To a very
1 = Not at all	small extent	3 = Somewhat	large extent	great extent

	1	2	3	4	5	
1. The business needs are well understood. Anticipated on-the-job results of the training are clearly defined and measurable.	☐	☐	☐	☐	☐	Define
2. The program design covers the entire process from invitation to on-the-job application and measurement of results.	☐	☐	☐	☐	☐	Design
3. The relevance of each section to the business is explicitly stated; application is stressed throughout, as is the expectation for action.	☐	☐	☐	☐	☐	Deliver
4. A robust process and sufficient time are provided for participants to set strong goals, plan for action, and prepare communications to others.	☐	☐	☐	☐	☐	
5. After the program, participants are reminded periodically of their objectives and opportunity to apply what they learned.	☐	☐	☐	☐	☐	Drive
6. Participants' managers are actively engaged during the postprogram period. They review and agree on objectives, and expect and monitor progress.	☐	☐	☐	☐	☐	
7. Participants continue to learn from each other after the program. Materials and advice are available to help them accomplish their goals.	☐	☐	☐	☐	☐	Deploy
8. Participants can easily engage coaches for feedback, advice, and support. The group is tracked and supported during the application (postprogram) phase.	☐	☐	☐	☐	☐	
9. On-the-job results are measured based on desired outcomes identified prior to the program.	☐	☐	☐	☐	☐	Document
10. An active, continuous improvement process is used to strengthen the preparation, program, and follow-through.	☐	☐	☐	☐	☐	

Total Score: _____

Exhibit I.1. 6Ds™ Learning Transfer and Application Scorecard, Cont'd.

Scoring Instructions:

Add the numeric value (1 to 5) of all boxes selected. The maximum possible score is 50. Use the table below to assess the readiness of the program to deliver valuable follow-through results.

Points	Assessment
>45	Excellent likelihood of measurable results and return on investment from program. Action: Continue disciplined approach to learning; strengthen lowest-scoring items.
33–44	Moderate likelihood for positive results, but return may be less than optimal. Action: Strengthen weakest items to raise score to >44.
<32	Valuable results and adequate return on investment is less likely. Action: Revise program in a systemic way.

Source: *Copyright © 2005 Fort Hill Company.*

For Line Leaders

- Think about critical business needs that can be addressed (at least in part) by a learning and development program, then complete the worksheet in Exhibit I.2.
  - In the first column, labeled "Critical Business Needs," write the most pressing business opportunities or challenges that training can help address.
  - In the second column, labeled "Conditions of Satisfaction," describe what people will be *doing* better and differently if the program is a success and the results this will produce.
  - In the third column, "Acceptable Evidence," describe how you will know whether the program is working; what kinds of data do you consider credible and relevant?
- Show the completed worksheet to your head of learning and development. Ask whether it is possible to deliver the results desired.
  - Work together to make it happen.

- If you are already investing in learning and development (through an internal unit or external vendors) use the 6Ds Scorecard (Exhibit I.1) to identify the most promising areas for improvement.

  - Ask your learning leader to do the same and compare your results.

  - Use the relevant chapter(s) of this book to jointly develop a plan for improvement.

Exhibit I.2. The Learning4Results™ Worksheet.

Critical Business Needs (that training can help address)	Conditions of Satisfaction (what will participants be doing differently in 3–6 months?)	Acceptable Evidence (what data are needed to decide whether the program is working?)

DEFINE OUTCOMES
IN BUSINESS TERMS

---

*Management must always, in every decision and action, put
economic performance first. It can only justify its existence and
its authority by the economic results it produces. There may be
great non-economic results: the happiness of the members of
the enterprise, the contribution to the welfare or culture of the
community, etc. Yet management has failed if it fails to produce
economic results. . . . It has failed if it does not improve,
or at least maintain, the wealth-producing capacity
of the economic resources entrusted to it.*

—Peter Drucker

IN AN EVERMORE performance-driven world, corporate education is
increasingly being asked to define, commit to, and then deliver relevant
business outcomes. Fred Harburg, senior vice president of leadership and
management development at Fidelity Investments, put it this way: "We
are not in the business of providing classes, learning tools, or even learning itself. We are in the business of facilitating improved business results"
(Harburg, 2004, p. 21).

The "finish line" for learning and development has been redefined. It
is no longer enough to deliver highly rated and well-attended programs;
learning and development's job is not complete until learning has been
converted into results that matter to the business. The new finish line is

results; and the only way to know whether it has been reached is to agree in advance on the definition of success. Thus, the first and critical discipline practiced by breakthrough learning and development organizations is that they clearly define, in partnership with business leaders, the desired outcomes in business terms.

In this chapter we underscore the importance of shifting the emphasis from learning outcomes to business outcomes and provide guidance for making this transition. Topics include

- Beginning with the end in mind
- Avoiding common pitfalls
- Mapping the impact
- Picking the right problem
- Managing expectations
- Besting the competition
- Action points for learning and line leaders

BEGIN WITH THE END IN MIND

Corporate learning and development initiatives should always be a means to an end. The "end" will vary according to the nature and drivers of the business, its needs, and its environment. But the essential goal will always be to improve the performance of the business. More effective leadership, best-of-class customer service, accelerated product development, enhanced teamwork, greater employee retention, and so forth all contribute ultimately to a company's financial health and performance. Ultimately, companies invest in learning and development to improve their ability to win in an increasingly competitive global marketplace.

Truly effective interventions, then, begin with the end in mind: the objectives of the business. Business results must be the touchstone for learning and development efforts, the "true north" against which programs are designed, implemented, and measured. Any other organizing principle is likely to get the initiative off course, as David Campbell put it: "If you don't know where you are going, you will probably end up someplace else" (Campbell, 1974). Berry Gordy, founder of Motown Records, said it this way: "People ask me, 'where did I go wrong?' My answer is always the same: Probably at the beginning."

That learning and development programs should be designed with the end in mind hardly seems like a revelation. Yet our experience suggests that it is difficult to accomplish well; it requires fixity of purpose and true collaboration between learning and line leadership.

Sony Electronics is a great example of the value of such collaboration. Sony uses a Talent Management Council that comprises both line and learning leaders to ensure firm linkage between learning and business objectives (see Case Study: Sony Electronics). The result has been greater strategic alliance, better programs, and deeper understanding of the value of learning and development.

•

Case Study: Sony Electronics—Linking Development to Business Results

Sony is a global leader in the discovery, development, and production of electronic components and entertainment and has more than 150,000 employees. Sony Electronics in the United States uses talent management councils to firmly link development programs to business needs and to ensure execution of learning transfer objectives.

The talent management councils were created three years ago to take talent management and leadership development far beyond typical succession planning. Sony recognized that to continue to prosper in a highly competitive and rapidly changing market, it had to increase its overall leadership pool, introduce new leadership ideas and skills, and increase its bench strength.

The senior talent management council comprises the president's direct reports, the senior-most leaders in the company. It is responsible for selecting high-potential leaders and guiding leadership development strategy. A junior council includes directors and vice presidents from Sony's pool of top talent.

According to Debby Swanson, national director, talent and organizational development, "At the start of each cycle, we talk to the talent management council, we review the current business objectives and the direction we are trying to take the company. Senior managers prioritize the business capabilities required to meet the business objectives. We then identify the leadership competencies that align with these business capabilities. There are also common culture issues that we focus on, like breaking down silos. These are also woven into the design of our programs; for example, having small cross-functional learning groups stay together to work on their goals."

The councils serve not only to ensure linkage between business objectives and learning but also as faculty in the development programs. Council members also play a critical role as the business reviewers of results reported by participants three months after the residential portion of the program. Their involvement ensures accountability for execution of learning transfer objectives and critical assessment of the results.

After three months of on-the-job follow-through and application, participants in leadership programs meet for a teleconference of one to one and one-half hours with a member of the talent management council. The teleconference includes

- A business update from the senior leader

- An update about the program from one of the learning leaders

- An analysis of the execution phase of the program based on data in the follow-through management system (*Friday5s*®) that includes which team had done what, which individuals completed all their updates, overall participation, and so forth

- A presentation by each team on their learning over time and their accomplishments, including full-year estimates of value created as a result

"Knowing that one of the senior talent management council managers will be on the call with an eye on their final results puts pressure on accountability and helps ensure that participants execute their objectives. The other huge benefit is that these calls allow members of the talent management council to hear directly what people are doing differently on the job. It has been very powerful," said Swanson.

"In the Executive Leadership Program, participants are asked to estimate the annual value created as a result of the program. We tally these and we show the results of what they have done as a group and for the program as a whole. They are self-reported estimates, not hard metrics, but when we have been challenged by one of the senior managers we say: 'These are your people and this is what they are saying.'

"And once the talent management council participates in a call and really hears the stories behind the numbers, they no longer question it. An example is one of our senior VPs who was attending a session in which one of the participants projected $300 million in value. If I had presented it, I might have been challenged, but when he heard the story first-hand, he said, 'Well, I can see how that could be even more.'"

Jody Grawey, manager, talent and organizational development, pointed out that there is value even in the absence of hard numbers: "For much of the leadership curriculum, we don't have hard metrics. Many of the reports are more anecdotal, but the teleconferences still serve to give the talent management council insights about where the investment in learning is going, what actual changes people make on the job, and the influence that participants in this program have on the business. We have received nothing but encouraging feedback from talent management council members about their experiences in the wrap-up sessions and how enlightening it has been for them to really see what happens and the results that can be produced."

Swanson agreed: "The wrap-up sessions appear, on the surface, to be entirely for the participants, but our other objective is to educate the senior people on the value of learning. It is very powerful when they hear real business stories from people who are in their business units—the actual things that people have done and why they think it has had this impact: 'Here is what I am doing. Here is what I tried. Here is what I accomplished.'

"I am starting to see that aligning learning and leadership development with business objectives is not as big a gap as it used to be in the minds of the business leaders. I attribute this to their participation on this council and hearing the kind of impact development can produce."

•

IN BUSINESS TERMS

Throughout this discussion, we will repeatedly emphasize that outcomes need to be defined in "business terms." Does that mean that the objectives of every program must be expressed in dollars and cents? Ultimately, yes.

Drucker's famous dictum with which we began this chapter is uncompromising: management's responsibility is to ensure that *every* investment a company makes yields a return because business is, in the end, about financial return. Even corporate philanthropy reflects business aims; good community relations, positive reputation, and enhanced employee loyalty contribute to the organization's value.

Training in leadership, ethics, diversity, and so forth are laudable in their own right, but they must also pay dividends in terms of lower operating costs, greater productivity, enhanced innovation, and improved consumer confidence. Programs that help participants improve their personal performance pay dividends in greater job satisfaction, motivation, and retention. Ultimately, every training initiative must produce a positive financial return, directly or indirectly; it is the only acceptable justification for investment by a for-profit business. That may strike some as crass and mercenary, but we are convinced that the ability to define and deliver business benefits is the only way for learning and development to prove its value and demonstrate that cutting the training budget ultimately hurts the bottom line.

Business Terms Include More than Just Finance

Defining results in business terms, however, does not require explicitly quantifying financial returns for every program. As we shall discuss in D6, the chapter on documenting results, such analysis is not always necessary or cost-effective. If a clear causal link has already been accepted between certain behaviors (for example, better coaching of subordinates) and financial returns (lower employment costs as a result of greater retention), then it is sufficient to promise and measure an increase in the desired behaviors.

When we say "in business terms," we mean *verifiable outcomes of relevance to the business* of the organization. We mean designing a program that will result in "subordinates receiving more frequent and more effective coaching" (for example) as opposed to "participants will learn coaching skills." The former is concrete, measurable, and linked to business needs. The latter, "learn coaching skills," could be measured, but that misses the point. The issue is not whether new skills are learned, but whether they are *used* in a way that benefits the organization. "[N]ew skills and knowledge alone do not add value; they must be applied, then nurtured until improved performance can be counted on consistently to produce an important job result" (Brinkerhoff and Apking, 2001, p. 6). A program that will increase customer satisfaction scores is worthy of investment; a program that delivers only attendee satisfaction is not.

Learning and development's task is complete only when learning has been transferred and applied in a way that produces results; the measure of its success is in *business terms*. "Effective training occurs when it is fully transferred and when performance achieves or exceeds business goals" (Wall & White, 1997, p. 169).

Linking Business and Learning Strategy at Honeywell

Honeywell is a leading global technology and manufacturing company with more than 100,000 employees worldwide. Linking learning and development initiatives tightly to the needs of the businesses is vital in Honeywell's highly competitive and rapidly evolving markets. Therefore, Honeywell uses an ongoing, multifaceted approach to ensure strategic impact of its learning and development efforts (Magee, interview):

1. *The management resources review process is used to identify common needs across the corporation and within specific management bands.* Honeywell has a robust process for assessment

of talent (management resources review process) that includes data from performance reviews as well as 360-degree feedback. The learning and development group leadership reviews these data annually to develop a hierarchy of needs across the company, as well as needs specific to particular management levels, functions, and regions. Especially important in this regard are the data that compare employees' strengths and weaknesses on the twelve core Honeywell behaviors.

2. *Learning is integrated into the strategic planning process.* The learning and development organization has visibility to the strategic plans of each of the businesses, their key objectives—growth, profitability, and so forth—and the major challenges to achieving them. The chief learning officer (CLO) and his team ensure that the learning and development strategy is aligned with the business strategy. They have face-to-face meetings with each of the business presidents to validate that what learning and development is offering continues to meet the strategic needs of the business.

3. *The CLO works directly with the CEO and senior management team to support new initiatives.* The chief learning officer has direct insight into the major initiatives of the chief executive officer (CEO) and his team and works to ensure that learning initiatives are designed, piloted, revised, and in place to support the business needs being addressed. A current example would be all of the learning and development needed to support the Honeywell Operating System initiative, a standardized way of doing work at the manufacturing level.

4. *Leaders teach.* "Leaders as teachers" is a core value at Honeywell. Senior leaders participate regularly as instructors and mentors in learning programs. Their deep knowledge and immediate credibility not only greatly enhance programs, but their participation also provides them with first-hand knowledge of the program objectives and what is being taught. This serves as a continuous check that learning and development is addressing the most important business needs.

AVOID PITFALLS

That outcomes should be defined in advance and linked to business outcomes is hardly a new idea. Brinkerhoff called it "the fundamental logic of training" (Brinkerhoff, 1987); it is discussed in every textbook of educational design; its merits are extolled at training and management conferences. Yet in our consulting practice, we continue to encounter programs that miss the point, despite the efforts of professional, experienced, well-intentioned design teams (Exhibit D1.1). How does this happen?

Exhibit D1.1. A Bad Example.

A major corporation recently consulted us about increasing the impact of a soon to be launched management development program.

We asked: "How will the company benefit by having someone attend the program? What will participants do differently as a consequence that will improve business results?"

There was an awkward silence.

The chief of learning turned to the program director. The program director deferred to the designer. "That's a good question," they all said. But no one had the answer.

They had a detailed plan—practically to the minute—of what was going to happen during the course. They knew which leadership models they were going to use. They had purchased a custom simulation and hired big name speakers. They had a list of learning objectives—what knowledge participants would acquire—but no one could explain how these were linked to the business of the business. They were about to launch the program to hundreds of mid- and upper-level managers, but no one responsible for putting it together could explain the key business drivers or how attendance would increase productivity, generate new revenue, or otherwise create value for the company.

This was a smart, dedicated, hard-working and talented team, yet they had fallen into the trap of focusing so hard on the how that they had lost sight of the why. Their experience suggests just how easy this is to do and why learning and line leaders alike must keep coming back to the business rationale—defining the intended outcomes in business terms.

Our experience suggests that there are five key pitfalls that must be avoided:

- Action without analysis ("We need a program")
- Confusion between means and ends
- Laudable intent
- No line leader input
- "Training results cannot be measured"

Action Without Analysis ("We Need a Program")

When the goal of having a program is defined as "having a program," the initiative is in trouble from the start. The problem typically begins when someone in upper management decrees that the company needs to have a program on some particular topic. Ideally, the impetus is a real business need, such as insufficient bench strength in the leadership ranks or a changing environment that demands a new strategy. But programs also spring from causes that are less results-driven, such as a business book extolling the latest theory, a consultant, a competitor's program (especially if it attracted media attention), or a pointed question from the board ("What are we doing to accelerate innovation?").

Whatever the inciting event, the assignment gets passed down the line as, "Put together a program on X." Well-meaning subordinates set in motion a whole series of events to fill the order. Experts are consulted; vendors are vetted; leadership models are debated. After the expenditure of much energy, a "custom" curriculum is designed; logistics are planned; speakers are hired. The only detail that has been overlooked is the business driver: What results are we expected beyond "having a program"? The program becomes an end in itself; success is defined as the number of attendees among the target audience and whether they enjoyed the process (as reflected on end-of-course evaluations).

The higher in the organization that the idea for the program originated, the less likely it will be challenged. "Having a program" will become an unquestioned organizational imperative. Jack Welch is reported to have said that one of the problems with being CEO is that "you ask for a cup of coffee and they go out and buy Colombia."

If the CEO wants a program, what human resources or organizational development staff member is going to have the temerity to ask: "Why?" or "What's the payoff for the company?" Yet those are exactly the kinds of questions that must be asked if learning and development is going to succeed. As Susan Burnett put it: "When I was being interviewed, the CEO said, 'I want Merchant University.' And I said: 'Why?' If I had not had that conversation, I would not know." (See From the Top: Susan Burnett.)

•

**From the Top: Susan Burnett, The Gap,
on Defining Business Outcomes**

When Susan Burnett became senior vice president of talent and development for Gap, Inc. she got some good news. "I came in on the day they were finalizing the budget and sat down with my new boss.

She showed me the budget and she said, 'Hey, I have some good news for you. The learning team got six million dollars in incremental funds to produce Merchant University, Design Academy, and a new on-boarding process.' I said, 'OK, cool, six million dollars, that is great. But why does the business need these programs? What business results are we supposed to produce for Gap, Inc?'

"And so I interviewed people, talked to managers. I am voraciously interested in how the business works and how we make money—always have been. It comes from years of line management. So here was the perfect opportunity. I was a new leader, in a new business, and I needed to really understand the drivers for success.

"I learned about Gap's business strategies for growth, operations, and people. As I talked with the executive team and their leadership teams, I learned that Gap's transformation would come from building new leadership capabilities in our people and new organizational capabilities in product development, supply chain, and IT. I learned that the merchant job was central to our brand's success, and that Gap had invented the role of the merchant in the late 1980s, evolving from buyer to merchant leader. I also saw that the current reengineering of the product pipeline would require the reinvention of the merchant role again. And I learned that turnover of our new employees and our key merchant talent was industry leading and unacceptable.

"I was so excited that my learning organization would have the opportunity to make a big difference in achieving Gap's business objectives. We could stem the new employee turnover tide with an awesome hiring to on-boarding process that improved productivity and performance in the first ninety days. We could accelerate understanding of the new merchant role, the new concept to customer pipeline, and build the new merchant general management capabilities desperately needed by our business."

Then she discovered the bad news. The learning team was not connected to the priorities of the business. They were not working on the right issues, but they were working hard to produce legacy programs. They had not had the opportunity to be connected to the business strategies and core changes the new leadership was driving.

"I got a proposal for Merchant U that wasn't connected to the transformation the business needed for success. I also saw that they didn't have the critical business relationships and connections that would get them the information they needed. They were working directly with the merchants, the folks who were the target for the changes. It was a recipe for failure."

•

The stronger the command-and-control culture of a company, the more likely everyone will exert best efforts to create a program without ever stopping to ask, "Why?" The result will be a learning initiative that lacks grassroots support. Line managers will grumble among themselves about the cost or wasted time, but most will go along in order to save their powder for bigger battles. A conspiracy of silence develops; the discussions of the program will all take place in what Connolly and Rianoshek (2002) call "pretense" mode—everyone saying the right things but no one addressing the real concerns. And the poor learning organization—having done its best to fulfill what it thought it was asked to do—will not understand why its contribution is not valued as highly as the management rhetoric should suggest.

Programs created for the sake of "having a program" are doomed to failure. Line managers and learning leaders must work together to create a climate in which it is acceptable to challenge the premise of proposed programs and in which the only acceptable rationale for learning and development initiatives is a legitimate business need.

Confusion Between Means and Ends

Just as "having a program" is inadequate as a rationale, "having given a program" is inadequate as an outcome. Many corporate learning and development departments still report the number of people taught, hours of instruction, and number of courses offered as though these were results. Learning management systems have contributed to the problem by making it easier to collect, generate, slice and dice these data, and turn them into PowerPoint® slides. But such statistics are measures of *activity*—not *productivity*. They are, as we shall see, measures of inputs, not outputs.

The well-known human resources consultant, Dave Ulrich, related a meeting he had with the chairman and top human resources leaders from a large bank. "The training person said that 80 percent of employees have done at least forty hours in classes. The chairman said, 'Congratulations.' I said, 'You're talking about the activities you're doing. The question is, What are you delivering?'" (quoted in Hammonds, 2005).

The real goal of learning and development—and the standard against which it will increasingly be measured—is the extent to which it contributes to a company's prosperity and competitiveness. That requires understanding the business drivers and designing for and measuring against them. The *activities* involved—courses, hours, instructors, coaching, action learning, and all the rest—are the *means* to an end, not the end itself.

Confusing means with ends is hardly peculiar to learning and development. In any initiative, it is easy to become so focused on activities that the original purpose is lost. "Having lost sight of our objectives, we redoubled our efforts." Activities are seductive; they are concrete, quantifiable, and easy to measure. But Bordonaro points out the danger of "paying disproportionate attention to the measurable simply because it is measurable" (2005, p. 214).

Writing about corporate change initiatives, Schaffer and Thomson (1992) said: "At the heart of these programs, which we call 'activity centered,' is a fundamentally flawed logic that confuses ends with means, process with outcomes." A focus on activity rather than results leads to a situation in which "[t]he performance improvement efforts of many companies have as much impact on operational and financial results as a ceremonial rain dance has on the weather" (p. 2).

The fault is management's. As the comic character Pogo said: "We have met the enemy and he is us." For years, learning and development organizations have been treated as pure cost centers rather than contributors to productivity. The result has been undue emphasis on efficiency (cost containment) rather than efficacy (cost benefit), on activity (programs or hours of training) as opposed to results (increased sales, greater efficiency, higher retention). Training departments, consultants, and vendors do not promise specific results because they haven't had to. As long as companies are willing to pay for activity, only a fool would offer more.

This is in stark contrast to the standards for line departments. If a sales manager requests funds to increase the size of the sales force, he or she must be able to demonstrate how this will be translated into more *sales,* not merely more sales calls. A sales manager is measured and rewarded for achieving the promised increase in revenue, not merely increasing the size of the sales force, even if that is an enabling intermediary milestone.

Line management and learning leaders must work together to ensure that learning departments are held accountable for demonstrating a return on investment, that they are subjected to the same rigorous scrutiny to which a well-run business subjects its line operations, and that they are recognized and rewarded for producing results. It is a manifest disservice to both learning leaders and shareholders to use a lower standard to evaluate educational programs than other business processes.

Laudable Intent

A third pitfall for learning and development programs occurs when they are positioned on the moral high ground. Challenging the value of leadership development, six sigma training, or a diversity program is akin to questioning the value of motherhood, patriotism, or equality. Managers who value their careers are reluctant to challenge programs with laudable intent.

The result is that learning and development initiatives on politically correct topics are not subjected to the same kind of rigorous examination and debate as other expenditures of comparable magnitude. The debate about a marketing program is rarely about whether more sales are good—that goes without saying. The debate is about whether the proposed plan is the best possible approach and whether it is likely to deliver the promised results. Likewise, debate about a proposed training program in leadership, diversity, total quality, or other laudable objective should be about whether the proposed process, objectives, and metrics have a high probability of delivering the desired results. Such debate has nothing to do with the merit of the objective, which is a given. To maximize the effectiveness of their organizations and programs, learning leaders should welcome debate about the best means of achieving laudable intents and should work with line leaders to encourage it.

No Line Leader Input

We continue to be surprised by the number of major programs, in otherwise well-managed companies, that are developed entirely within the human resource or training organization and go forward with little or no input from line leaders. Although it is true that human resources, organizational development, and learning organizations have deep expertise in their respective disciplines, they are not the consumers of the program or directly accountable for the bottom line. Their perspective on the business is different from that of line leaders; they have less hands-on experience managing hard business metrics. If they consult only among themselves, they may design a program with strong learning objectives but only weak links to key business measures.

In their book, *Performance Consulting*, Robinson and Robinson (1996) underscore the importance of aligning people strategies with business goals. They argue that learning professionals must transform themselves from traditional trainers to performance consultants. "Someone in the role of Performance Consultant thinks in terms of what people must *do* if business goals are to be achieved. This is different from the traditional training process of focusing on what people must *learn*" (p. 10, emphasis in original).

•

From the Top: Al Vicere, Pennsylvania State University, on Business Links and Sponsorship

Al Vicere is Executive Education Professor of Strategic Leadership at Penn State University and president of Vicere Associates, Inc. He has worked with top leadership teams and development programs in the world's leading companies. When he was asked to think of a program that he was really proud of and that was producing results, he thought immediately of 3M. He stressed the importance of active senior sponsorship, linking learning to strategy, and thinking systemically about change.

"From the outset, the CEO, Jim McNerney, really believed in learning and development as a pathway to change. There is a staff of people who are extremely competent and understand learning processes. Between that staff and McNerney with his excitement, they now have an entire senior leadership team who have made the learning process a platform for change. They have embedded it into the organizational processes of their culture."

Vicere acknowledged that "it certainly helps when you have a CEO who gets it and who understands the power of learning," but the key was McNerney's visible and active support that went far beyond words: "Not just putting people in a room, communicating a message, and hoping it sticks. But really communicating with people, engaging them in an active process where they can see and experience how learning is used to start to frame the next stages of the organization's evolution. Not only did he have the perspective, but the teams that were put in charge of designing the initiative were in constant touch with him. He wanted not just to be 'briefed' as they say, but to talk about the process, look at some alternatives, generate ideas.

"The next success factor was the internal team at 3M who put the process together. It was a diverse team of people who were open to the idea of linking the learning platform to the strategy. They were very, very open to the idea of looking at the strategy and learning systemically. 'Let's build the initiative around the strategy. Let's link the initiative tightly to the workplace so that it is not just words, but a set of practices. Let's make sure that people recognize that the skills that they are practicing are actually the skills they will need to achieve the business metrics. And let's make sure that they see that achieving the metrics is critical to success, rewards and advancements.'

"The third success factor was that team was smart enough to know that a team of people from HR cannot create a platform like this. It has to be embedded in the operating management of the firm. So the team spent an enormous amount of time interacting with senior management in 3M, bouncing ideas off them and engaging them in the process. As an example, in the Accelerated Leadership Development program 75 to 80 percent of the teaching was done by 3M executives.

"The last big meta-piece is that the learning in all of the initiatives is very, very relevant to the strategy, to 3M's strategic imperatives. It is abundantly clear where the company is trying to go and that learning is directly tied to getting there."

The business impact and importance of the resulting model were independently confirmed in a recent article in the *Harvard Business Review,* "Turning Great Strategy into Great Performance": "Soon after he became CEO of 3M, Jim McNerney and his top team spent 18 months hashing out a new leadership model for the company. Challenging debates among members of the top team led to agreement on six 'leadership attributes'—namely, the ability to 'chart the course,' 'energize and inspire others,' 'demonstrate ethics, integrity and compliance,' 'deliver results,' 'raise the bar,' and 'innovate resourcefully.' 3M's leadership agreed that these six attributes were essential for the company to become skilled at execution and known for accountability. *Today, the leaders credit this model with helping 3M to sustain and even improve its consistently strong performance*" (Mankins & Steele, 2005, p. 72, emphasis added).

•

Programs that are clearly linked to business strategies and that have support from senior line leaders can have profound and long-lasting impact on company performance (see From the Top: Al Vicere).

One way to ensure line leader input is to create a steering committee of both business and learning leaders to provide oversight and insight to key development programs. At Sony, for example, senior business leaders serve on Sony's Talent Management Council, which helps design and evaluate Sony's Integrated Leadership Curriculum. An executive from the council attends the virtual wrap-up session in which participants report the business impact of working on their leadership goals. The involvement of senior leadership in not only the design process but also the ongoing rollout ensures that the program has legitimacy and remains focused on business outcomes. A side benefit is that senior leaders hear first-hand the impact it is having.

Scott Saslow, writing about best practices in executive education, summarized the benefits of forming an advisory board as follows: "Senior executives, from multiple business units and corporate functions, should regularly meet and provide input on what needs to be done (and win implicit buy-in in the process). They will help push programs through the approval and budgeting process and provide timely and accurate feedback on program effectiveness. Educational programs will carry significant weight if they are supported by the advisory board and board support will increase the credibility of the entire executive education function" (Saslow, 2005, p. 45).

"Training Results Cannot Be Measured"

A frequent excuse for failing to define the expected results of learning and development is that "it cannot be measured." We do not deny that it is difficult to isolate and quantify the specific contribution of training. Many factors influence business results: overall economic climate, success of marketing, competitors' actions, new market entrants, even the weather. But those factors also confound the evaluation of sales, marketing, and other business activities, which are nevertheless held accountable for delivering on their promises.

That something is difficult to measure with precision, or that it is influenced by numerous extraneous factors, is no excuse for not defining objectives. When a pharmaceutical company develops a new drug, it must specify the drug's claims—what it supposedly treats or cures. The company must provide the Food and Drug Administration with a plan to prove beyond a reasonable doubt that the drug does, in fact, what it claims to do. Data must be obtained from real patients. But the effect of the drug in real patients is influenced by many other factors—lifestyle, concurrent diseases, stage of illness, and genetic background. Patients may not have even taken it according to directions (Figure D1.1), and the outcome may be quite hard to measure. No matter. If a company wants the rights to market a drug, it has to design and execute an evaluation scheme that unequivocally documents the drug's benefits in spite of these difficulties.

Before the FDA was established, drug producers were allowed to make whatever claims they wanted. The result was the "snake oil salesman," who sold extravagant claims for quack remedies to the gullible for whatever ailed them. It is precisely to avoid promulgating unsupported remedies that the "Standards for Educational and Psychological Testing" were prepared by a committee of the American Educational

Figure D1.1. Many Factors Besides Training Affect Business Results, Just as Many Factors Besides a Drug Affect the Medical Outcome in a Patient. Nevertheless, Both Can and Must Be Measured.

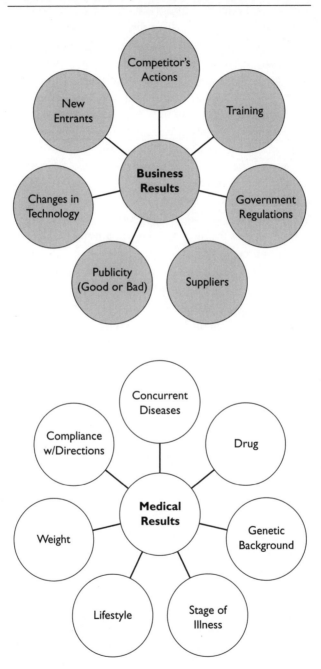

Research Association, American Psychological Association, and the National Council on Measurement in Education (1996). The standards require that measures (and by inference, human resource programs based on these measures) be reliable and valid predictors of the value to individuals and organizations. The difficulty of reliably defining and measuring the outcome of educational programs is acknowledged, but difficulty does not provide an exemption from the standards.

"[E]xperience with several CEOs and top teams and regular discussions with their advisors convince me that the rejection of measures in learning fundamentally is a dead end. Measurement is an integral part of human endeavor, and its power can't be cancelled out by high-sounding sentiment" (Bordonaro, 2005, p. 229). To claim that the effects of learning and development cannot be measured is wrong-headed and potentially dangerous; if the positive effects of learning and development cannot be measured, then presumably neither can the negative effects of reducing or eliminating it. Failure to measure outcomes no doubt contributes to the fact that training budgets are among the first to be cut in periods of belt tightening.

The discipline of defining outcomes in business terms is an important safeguard against this pitfall because it defines in advance the measures of success that matter to management.

MAP THE IMPACT

Ultimately, there are only two ways to increase profitability (the ultimate measure of corporate performance): (1) increase revenue; (2) reduce the cost of producing goods and services (Figure D1.2).

Figure D1.2. Pathways to Improving Business Results.

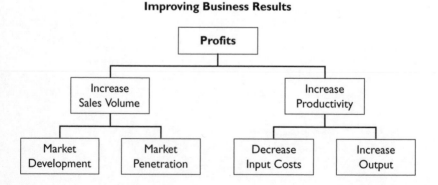

For learning and development programs to add value, they must contribute to one or both of these pathways by helping employees take better, more effective, or more efficient actions on the job. Improved actions and changed behaviors must necessarily precede business impact—and therefore will be evident first (Figure D1.3).

Figure D1.3. Learning and Development Produces Results Through New and More Effective Behaviors of the Participants.

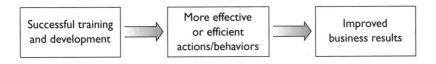

Because the flow of causality is from left to right, from training to behaviors to results (Figure D1.3), learning and development programs must be planned in the opposite direction, from desired results to the behaviors required to produce them to the sorts of exercises and experiences needed to create the capability for action (Figure D1.4).

Figure D1.4. Learning and Development Programs Should Be Designed Beginning with the Desired Business Outcomes and the Changes in Behavior Required to Produce Them.

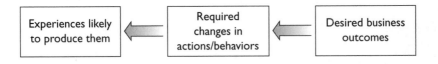

Impact Mapping

Brinkerhoff developed the concept of *impact mapping* as a powerful tool for ensuring linkage between learning initiatives and the ultimate goals of the business (Brinkerhoff & Gill, 1994; Brinkerhoff & Apking, 2001). The three core elements of impact maps are capability, performance, and results: "[I]f we learn how to do something, we have the capability to perform in a new way. For value to occur, we have to change our behavior and use the new capability in performance. Further, our performance must be aimed at worthwhile results" (Brinkerhoff & Apking, 2001, p. 63).

We have found the planning tool in Figure D1.5 helpful in guiding the discussion between line leaders and learning providers to map the desired impact. It begins by asking managers to define the business needs that will be met if the course is a success; in other words, how will value be created? The second question helps translate these overall goals to what, specifically, participants need to do better or differently following the program to achieve the business results. The third question gets at process measurement. That is, what will be the early indicators that the program is working? The final question is important because it defines the scorecard by which success will be judged.

Figure D1.5. A Tool for Helping Line Leaders and Learning Providers Reach a Common Understanding of the Required Outcomes.

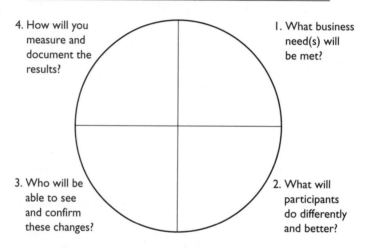

Use the input from interviews with line leaders and discussions with the advisory council, steering committee, and other stakeholders to construct an impact map that makes explicit the links between capabilities (specific skills and knowledge) and the ultimate objective: improved business results (Figure D1.6). Share this impact map with the key stakeholders and revise as necessary. Begin planning the actual developmental experiences only after consensus has been reached on the outcomes, the capabilities, and the performance needed to achieve them.

Human Performance Technology

The International Society for Performance Improvement (ISPI) has defined human performance technology (HPT) as a systematic approach to solve practical problems of performance by the individuals and groups in organizations. They have defined a set of governing principles that

Figure D1.6. Two Examples of Impact Maps That Relate Capabilities to Be Developed to Performance and Overall Business Objectives. Note That at This Point, Neither Is Concerned with *How* the Capabilities Are to Be Developed, yet Both Immediately Suggest Intermediate and Ultimate Measures for Results.

Target Population	Capability Needed	On-the-Job Performance	Work Unit Result	Overall Business Objectives
District sales manager	How and when to coach for greatest benefit	Uses coaching language and techniques when interacting with sales representatives	Increased sales performance by reps Lower turnover	Growth Improved profitability

Target Population	Capability Needed	On-the-Job Performance	Work Unit Result	Overall Business Objectives
Newly promoted supervisors	Ability to recognize developmental level and adjust leadership style for maximum benefit	Use concepts and methods of situational leadership	Greater unit productivity Greater job satisfaction Lower turnover	Improved profitability Greater management bench strength

reinforce the importance of clearly defining desired outcomes and performance gaps before designing interventions:

- Focus on outcomes.
- Be systematic in the assessment of the need or opportunity.
- Be systematic in the analysis of the work and workplace to identify the cause of factors that limit performance.

"The HPT process begins with a comparison of the present and the desired levels of individual and organizational performance to identify the performance gap. A cause analysis is then done to determine what impact the work environment (information, resources, and incentives) and the people are having on performance. Once the performance gap and the causes have been determined, the appropriate interventions are designed and developed" (ISPI, n.d.).

PICK THE RIGHT PROBLEM

In most fields of human endeavor, half the solution is defining the right problem. The key to maximizing the return on learning and development is to pick the right need to address. Which improvement target offers the greatest potential for return is very much situation-specific. It depends on a company's history, environment, market, competitors, product life cycle, and cost structure. Moreover, circumstances change over time, so the most pressing need of a prior year may no longer be the best current investment. Corporate educators must continually scan the environment, reassess their offerings, and adjust to changing needs just as product development, sales, and marketing leaders must.

Picking the right problems and delivering the right solutions require ongoing dialogue between general managers and educators that is characterized by open-minded questioning, active listening, and a real interest and passion for the business.

Discover the Highest-Value Needs

Successful companies invest substantial time and effort to discover their customers' most important unmet needs. In *The Innovator's Solution*, Christensen and Raynor (2003) explain: "When customers become aware of a job that they need to get done in their lives, they look around for a product or service that they can 'hire' to get the job done." Therefore, "companies that target their products at the *circumstances* in which customers find themselves, rather than the *customers* themselves, are those that can launch predictably successful products" (p. 75).

In effect, line organizations "hire" learning and development to do a job they need done. The better the learning and development group understands the *circumstances* that line managers face—the business ends they are trying to achieve—the better they will be at delivering solutions that produce valuable results. Learning and development organizations must invest more in market research to be certain they continue to discover and address the highest-value needs.

Put a Price on It

The impact of learning and development in business is ultimately measured in financial terms. It makes sense, therefore, to target programs to opportunities with the greatest potential for payback. Spencer (2001) recommends developing a business case for each proposed intervention to ensure that it has sufficient potential to merit the effort. The steps are to calculate the overall value of the opportunity by analyzing the difference between the value of average and above-average performance, estimate the percentage of the performance variance that training can affect and the likely magnitude of that impact, and use these to project an expected economic value added and return on investment from the proposed program.

Spencer (2001) used this approach to evaluate the expected benefits and return on investment for a program designed to enhance emotional intelligence of branch managers in a multinational technology company. Using company financial records, he showed that the profitability of branch managers who were performing one standard deviation above the mean was $1.7 million better than average performance. Thus, even if the training program improved performance just a fraction of a standard deviation, it had enormous potential for return. Based on this analysis, the program was approved, implemented, and evaluated. Although the actual impact was smaller than projected, it still produced a very strong return on investment.

This technique can be used to estimate the probable value of proposed programs. Depending on the nature and complexity of the job, employees whose performance is one standard deviation better than average produce up to one and a half times more value than average performers. The specific values of differences in performance for many different job types have been researched and published. These can be used to adduce the relative value of different training proposals.

Do Your Market Research

How does a company decide which customer needs offer the most attractive opportunity for its products and services? Market research. Multiple sources of data are consulted. Studies, interviews, and focus groups are conducted to understand what customers want, what they are willing to pay, how they will judge success, and how they should be segmented and targeted.

Defining customer needs for a learning and development initiative should be less rigorous than defining customer needs for a new automobile or laptop computer. Many of the same techniques should be used. Since most key customers for learning and development are internal, the needs analysis should be faster and less expensive to conduct than for a consumer product, but for a major program it should be no less thorough.

Do Your Homework

There are two key sources of information from which to identify the most valuable training interventions: "explicit" knowledge contained in business plans and reports, and the tacit knowledge of leaders, managers, and employees. Both will be needed to make an informed decision. Program designers and teams should begin by reviewing all of the available written information before taking busy managers' time for interviews or focus groups.

There are three reasons for this. First, it demonstrates respect for others' time and the pressures they face. You should never waste a manager's time asking him or her to go over things you could have easily read for yourself. Second, you will be afforded more respect—and probably more time—if it is clear that you have done your homework and have generated ideas of your own. Third, with the business plan as background, you will be able to ask more intelligent and penetrating questions and thus reach a deeper level of understanding than if you simply show up and ask to be enlightened.

Get a copy of the business unit's plan and read it carefully. Review any other relevant company documents, such as a strategic plan, consultant's report, and competitive analysis. Read actively with an inquisitive mind. What is the business unit trying to accomplish? What are their key objectives and initiatives for the year? What do they list as the competitive threats or downside scenarios? What keeps them up at night worrying? Where could an effective training or development program reduce the risk and improve the likelihood or magnitude of the success?

Once you have reviewed the available documents and formulated ideas about key needs, it is time to get out and speak with line leaders. The goal is to elucidate and understand their greatest unmet needs, their pain and frustrations. What are the causes of suboptimal performance that education could resolve? Where are there inefficiencies or inconsistencies that waste significant amounts of time and money? These are the problems to attack first. Suggested interview guidelines are given in Exhibit D1.2.

Avoid the temptation to interview only other learning leaders or the heads of human resources; the information you gather will be insufficient. However well-informed and well-intentioned they may be, they are one step removed from the action. You have to talk to the people who are in the arena, the people whose careers depend on delivering results. If learning and development can achieve real alignment with the

Exhibit D1.2. Interview Guidelines for Discovering Business Needs.

Preparation

- Do your homework; read the relevant business plans, reports, and related materials.
- Schedule your interview with the business leader in advance; state the objective and time required.
- Know what you want to get out of the interview before you begin.

The Interview

- Follow the classic sales opening: meet and greet, state the value, propose an agenda, check for agreement.
- Start on time and end on time.
- Use open questions, check for understanding by restating, and probe for the deeper issues.
- Summarize what you understood from reading the plan and check for understanding: "From what I was able to read, it seems like the most important things you are trying to accomplish are.... What have I missed?"
- Ask for help in identifying the links among overall business goals, the specific objectives of the person or unit, what performance looks like, and what capabilities are needed to achieve them.
- Identify the main gaps between current and desired performance. Are there areas in which people lack key skills or capabilities that will make it difficult to achieve the objectives? What one improvement in terms of people's skills or behaviors would most help achieve the objectives?

Follow-up

- Immediately following the interview, summarize what you heard very succinctly in writing.
- Construct and enclose an impact map; it is an excellent way to set out your understanding of the linkages between the results desired and the capabilities needed to support them.
- Send a thank-you note to the person you interviewed and include a copy of your summary ("Thank you very much for your time. I found our discussion very helpful and enlightening. I have attached a brief summary of the key points. Please let me know if I missed or misunderstood anything").
- The purpose is fourfold:
  1. Summarizing your notes will encourage you to reflect on what you have learned and better cement it in your memory.
  2. The document will be a useful reference as the planning process proceeds.
  3. Your summary acknowledges that you valued the person's time and input.
  4. Finally, sharing your summary with the person you interviewed provides him or her with the opportunity to correct any oversights or misunderstandings, which will help you create a superior solution.

needs of the business and help line leaders deliver results, it will have strong support, even in the face of financial exigencies (see From the Top: Ray Vigil).

•
_____

From the Top: Ray Vigil, Chief Learning Officer, Humana, Inc.
Ray Vigil is the chief learning officer for Humana, Inc. Health care is a rapidly changing industry that places unprecedented demands on its leaders. Skills and approaches that were successful in the past are no longer adequate; new leadership competencies and insights are needed. Vigil explains how the leadership development strategy must be an integral part of the overall business strategy and how it must begin with the end in mind. Because these conditions have been met at Humana, the Leadership Institute is viewed by the top management as an important enterprisewide tool with tremendous positive business impact.

"The CEO wanted to take a very traditional company and move to a consumer-centric point of view, approaching problems and the industry very differently, so that we produced competitive advantage by a disruptive change strategy in the way we go to market. But historically, leaders in health care have not had the same kind of leadership development focus that other industries have had. So, the big challenge we had initially was how to take a management team that had been successful with very traditional functional skills and get them to realize that they needed to embrace a very different vision; they had to develop the capability to work across the enterprise, not just in their function.

"Our CEO had been working with the senior leadership team to develop an enlightened view and a strategy for becoming a consumer-centric company. While leaders understood the strategy intellectually, they were having difficulty understanding what they had to *do differently.*

"Most people would say, 'Gee, if you understand something, it ought to be obvious that you take action on it.' But I think it is a very big challenge for people to *execute* a strategy that is very different from the mindset and skills that brought them success in the past.

"From the beginning, when our CEO said, 'I know I need a chief learning officer,' I interpreted that to mean that he had a business strategy that was going to require a great deal of change leadership, and he needed a learning strategy to complement the business strategy. I was able to convince my team that we needed to think about what we were doing in a strategic sense. We needed to really drill down on where the CEO wanted to take the business and what it was going to take to get us there. What did the future state look like?

How do you implement and execute that strategy with the human capital we have?

"We devised something we called the touch-point program to identify the key intersections, the key leverage points with the organization that could make a difference. We identified the key stakeholders and made them part of the design team. They helped us design the whole process, including the evaluation and after-action review. When it came time to implement, everybody was shocked that there was such great acceptance, but that was because we had identified the key leverage points and through the touch-point campaign had incorporated their interests and thinking into the program. Because we started with an outcome of use and what the end state was supposed to look like, we were able to integrate all the pieces into a coherent strategy and an integrated experience for the participants."

•

APPLY MARKETING PRINCIPLES

Most likely, market research on learning needs will discover a target-rich environment—a large number of situations in which learning and development could contribute to the success of the enterprise. By no means should all of these be pursued. Learning and development organizations need to pick their targets carefully. No enterprise has sufficient resources to pursue every market opportunity; no learning and development group can take on all the potential teaching opportunities. The more limited your resources, the more important it is to target your efforts where they will produce the greatest return.

Segment and Target

Targeting educational efforts is analogous to targeting marketing campaigns. Successful marketers understand that all customers are not created equal. Customers' circumstances differ, their needs differ, as do their definitions of quality, willingness to pay, and how much it costs to serve them.

Marketers divide potential customers into *segments* according to what kind of product, service, or offer it takes to satisfy their needs. For example, the circumstances of a young family with children are very different from those of a successful executive with an "empty nest." As a result, the features that the young family values (is willing and able to pay for) in a car will be very different from the features sought by the corporate executive with grown children. The executive is unlikely to be in the market for a seven-seat minivan with juice-box holders, and the young family isn't going to buy an expensive, red, two-seat convertible.

Groups of customers that share similar circumstances, needs, and perceptions of value constitute a market segment; those with different needs and values form a different segment. Every market has multiple segments; no one product or service can satisfy them all. The key to success is to target the most attractive market segments with an offer that matches their circumstances and needs. Attractive segments are those who are large enough to support the organization's ambition, need the product or services, and perceive sufficient value to overcome the price barrier.

Customers who place little value on the product or service, are expensive to reach, impossible to satisfy, or unable to pay are unattractive segments and should be avoided. Trying to capture 100 percent of potential customers results in a Pyrrhic victory; the cost of winning some customers is so great as to be worse than a loss.

Learning and development needs to segment its potential customers by circumstance, need, value perceived, and ability to pay in the same way that the marketing department segments the company's customers. Picking the right problem means targeting finite resources where learning and development has the best opportunity to make a significant contribution. It means saying "no" to lesser opportunities and being prepared to defend the selection criteria—another place in which a joint advisory council or steering committee can be invaluable.

Is Training the Answer?

Not every problem is amenable to training. Indeed, as Senge (1990) showed in *The Fifth Discipline,* most business problems are system problems and require systemic approaches. One of the most common reasons that training fails to deliver satisfactory business results is that the problem was not a training issue in the first place (Phillips & Phillips, 2002). If the productivity of customer support personnel is low because the customer support software is slow and unreliable, no amount of training will noticeably improve the situation; better results will be achieved by expending resources to upgrade the software, equipment, or both. If, on the other hand, productivity is low because individuals do not know how to use the software efficiently or take advantage of shortcuts, the right training can produce a significant improvement.

Even when training is clearly *part* of the solution, it is rarely *all* of the solution. In the next chapter (D2), we will consider the criticality of designing the complete experience, which includes the systems and environmental factors that affect the success or failure of a program to deliver its objectives. Because learning and development is increasingly being held accountable for return on investment, it must work with line management to understand and optimize *all* of the factors that contribute to success and it must eschew assignments in which training is not the best answer.

MANAGE EXPECTATIONS

People buy products on the promise of desired outcomes. People do not buy quarter-inch drills; they buy the expectation of making quarter-inch holes. Management doesn't (or shouldn't) buy courses; they buy the expectation of improved performance. Whether or not they are satisfied with their purchase depends on the relationship between their expectations and the actual outcome. Therefore, learning and development organizations need to manage the expectations of their customers to ensure that expectations are in line with what can be realistically delivered.

Exactly the same level of performance will produce delight in one customer whose expectations were low and dissatisfaction in another whose expectations were high. Consider your own reaction to exactly the same meal if it were served to you in a modest diner for $9.95 or in the Plaza for $49.95. In the first case you would be delighted; in the latter, disappointed.

Those who decide how much to invest in learning and development will do so based on their anticipation of the value it will deliver. As with the restaurant example above, the greater the cost, the higher the expectation and the greater the benefit required for the purchasers to feel they have gotten their money's worth. The challenge for learning and development—as for anyone selling a product—is to promise enough to get the order but not so much that it cannot be delivered. And the best way to find the right balance is to agree in advance on the measures of success.

Agree on What Defines Success

Sporting events are fun to watch because everyone knows the rules, how points are scored, and what "winning" means. No one would pay to attend a football game if the rules for scoring were decided after the game was over or winning was based on which team enjoyed the game more. Likewise, learning and development can never truly claim success if the goalposts are not defined, fixed in position, and agreed to in advance. Management and the learning organization need to work together to define the "Conditions of Satisfaction" (see Exhibit D1.3).

Exhibit D1.3. Conditions of Satisfaction.

Richard Leider is a consultant and award-winning coauthor of *Whistle While You Work* and *Claiming Your Place at the Fire*. When asked about the importance of defining objectives, he said: "We teach leaders how to create what we call COS—conditions of satisfaction.

"What are your conditions of satisfaction? What is it that we are supposed to do differently after this and by when? What is it that you want delivered by when? Or created by when? You could call it accountability, but when leaders lead, they are customers. For leadership development, the line leader is a customer. She makes a request, she puts out certain conditions of satisfaction. And so this whole notion of leader as customer translates into the training, and therefore the follow-up practice; leaders have certain conditions of satisfaction for training.

"So often leaders are not clear about their conditions of satisfaction. There is a certain language and a certain rigor that leaders need to learn in order for meetings and training and transactions to be effective. It really clears up all that murkiness. You could say it is common sense; well, the fact is—look where the breakdowns are."

A good commission plan drives sales behavior because it spells out how salespeople can increase their financial success. Contracts include specified performance levels to avoid future disagreement about deliverables. In drug development, the evidence required to support a specific claim is agreed upon with the FDA *in advance* of clinical studies. Management by objectives is effective when individuals meet with their manager to define goals that are specific, measurable, achievable, relevant, time-bound, and agreed to in advance.

The objectives for a learning and development initiative should be no different. The promised results *and the way in which they will be measured* should be agreed to as part of the design, not as an afterthought. Only then do those responsible for implementation have the opportunity to excel.

Best the Competition

For companies to succeed, they need to ensure that the products and services they deliver provide more value for the money than the competitors'. For learning and development, the alternatives include not only other providers and delivery systems but also the lowest-cost and most serious competitor of all: "non-use," that is, no training at all. Learning and development organizations must demonstrate that they deliver substantially more value than no training at all, or it will continue to be the competitor of choice in times of fiscal restraint.

•

Case Study: British Broadcasting Company

When Nigel Paine took over as the director of training for the BBC, he discovered that the company was investing £1.5 million a year in executive education of one sort or another. But when he searched all the available records, he could find no evidence of return on investment (Paige, 2003). People who attended such programs did not necessarily advance more quickly, stay with the firm longer, or generate more business value. There seemed to be no rationale for why some employees were sent to training programs and others not, no explicit expectations of what would be gained, no follow-through. Therefore, he placed a moratorium on all educational spending.

Needless to say, there was a great hue and cry among providers, both internal and external. But no one, however, could present evidence that their solution provided more value than the alternative of doing nothing. One and a half million pounds is real money, even for a corporation the size of the BBC. An investment of that magnitude will and should be scrutinized. Management has a fiduciary responsibility to be sure that an investment in learning and development is the best possible use of the money and that it could not be more profitably deployed elsewhere.

This is a key point with respect to the first discipline of defining outcomes: learning and development programs compete for resources not only with alternative educational providers and formats, but also with other departments and other uses for the money. Canceling a £1.5 million expenditure, for example, drops £1.5 million straight to the bottom line. Learning and development leaders are at task to show how shareholders are better served by investing the £1.5 million in learning and development rather than having it reported as profit and paid out as dividends. To do that, learning and development must concentrate on issues and needs with the highest potential payout, define the outcomes in business terms, and develop a clear "line of sight" between the program, the capabilities participants will gain, the new behaviors they will practice, and the results these will produce.

•

SUMMARY

The first, crucial, and frequently overlooked step in successful learning and development is to define expected results in business terms. The most successful programs begin by identifying the highest value needs of the business that training can address. They define the outcomes that can be expected from an educational program and communicate them to the key stakeholders in the language of business. They agree in advance on the measures of success and then design the program and follow-through environment to overdeliver on the promise.

If this first critical discipline is skipped—if program designers fail to define expected results in business terms—no amount of effort in subsequent stages will fully compensate; the future of the program, and perhaps the company itself, will be at risk.

•

ACTION POINTS

For Learning Leaders

- Never offer a program simply because you were asked to offer a program.
- Always ask, *Why? What is the benefit to the company?*
  - If you do not clearly understand the business need and the linkage between the training and filling the need, you cannot possibly design an effective intervention.
  - Stand your ground when you do not believe training is the solution or when training will fail unless accompanied by concomitant changes in systems, rewards, and so forth. Use the power of your expertise.
- Read and understand the business plan. Be proactive in identifying areas in which learning and development could contribute.
  - Test your ideas with discerning line leaders. Make them your allies.
- Once you have decided to address an appropriate need with training, negotiate a clear "contract" with management that specifies *in advance* the objectives, methods, and how success will be measured.
- Review all the programs for which your group is responsible to be sure each has a set of objectives that are credibly linked to business imperatives.

- Be proactive in managing the training portfolio; propose to management realignment or even reduction of resources if appropriate.

For Line Leaders

- Review the key learning and development initiatives in the business unit for which you are responsible.
  - Are they clearly aligned with the most pressing needs of the business?
  - Are there critical needs that are not being addressed?
  - Are time and resources being spent on worthwhile but lesser-value issues?
- If you conclude that the current learning and development initiatives are not aligned with the most important needs of your business, you and the learning leader share the responsibility for ensuring that they are.
- Write down the business need that you would really like to see learning and development address and the results you want. Then schedule a discussion with the head of learning and development.
- Ask whether it is possible to address your needs with training. (Keep in mind that many issues in business are systems or process issues that cannot be solved by training or can be solved more quickly and less expensively in other ways. If the head of your learning organization is any good, he or she will tell you whether it is realistic to try to achieve the results you want through training.)
- Work through Figure D1.5 with the head of learning and development.
  - Agree on the behavioral changes that are needed to achieve your objective and how they can be assessed.
  - Ask learning and development to propose a plan for achieving these results and review it critically, using the 6Ds as a framework.
  - If necessary, rebalance your learning and development portfolio to redirect resources to the initiatives with the greatest potential payoff.

D2

DESIGN THE COMPLETE EXPERIENCE

The only competitive advantage the company of the future will have is its managers' ability to learn faster than their competitors.

—Arie de Geus

COMPETITION IN VIRTUALLY EVERY field is now global and accelerating, and knowledge workers in developed countries must now compete for jobs with workers throughout the world, as Friedman (2005) points out so powerfully in his landmark book, *The World Is Flat.* The pace of technological, environmental, social, and economic change has made "learning agility"—the ability to learn, unlearn, and relearn rapidly—a critical survival skill for both companies and individuals. Learning and performance go hand in hand; business units that learn rapidly outperform those that learn and develop at a slower pace (Wick & Leon, 1993).

Therefore, investing in learning makes sense. But learning is not an event, it is a process as John Alexander, president of the Center for Creative Leadership, likes to say (see From the Top: John Alexander). It is a process that takes place over time in the challenging business environment, replete with competing priorities and time pressures. Breakthrough learning and development organizations acknowledge this reality by practicing the second discipline: they design and manage the *complete experience,* not just what happens during the period of instruction.

In this chapter we examine what it means to think holistically and systematically about the learning experience—to actively manage what happens before as well as after the traditional boundaries of corporate education—and the benefits that accrue by doing so. We focus on

- Many factors influence outcomes
- A new paradigm
- The three phases of corporate learning
- Evaluation
- Check for completeness
- Action points for learning and line leaders

•

From the Top: John Alexander, Center for Creative Leadership, on Learning as a Process
John Alexander is the president of the Center for Creative Leadership (CCL®), which is ranked among the overall Top 10 providers of executive education worldwide by the *Financial Times*. He spoke about the importance of regarding learning as a process that takes place over time and requires feedback.

"'Learning is a process and not an event' is something that we believe in, based on our research and experience. It is the way we learn as adults. You get an idea and you try it out. Then you need feedback about how it went. You make adjustments, try again, and then get more feedback.

"Our original research showed that some of the most powerful learning you can have is from your own experience, whether in your job or in your personal life. This kind of learning happens over time and, therefore, is a process. We like to teach here that good leaders are good learners. You learn best by putting your ideas into action and then asking for feedback. It may begin with a burst of insight, but you still have to test out your assumptions and get feedback. That is why it is important to take the time for learning and to take action to try new things. Otherwise, you don't change and you don't get better.

"The ability to learn from experience makes leaders far more effective. The more they try out and test out their ideas, the more effective they will be. A lot of what we do here at CCL is to help leaders get better. That is our goal.

"We have been helping people improve the way they learn for many years. Preparatory work is standard in our programs so the process starts before they even get to our classrooms. Then it is extended after the session with coaching by telephone and increasingly the Internet.

"In our customized programs we work with people over time by using action-learning techniques. We extend the learning by using a project sanctioned back home. Then participants come back and do a check-in. We have cohorts that last many months. It is about deepening the learning and extending the learning journey to make it more impactful.

"We also use other means, such as *Friday5s*, content on our website, CCL publications, and guidebooks to reinforce what happens in the classroom. We have alumni gatherings to bring people back together for a refresher—to recharge their spirits and replenish their energy, to think about their goals and how they are doing.

"My advice to people who want to facilitate learning is to put yourself in the shoes of the learner. Ask the question, 'If I were in the class or learning group, what would I want, how would I want to receive information, and how would I want to become a learner?'

"Try to see the learning through the eyes of the participant. Ask for suggestions on how to better carry this learning journey forward. Survey individuals to find out what they want. Use a variety of learning techniques. Some like face-to-face activities, some the Internet (particularly younger people). And some need personal time to reflect. I would give them a menu of choices about how to learn. One size does not fit all."

•

MANY FACTORS INFLUENCE OUTCOMES

What a person takes away from a given learning experience is shaped by many things, including prior knowledge and life experiences, belief structure, natural learning style, aptitude, and emotional state. Similarly, numerous factors influence the extent to which people subsequently transfer and apply their knowledge, including opportunity, encouragement, reinforcement, and early success (Figure D2.1).

Because the success of corporate learning and development programs (the generation of meaningful business outcomes) requires both learning *and* learning transfer, the design of any such initiative must comprehend the complete learning experience—not just what happens in the formal classroom, e-learning sessions, or simulation. Research has shown that what happens before and after the formal program is as important, if not more important, than what happens in the course itself (Broad, 2005, p. 82–93).

Figure D2.1. A Few of the Many Factors That Compose the Learner's Experience and Affect Learning and Learning Transfer and, Therefore, Results. Effective Program Design Takes These into Account.

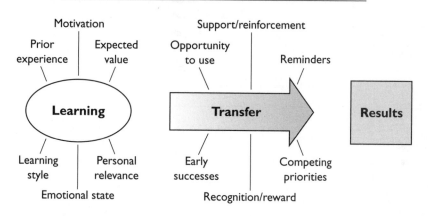

A NEW PARADIGM

The classroom, or its electronic equivalent, is a box, both literally and figuratively. As long as educators and managers think of learning as only what goes on in the "box," they place artificial limits on both the potential and the return of educational programs. Writing in the *Journal of Organizational Excellence,* Teresa Roche of Agilent Technologies and her colleagues explained: "At Agilent, every department is expected to innovate, learn continuously, and deliver bottom-line results. Global Learning and Leadership Development knew it could not fulfill these expectations simply by delivering traditional programs in traditional ways—no matter how high the end-of-course ratings. To reap the full benefits of corporate training investments, it needed to broaden its perspectives about when, where, and how learning occurs" (Roche, Wick, & Stewart, 2005, p. 46).

Broad and Newstrom (1992) introduced a key concept: the transfer matrix. They defined three periods—before, during, and after the program—and three learning partners: the manager, the trainer, and the trainee (Figure D2.2). The matrix was an important step forward in that it challenged organizations to think more broadly about the learning experience both in terms of time and key influences. It recognized that learning transfer is affected by what happens before and after the program and by interactions with managers and others, in addition to interactions between learners and instructors.

Figure D2.2. The Transfer Matrix:
Transfer Partners and Time Periods.

Partners	Time Periods		
	Before	During	After
Managers			
Trainer			
Trainee			

Source: *Adapted from Broad and Newstrom (1992). Used with permission.*

Subsequent work has refined the model. It now recognizes that many other stakeholders, in addition to the manager and trainer, significantly influence both learning and learning transfer (Broad, 2005, pp. 29–30). The support or lack of support from peers, direct reports, executives, and others influences participants' attitudes toward learning and its subsequent use, as does the overall climate and culture of the organization. The impact of such influences, though outside the traditional role of learning and development, needs to be considered as part of the overall design and managed to maximize program effectiveness.

The International Society for Performance Improvement (ISPI), for example, calls specific attention to the need to think holistically and systemically about human resources interventions in its standards for Human Performance Technology: "Taking a systems view is vital, because organizations are very complex systems that affect the performance of the individuals that work within them. . . . A systems approach considers the larger environment that impacts processes and other work" (ISPI, 2002, p. 3).

THREE PHASES OF CORPORATE LEARNING

Traditionally, the phases of corporate learning and development were described as "before," "during," and "after" training. There is a growing trend, which we support, to replace these terms, since they place undue emphasis on the training-event portion of the overall learning process. Pfizer refers to the three phases of its Advanced Transition program as the "on-ramp," "residential," and "on-the-job application" phases (Blee, Bonito, & Tucker, 2005, pp. 261–264). Programs such as Cisco's Strategic Leader program, Unilever's Leading People for Growth, and Sony's Integrated Leadership Curriculum have begun using the terms

Phase I, Phase II, and Phase III, as have a number of writers (Zenger, Folkman, & Sherwin, 2005) to emphasize that they are simply stages of an ongoing, coordinated learning process.

Likewise, program directors are increasingly adamant about avoiding the term "pre-work" for the learning that needs to occur in Phase I. They argue that the very name "pre-work" suggests that it is not real work and therefore not that important to complete. Yet in a properly designed program, completing the Phase I learning exercises is essential to participate fully and extract maximum value from the rest of the program; hence the concern about finding a less pejorative term.

In the subsequent discussion, we adopt the three-phase model and the neutral terms Phase I, Phase II, and Phase III. Although these terms are not very catchy or memorable, they have the advantage of being broadly applicable to a wide range of program types, delivery formats, and objectives. As the three-phase model is not yet in widespread use, we append the course-centric terms "before, during, and after" to provide links to earlier work. For each phase, we examine the evidence of its importance and provide suggestions for strengthening it as part of "designing the complete experience."

PHASE I

What participants take away from a learning and development program, what they are able to transfer, and therefore ultimately the results they are able to achieve, are influenced by what happens during the Phase I preparatory period, long before the formal coursework begins. This is true even for programs that have no specific Phase I assignments. The participants' prior education and experience form the foundation on which to build new capabilities; their expectations of the program—and their managers' expectations of them—set the bar.

Expectations Influence Outcomes

Participants do not arrive at corporate educational programs like blank sheets of paper. They come with opinions, biases, and expectations. They may have read about the program in a course catalog or online and may have formed an opinion; they probably heard something about it from colleagues who have already attended. Even if the course is being offered for the first time, they will have expectations based on their experiences with similar courses in the past. And their opinions will be strongly influenced by their managers' level of interest or indifference.

Whatever the sources of influence, participants enter learning and development programs with (often strong) preconceived notions about the value they will derive. These "going-in" opinions cannot be ignored because, to a surprising extent, they are self-fulfilling prophecies. Participants get out of a program pretty much what they presume they will. That is, if they expect it to be a high-value, worthwhile learning experience, then that is usually what they experience. If they expect it to be a waste of time, it almost always is, for them. Two participants who come to the same program with very different expectations will have very different experiences and leave with very different perceptions of the value they received (Figure D2.3).

Figure D2.3. The Experience of Different Participants in the Same Program Is Strongly Influenced by Their Assumptions Going In.

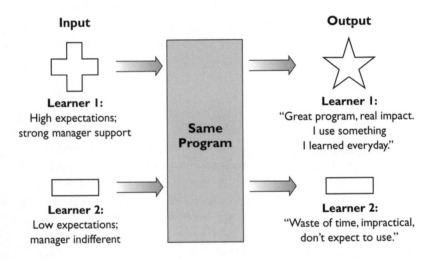

Input

Output

Learner 1:
High expectations;
strong manager support

Same Program

Learner 1:
"Great program, real impact.
I use something
I learned everyday."

Learner 2:
Low expectations;
manager indifferent

Learner 2:
"Waste of time, impractical,
don't expect to use."

This phenomenon is so strong that learning and development planners ignore it at their peril. That is not to say that a great program cannot convert the skeptics, or that a truly awful program will not disillusion even "true believers." But it is much easier to achieve business results when people enter programs with high expectations of value and learning intentionality because they know they will be held accountable for results. Thus, designing the complete experience (D2) involves managing the expectations and shared knowledge created in Phase I—before what has traditionally been considered the start of the program.

Influence of the Manager in Phase I

When Broad and Newstrom (1992) polled trainers about which time-role combinations had the greatest impact on training, they concluded that the manager's involvement in Phase I *prior to the formal course-work* was the single most powerful influence on whether learning transfer would occur. This perception has been confirmed by others. For example, Brinkerhoff and Montesino (1995) found that participants who had discussion with their managers before and after training reported significantly higher levels of skill application and felt more accountable for applying new learning. (See From The Top: Kevin Wilde).

Feldstein and Boothman (1997) compared high- and low-performance learners and identified eight factors that characterized high-performance learners. Half of these were related to the influence of the manager. For example, 75 percent of the high-performance learners reported that their supervisors had expectations of improved performance following training, whereas only 25 percent of low-performers did. In a follow-up study, a system was implemented to increase the pre- and postcourse interaction with managers. The result was that both the learners and their managers reported much higher rates of transfer.

•
_____

**From the Top: Kevin Wilde, Chief Learning Officer
for General Mills**
Kevin Wilde, chief learning officer for General Mills, underscored the importance of Phase I and manager involvement: "You need to prepare the students much more before the program. You need to inform the manager of the participant what is going on and you have to clearly indicate that the classroom piece is a small part of what we are expecting.

"We looked at our Management Institute and did a series of follow-up studies. We surveyed participants as well as the participants' managers to determine whether we achieved the specific objectives of the program. We looked at the data to see which ones improved and which ones did not.

"One of the things we do now is put a conference call on the front end, two to four weeks before the program and we mandate that all participants of the upcoming course attend it. I have a consultant or program manager preview the program and go through the pre-work. More importantly, we send the signal that we want them to integrate it and make it part of their job follow-up.

"We also send documents and a letter to the manager on what the program is about and how they can reinforce the learning of the program. We do a follow-up conference call with the participants thirty to sixty days later. How are you doing in your learning? What is working? What more help do you need? How are you doing on your project?"

•

Strengthening Phase I

What happens in Phase I is critical in the overall value chain created by learning and development. Three actions are key: ensuring high expectations, laying the groundwork, and engaging managers.

ENSURE HIGH EXPECTATIONS The effectiveness of a program is shaped by the participants' expectations. How they perceive the program—as essential for their success, as a reward, a mini-vacation, or a waste of time—influences how seriously they approach it and therefore its chance of success.

Corporate education can ensure higher expectations by applying marketing principles when communicating its programs to potential participants and their managers. Marketing departments spend a great deal of their time and money worrying about their product's *positioning*—what customers think when they hear the product's name. Which ideas do they hope will spring into a prospect's mind? Innovative? High-quality? Sexy? Time-saving? Strong brands like Coca-Cola®, Crest®, Lexus®, and LaserJet® have strong positions. Their key attributes come immediately to mind; shape perceptions of value, price, and alternatives; and influence buying decisions. An effective marketing organization uses all the communication vehicles at its disposal to ensure that the desired brand attributes become firmly embedded in prospective customers' psyches.

We believe that corporate education can do a much better job of marketing its offerings by developing strong "brands" that are perceived as integral to the business and essential to one's career. These efforts will pay dividends: a program that is perceived to be vital and integral to the corporate strategy has a greater chance of success than one that is perceived as a reward, a human resources initiative, or yet another "flavor of the month" from management. Building a strong, credible, and trusted brand takes time, effort, and consistency, but the payback is significant.

SECURE EFFECTIVE MANAGEMENT SUPPORT Strong management support greatly increases the probability of success. Employees at all levels are pressed for time. Overwhelmed by competing priorities, they look to their managers for indications of what is most important, and then apportion their efforts accordingly. If they perceive that a program has strong managerial support, it will get more effort and attention. If management appears indifferent or skeptical about the value of the training, attendees will spend the minimum possible amount of time and effort in all three phases.

Therefore, securing visible managerial support at all levels is a crucial task of Phase I. Ensuring that participants know, feel, and believe in management's support is crucial to maximize the return on educational investments. Obviously, credible support is easier to recruit and sustain if the first discipline—defining the outcomes in business terms—is followed. Line managers will be more willing to have their people attend and be more supportive of application if they are consulted during the program's creation, feel they have ownership of its objectives, and can see that their needs are being addressed. At Humana, for example, line leaders are part of the design team; Sony includes senior line leaders on its Talent Management Council; 3M's top management drove its leadership initiative.

Louis Carter, founder and president of the Best Practice Institute, recently completed a study of organizations that achieved sustainable results from leadership and development. Over a hundred interviews were conducted. Support and participation of senior management was the highest ranking critical success factor (Carter, Ulrich and Goldsmith, 2005, p. 421). "The Best Practice Companies' internal role models are managers who are teachers," said Carter (Carter, interview). Critical senior leadership behaviors for success identified in the Best Practice Institute study (Carter, Ulrich, & Goldsmith, 2005, p. 444) included

- Allocating funds for the initiative
- Modeling behavior consistent with strategy
- Integrating the initiative into the strategic plan
- Facilitating education or training

Support needs to go beyond words. If a learning and development program is to be effective in bringing about organizational change, the most senior and most visible leadership must model its precepts. Senior

managers need to complete the program themselves, embrace its principles, use the recommended approaches to management, and incorporate
specific concepts from the program in their day-to-day activities. If they
do not, they seriously undermine the program's impact and education's
credibility (see Case Study: When the Video Doesn't Match the Audio).

•

Case Study: When the Video Doesn't Match the Audio
A biotechnology firm had experienced dramatic growth over a number of years. Managers had been rapidly promoted as the business
grew but with very little formal management training and, because
of the pace of growth, limited on-the-job experience and mentoring.

As a result, most middle managers led by the seat of their pants,
mimicking the entrepreneurial style of the founder. The company encountered market turbulence, its stock dropped precipitously, and senior management realized that the lack of professional management
was a serious impediment to continued prosperity. They had human
resources design and implement a five-day program to help managers
increase the efficiency of teamwork, foster innovation, and improve
efficiency and ownership through delegation.

The senior management team strongly endorsed the program and
made stirring speeches about its importance for the future of the
company. When it came time to attend themselves, however, they
asked organizational development to put together a special half-day
"executive edition" that had neither preparatory work nor follow-
through. They were "too busy" to attend the full program.

The result was predictable. The senior managers never mastered the
material. They failed to incorporate the processes or terminology into
their own leadership. So, for example, while middle managers were
exhorted to expand creative thinking by conducting brainstorming sessions in a particular way, their own managers failed to do so.

In fact, the actions of the company's senior leaders failed to reinforce any of the program's concepts or principles. Needless to say,
the program failed to create the hoped-for change or generate a return on investment. Indeed, the "do as I say, not as I do" attitude of
the senior leaders not only undermined the program's effectiveness,
it also contributed to cynicism among middle managers regarding
both the senior leadership and the value of training and development.

•

Finally, the reward and recognition structures must be in alignment:
"It is top management, through the organizational climate or reward
structure it creates, that is *really* doing the training, regardless of what

the training staff does. The training administered by the training staff 'sticks' only if it coincides with what top management is teaching every day" (Mosel, 1957, emphasis in original).

The bottom line is that learning and development programs must have wholehearted support from the most influential leaders in the organization before they are launched. The support must go beyond rhetoric; managers of attendees must be prepared to support the program *in action* by using the concepts, tools, and methods themselves and by ensuring that their subordinates do so. If senior managers are unwilling to make the commitment to provide this level of support, the whole premise of the program needs to be reexamined. Designers need to question whether they have truly defined their company's most pressing needs and developed a program to address them. Launching a program in the absence of strong management support undermines its probability of success and potentially damages the overall educational effort.

SET THE EXPECTATION FOR FOLLOW-THROUGH An important objective of Phase I should be to leave no doubt in participants' minds about what management expects from them. They should come to the course with the clear understanding that the *privilege* of attending an educational program carries with it the *responsibility* to follow through by applying, improving, teaching, and producing evidence that the investment in them was a sound one. At Honeywell, for example, Jim O'Hern, director of leadership development, challenges the participants in the Strategic Leadership program "to leave a legacy" of results as an example to subsequent generations of participant leaders (O'Hern, interview).

In subsequent chapters, we discuss specific ways to facilitate follow-through, transfer, and application. All these methods are more effective, however, when the expectation for follow-through has been clearly established at the beginning. Ideally, follow-through should be part of the corporate culture, what Bossidy and Charan (2002) call a "culture of execution." Everyone should understand, without having to be told, that they will be expected to follow through on the investment in their education, just as they do on business objectives.

Imagine the quantum jump in performance that would result if everyone who attended a development program knew that they would be expected to learn as much as possible and prove it by putting the new learning to work. Imagine the change in mindset of participants if the last item on every course agenda was "begin transfer and application" instead of the typical "program ends" or "adjourn."

The real work begins when the formal instruction ends. How to make that expectation clear is part of designing the complete experience; the time to set the expectation is early in Phase I.

GET THE RIGHT PEOPLE INTO THE ROOM A key difference between teaching adults and teaching children is that adult learners bring much richer and more varied experiences to their education. These experiences are a powerful framework on which to build and a source of practical examples and real-world knowledge. Helping participants draw on and extend their experience and share their lessons learned are important precepts of adult education.

The very richness and variety of experience, however, presents a significant challenge for corporate educators. In high school or even college, educators can assume a much more homogenous set of experiences and educational backgrounds. In corporate education, however, groups frequently include learners who differ widely in age, years of experience, educational background, work histories, and, in an increasingly global marketplace, even mother tongue. Although this diversity offers fertile ground for discussion and insight, it also increases the difficulty of delivering an effective learning experience. Designing the complete learning experience, then, includes defining the background participants need to have to benefit from the program, as well as the Phase I learning needed to establish a common foundation.

In academic universities, upper level courses have clearly established prerequisites for enrollment, such as, "students must have successfully completed calculus 101." This is much less frequent in corporate universities and executive education programs at business schools—perhaps for fear of limiting enrollment. The danger of having no prerequisites, however, is that the program must necessarily be taught at the "one-size-fits-all" level with the result that the program fits no one perfectly—too elementary for some and too advanced for others.

Recognizing this dilemma, a number of companies are moving toward courses offered in sequence. This allows them to offer introductory courses to those new to a field or leadership pipeline level, as well as advanced programs that explore topics in greater depth. For example, Hewlett-Packard offered Dynamic Leadership I and Dynamic Leadership II. Pfizer's Learning Center structured its introduction to leadership for first-line managers into the "Leading Edge," followed nine to twelve months later by a more in-depth program called "Sharpening the Edge." Unilever has a five-part leadership series, and Sony has a four-level Integrated Leadership Curriculum modeled after the phases of *The Leadership Pipeline* (Charan, Drotter, & Noel, 2001).

Corporate educators can better meet the needs of their learners and take advanced programs to much higher levels of excellence by dividing learning and development into sequential programs with prerequisites. Prerequisites might include specific coursework but should also encompass specific work experiences, such as having led a project team or managed those who manage others. The shift toward measuring outcomes instead of activity will encourage training programs to define and set requirements, since allowing the wrong people to attend a program will dilute its effectiveness and ability to produce results.

GET PEOPLE ONTO THE SAME PAGE In general, the more preparation before a learning experience, the better. Preparation allows the instructors to go further and faster. But the amount of preparation to get people on the same page must be weighed against the time available. If there are too many assignments to complete, or more reading than can reasonably be done by managers who already have more than full-time jobs, the value of the preparation will be diminished. The time pressures acting against completing the Phase I preparation must be counterbalanced by incentives for completing it and by persuasion regarding its value. Here are some tips from best practice companies.

If participants are expected to complete reading or other assignments in Phase I, it is incumbent upon the instructors to make good and explicit use of them in Phase II—ideally in such a way that those who did not do the assignments wish they had. If Phase II is structured in such a way that completing the preparatory work makes the program much more valuable (or if the lack of preparation becomes embarrassingly obvious), the whole organization soon learns this. Subsequent groups will be better prepared, having gotten the word to be sure to do the homework. This is just like the reputation that specific courses and professors acquire in college. ("She is a great professor, but don't go to class if you haven't done the reading.")

Preparing learners to maximize course time in Phase II needn't be confined simply to reading assignments. The range of potential experiences is much richer. Think beyond traditional reading assignments to more experiential learning. For example, have learners interview a number of customers and record their perceptions, spend time in manufacturing or customer service, interview leaders of other divisions about successes or failures in collaboration, visit a competitor's store, or work with the competitor's products. Take advantage of technology and have participants work through an online simulation, assessment, or other e-learning module. Look for opportunities to stimulate their imagination or shake them out of their current comfort zone. One organization we worked with challenged its marketing managers to spend just two hours on the phone as a customer service representative trying to explain sales incentive programs. It was a real eye-opener: they came away with a whole new perspective and a commitment to design offers that were easier to explain.

There are so many interesting and innovative Phase I learning opportunities that the challenge is not to get carried away. Program designers need to weigh the time required to complete Phase I against the value delivered. A leadership transition program at one company had eight Phase I assignments that included reading a complete book and conducting a half dozen interviews. Needless to say, when surveyed, participants indicated that they rarely completed all of the scheduled activities. Assignments need to respect the time pressures of today's business environment; every minute spent needs to add value. Do not, for example, ask people to read an entire business book. Few have time, and the size of the task alone will deter some from starting. Identify the sections that will be discussed and assign those only.

Phase I work, no matter how relevant and well-focused, produces no learning unless it is done. Therefore, designing the complete experience includes designing incentives to help ensure that preparation is completed and its importance is appreciated. Here again, managerial support is vital. The managers of participants need to be aware of what preparation is expected and buy into its importance. Ideally, they ought to meet with their direct reports before they attend to discuss the preparatory exercises, goals for attending the program, and expectations for outcomes.

As a step in this direction, many companies now require the manager to approve attendance at educational programs. Some go further and encourage the participant and manager to sign a learning contract in which both agree, in advance, on the key learning objectives and how progress will be assessed—similar to performance management (management by objectives) for business initiatives. In the learning contract, the manager also makes a commitment: to provide ongoing advice and support as needed to achieve the agreed-upon goals. Where such contracts are taken seriously, all three phases of the program are enhanced.

There is also a role for technology in Phase I. Many 360-degree feedback instruments are now available online. Pfizer, as part of its Advance Transition program, has participants complete a unique leadership assessment survey to establish a baseline for transition performance (Blee, Bonito, & Tucker, 2005, p. 261). Advance Transition also includes a Web-based system to facilitate and collect Phase I learning, which is then used in the opening session.

Cisco Systems has adapted the *DevelopmentEngine*® follow-through management system for use in Phase I of its Emerging Leadership and Global Leadership programs. The system is set up to provide automated reminders about the preparatory assignments far enough in advance to facilitate their completion. Reminders have proven especially useful for assignments that cannot be done at the last minute, such as having participants define learning objectives jointly with their managers, interview a senior leader, or listen to customer service calls. (In programs without Phase I reminders, some participants inevitably postpone their preparation until the last minute—about as productive as trying to read *War and Peace* the night before a final in a Russian literature class.)

Participants are asked to record the insights from their Phase I preparation in a shared learning space. Instructors are able to access the database to review the results and select relevant examples for use in Phase II of the program. The shared visibility (the author of each entry is identified) provides clear accountability; it is apparent to everyone in the program who did, and did not, complete the preparation required. The use of group-specific examples during Phase II adds relevance and credibility to the content.

PHASE II: THE COURSE

We discuss Phase II (the *course* or structured education) in detail in the next chapter. In terms of planning the complete experience, the critical issue in Phase II is to ensure complete congruence between the desired business outcomes and the planned learning experiences. In other words, there should be a "golden thread" that links every course activity to one or more of the expected business outcomes.

Link Tactics to Strategy

One way to construct an explicit chain of inference is to ask a series of if-then statements beginning with the end in mind and working back to the kind of learning exercises needed (Exhibit D2.1). That is, *if* this is the outcome we are trying to achieve, *then* what do employees need to do to achieve it? If they are going to be able to do these things, what knowledge, skills, and attitudes do they need to have? If they are to become proficient in a particular skill, then what sort of learning experiences do they need? Finally, if these are the kinds of learning experiences required, then which are best accomplished in Phase I, which in Phase II, and which in Phase III?

Exhibit D2.1. Example of a Strategy Tree for Converting Impact Maps into Learning Exercises (from *What* to *How*).

IF we want to increase sales,

 _THEN our sales managers need to do a better job of coaching.

  _IF our sales managers are going to do a better job of coaching,

   _THEN they need to see what good coaching looks like and practice it with guidance.

    _IF they are going to practice it with guidance,

    _THEN we need to schedule time in the training session for practice in front of a skilled coach of coaches.

Each IF-THEN pair states what needs to happen (THEN) to accomplish a desired outcome (IF). Arrayed this way the business purpose of each exercise is clear, as is the logic of the program design. Obviously, there are many possible ways to achieve any given objective (increase sales, for example) but this format makes it clear that if one of the strategies the organization chooses to pursue is to improve coaching, then the specific training strategies and tactics need to be in accord.

This approach to the design of course content has a number of advantages. It ensures that the ultimate business objective is the criterion for weighing what to include and what to leave out. It helps ensure alignment between exercises and the desired behaviors and ways of thinking. In other words, if the goal is to improve strategic planning, and strategic *analysis* is identified as a requisite skill, then merely listening passively to lectures is incongruous with the goal. Participants need to be given the opportunity to practice their analytical skills with expert guidance and feedback.

When learning and development programs are designed this way, it is much easier for participants to see the relevance of what they are learning. The latter is important. As we shall see in the discussion of D3: Deliver for Application, adults learn most effectively when the relevance of what they are learning is clear (Knowles, Holton, & Swanson, 2005). Therefore, make the rationale for each learning exercise readily apparent. It should be possible to explain the decision for including each topic or exercise to learners, managers, sponsors, and other stakeholders in a short series of "so that" statements: "We included a business simulation *so that* you would have the opportunity to practice analyzing strategic alternatives, see the results of your decisions, and get expert feedback *so that* you will be better able to analyze strategic alternatives on-the-job."

Employ Adult Learning Principles

Other important principles for designing Phase II of the complete experience include the following:

- For maximum effectiveness, the three phases of learning must integrate seamlessly. That is, Phase II must use and build on the preparatory learning of Phase I and continue without interruption into the follow-through, transfer, and application period (Phase III). All three phases should be in alignment and mutually supportive; discontinuities undermine effectiveness.

- Support and involvement of respected managers is important in Phase II, just as it is in Phases I and III.

- Phase II must conform to the principles of adult learning. It must address adults' need to understand why they should learn something. Instruction and learning exercises must acknowledge and build on participants' experience and expertise.

- Teaching methods and exercises need to be designed to stimulate the kind of thinking required (analysis, synthesis, empathy) and recognize differences in learning styles.

- Less may be more. Dense-pack education—the tendency to cram every conceivable topic into a program of a few days— compromises the quality of learning and its transferability. It will be of greater benefit to the organization if people leave a program doing a few things well, rather than many things badly.

PHASE III: FOLLOW-THROUGH LEARNING

Enhancing the third phase of learning—follow-through transfer and application—has tremendous potential to enhance the overall effectiveness of corporate education. What does or does not happen in Phase III determines the results. Planning and facilitating follow-through (Phase III) is in everyone's best interest—the individual, the learning and development function, the participant's manager, and the company as a whole. It deserves much greater attention than it has received in the past. Follow-through management is a real breakthrough for improving results from corporate learning.

The Real Work Begins When the Course Ends

The literature on transfer of learning is clear: the postcourse environment has a profound effect on whether learning gets translated into results. Early on, Newstrom (1986) studied the barriers to effective learning transfer. Of the top nine barriers that Newstrom identified, only three were related to the content and delivery of the course, while more than half were related to the postcourse environment and support (Exhibit D2.2). The single greatest barrier to learning transfer was *lack of reinforcement on the job*.

Exhibit D2.2. Impediments to Training Transfer.

Rank	Barrier
1	Lack of reinforcement on the job
2	Interference from immediate (work) environment
3	Nonsupportive organizational culture
4	Trainee's perception of impractical training programs
5	Trainee's perception of irrelevant training content
6	Trainee's discomfort with change and associated effort
7	Separation from inspiration or support of trainer
8	Trainee's perception of poorly designed or delivered training
9	Pressure from peers to resist changes

Source: *Republished with permission, Emerald Group Publishing Limited. www.emeraldinsight.com/jmd.htm.*

Similarly, of the eleven reasons that training fails, as cited by Phillips and Phillips (2002), seven were related to the postcourse environment:

- Training was regarded as an isolated event
- Participants were not held accountable for results
- Failure to prepare the job environment to support transfer
- Management reinforcement and support was missing
- Failure to isolate the effects of training
- Lack of commitment and involvement of executives
- Failure to provide feedback and use information about results

Education Is a Process, Not an Event

Corporate education is not an event, like a play or a concert or three-day cricket match. Instead, it is a *business process* that is expected to yield *business results*. Every process has inputs and outputs. Phase I preparation and Phase II coursework both require significant inputs—investments of time and money by the corporation. Output is generated only by application in Phase III. For a program to be considered a success, the output needs to be sufficiently better than the status quo (had no training occurred) to repay the investment in facilities, trainers, planning, travel, time out of office, and so forth (Figure D2.4).

Figure D2.4. The Cost of Creating and Delivering a Training and Development Program Must Be Offset by Improved Productivity and Business Results. *Learning Transfer* Is the Critical Link Between Inputs and Outputs.

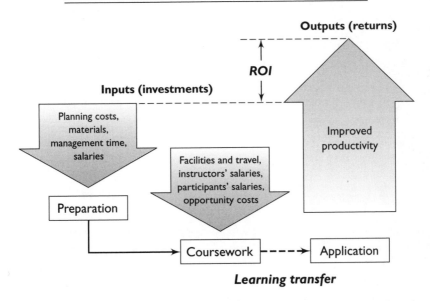

Transfer and application (Phase III) is not something that happens *after* a program; it is *part* of the program, an integral part of the process. Since it is the only phase of the process that generates value to justify the cost, it must not be left to chance or individual initiative. The entire learning process, including follow-through, must be managed from beginning to end like any other business process that is critical to an organization's success. The program doesn't end until the learning is translated into results. If mementoes of achievement are to be distributed, they should be given to participants who successfully complete transfer and application in Phase III, not merely who attended the course. Indeed, the president of Home Depot Canada, Annette Verschuren, did exactly that in her learning forums for store managers.

Plan Ongoing Support

When NASA launches a satellite to the moon, they do not simply aim the rocket, fire it off, and forget about it. The odds of hitting the target would be one in a million. Instead, they constantly monitor the flight path and make mid-course corrections to ensure that the objective is met.

Learning and development need analogous tracking and course correction processes to ensure that educational programs achieve their targeted rates of return. Participants can't be simply shot back into the workplace to pursue their own flight paths. They need ongoing support in Phase III to help them stay on course and hit the target. Designing the complete learning experience includes planning and providing Phase III guidance systems. Five factors should be considered:

- Planned points at which to assess progress and provide guidance
- Management support
- Coaching
- Supporting materials or media
- Critical mass and peer support

Specific suggestions for implementing ongoing guidance and support are discussed in D5: Deploy Active Support. The point to be made here is that Phase III support must be a conscious part of the design and be planned and executed with the same care as that traditionally afforded instruction.

Program designers should address the following questions for each of these five factors. We recognize that financial and organizational constraints will preclude addressing every issue. We recommend compiling the complete list of potential improvements and then investing time, energy, and dollars in the areas that have the greatest potential for return.

1. How will we ensure that the outcomes defined in D1 are kept in view, that individuals' objectives are not simply forgotten? When will Phase III progress be assessed so that course corrections can be made if necessary?

2. Given the profound impact of participants' managers, how will we involve them? What information, tools, and incentives can we provide managers to help them fulfill their role? How can we motivate them and persuade them of the value they can provide?

3. Beyond the manager, what other coaching support will help maximize the value of the program? Will instructors be available for consultation? If so, how much time should be allocated to this activity, and how can we maximize efficiency? Is peer coaching appropriate? If so, how will we encourage and support peer coaching and interaction both during the program and after? Is there a role for human resource specialists? If so, what sort of training and preparation do they need? Would external coaches provide value exceeding their cost? What special attributes are we looking for? How will we monitor and manage the quality of the coaching being provided?

4. What materials or online content do participants need to reinforce what they have learned and apply it effectively? What formats (paper-based, electronic, and so forth) are most useful? Is there content already available, or do we need to develop our own, specifically tailored for this program? What are the tradeoffs between make versus buy? How will we encourage use and avoid the "notebook on shelf" syndrome? What has been the pattern of use in other organizations?

5. How do we ensure that enough people in any given unit have been trained so that there is a critical mass of support for new ideas and change? One of the barriers to learning transfer is peer pressure to resist change. It is difficult for individuals to implement what they have learned if none of their colleagues are familiar with the concepts and methods. The rollout should be planned so that there is a critical mass of peer support for individuals when they return to work. How can we foster peer-to-peer interchange during Phase II and facilitate its continuation in Phase III?

EVALUATION

The final aspect of D2: Design the Complete Experience is to design the evaluation—how the program's impact will be measured. Planning, implementation, and evaluation should be part of a continuous process (Figure D2.5).

Figure D2.5. Planning, Implementation, and Evaluation
Should Be Part of an Ongoing Cycle in Corporate Education.
All Three Are Part of Designing the Complete Experience.

Key metrics and methods should be agreed upon with management at the very beginning as part of the needs assessment (see D1) and should guide subsequent planning. Participants should be told how the program will be assessed so that they know what to expect and what will be expected of them. As the old adage goes: "What gets measured gets done." Letting participants know how their performance will be assessed will itself beneficially influence that performance.

The sixth discipline, Document Results, is discussed in detail in D6. The key point to be made here is that the evaluation system *is*, in our view, also part of the complete experience. How the results will be documented and analyzed is an essential part of the design; program plans that do not include an assessment plan should be considered incomplete.

CHECK FOR COMPLETENESS: STAPLE YOURSELF TO THE LEARNER

How do you decide whether the learner's experience will be "all of a piece," and whether the design includes the complete experience? We have found the concept of "stapling yourself to the learner" to be a very useful exercise.

The idea grew out of a landmark article by Shapiro, Rangan, and Sviokla (1992) in the *Harvard Business Review*. They argued that the only way to really understand your customer's experience (and how to improve it) was to figuratively "staple yourself to an order." That is, physically follow an order through all the steps in your company to see how many times it was handled, how often it was set aside, how hard it was to find its status, where mistakes occurred, and so forth.

The application of this idea to learning and development is to imagine yourself stapled to a learner as he or she goes through all the phases of the program (not just the detailed agenda of Phase II) from the invitation until three to six months later. At each stage, imagine yourself as the learner, and ask

- Would I understand what is expected of me?
- Would I understand how this relates to other systems, slogans, and corporate initiatives?
- Is it clear how the learning initiative relates to my work? Would I know how to actually use what is being taught?
- Can I see the benefit for me personally? Why are they asking me to do this?
- Could I connect each exercise to things I already know or learned in other parts of the program?
- What would influence my opinions and actions at this point in the process?
- Where would I turn for help if I needed it?
- What does my manager think? Does she support it? How do I know?
- What is expected of me? How will I be evaluated? Will anyone know or care if I try to use this stuff?

Whenever we have done this exercise with a client, they have discovered places to make improvements that strengthen the overall process.

SUMMARY

The second discipline practiced by the most effective corporate education programs is planning for the *complete* learning experience, from how the program is positioned at the beginning of Phase I to how the results are documented at the end of Phase III, including how the contribution of key players outside the learning and development organization will be coordinated and encouraged. Designing the complete experience goes well beyond the traditional scope of corporate educators. It will require learning new skills and abandoning long-standing paradigms. It is, in our experience, the only way to achieve a real breakthrough.

The evidence is clear: adopting this holistic approach to learning and learning transfer dramatically increases output and both the perceived and real value of educational efforts. Redefining the finish line as the delivery of results, instead of the last day of class, is an invigorating challenge that offers substantial rewards.

•

ACTION POINTS

For Learning Leaders

- Review the programs for which your group is responsible to ensure that the designs truly encompass the *complete* experience from the learner's point of view.

- Use the "staple yourself to the learner" exercise, or a similar approach, to affirm that all three phases and all 6Ds have been included in the planning.

- Be vigilant for mixed messages—where what is taught in the program and what is practiced in the business are inconsistent or where one phase does not support another.

  - Such inconsistencies discourage participants from trying to transfer their knowledge and, if glaring, lead to cynicism.

- Emphasize to general management the importance of their support in all three phases of the program.

  - Explain how partnerships between line management and training and between learners and their managers are required to achieve optimal return on investment from learning and development programs.

- Pay particular attention to Phase III plans. This period has been traditionally ignored and offers ripe opportunities for improvement. Effective management of the follow-through period offers tremendous leverage for improving results.

For Line Leaders

- Ask learning and development to prepare strategy maps for proposed new programs and critical ongoing programs.

- Review the maps for clear links among the business objectives, the kinds of behavioral improvements expected, and the learning initiatives designed to produce them. If such linkages cannot be drawn or are suspect, the strategy needs to be reconsidered.
- Ask line managers what they are doing to ensure that development programs are reinforced so they "stick."
- Devise systems to hold line managers accountable for their role in getting results from learning and development.
- Measure and reward managers' involvement in Phases I and III, in particular.
- Ensure that "the video matches the audio." That is, be certain that what management says, what managers do, and what the system rewards are in alignment.
  - If not, you are wasting the time and money being invested in learning and development.
  - Education augments and facilitates change; it rarely initiates it or succeeds as a change strategy unless other elements of the system are brought into alignment.
- Make the necessary changes in the environment to support what is being taught and maximize the impact of learning and development.

D3

DELIVER FOR APPLICATION

---

*The real question is what can you do on Monday,
what can you do Monday six weeks from now, six months
from now, and what kinds of reinforcement mechanisms are
needed in order to really build a set of new habits.*

—Leo Burke

THE VALUE DELIVERED by a corporate educational program is proportional to the extent to which new knowledge and skills are *applied* to the work of the organization. Unused knowledge is like ungerminated seed; it will never bear fruit. Therefore, the job of corporate learning and development is not merely to *impart* knowledge, but to be sure that it is *put to work* so that its benefits can be harvested. Hence, the third discipline of effective learning and development is to *deliver for application*.

In this chapter we focus on ways to narrow the learning-doing gap and accelerate the transfer and application of new capabilities to business matters. These methods include

- Create a desire to learn
- Make relevance clear
- Provide know-how
- Maximize retention through connections
- Plan for transfer

- Communicate the objectives
- Check the process
- Action points for learning and line leaders

NARROW THE LEARNING-DOING GAP

We have characterized the challenge for corporate educators as the need to bridge the learning-doing gap, that is, to help learners make the leap between knowledge acquisition in the program and knowledge application on the job (Wick & Flanagan, 2005, p. 10). The breadth of the chasm between learning and doing is influenced by the way in which the material is presented. Relevant examples, active learning, simulations, practice sessions, and other application-focused delivery techniques narrow the gap by making it easier for participants to connect their learning to their work. Passive listening, endless PowerPoint slides, and theory without examples widen the gulf.

For participants to generate business results by applying what they learn from a corporate educational program, three conditions must be met:

- They must *see value* in applying what they have learned.
- They must *know how.*
- They must be *given the opportunity* to do so.

The goal of the third discipline, Deliver for Application, is to be sure that participants leave learning and development with the desire to apply their new knowledge and clearly identified opportunities to do so. Methods to achieve these outcomes are discussed below.

CREATE A DESIRE TO LEARN

Motivation to learn is a *sine qua non* for effective education of adults. And what drives motivation for most people is the expectation of future benefits that they value—in other words, "What's in it for me?" Program participants will be motivated to learn and, more important, apply what they learn if they are convinced that doing so will produce an outcome that they personally value. The specific benefit that an individual values most is a matter of personal choice. But most employees are motivated to learn and use skills and processes that make their work demonstrably easier or faster, improve their working environment, and increase their chances for promotion, recognition, and so forth. As Richard O'Leary, director of human resources and diversity for science & technology at Corning, said: "A design criterion should be that the program feels integrated with how you get results. Make sure you are designing learning or applying learning that people have a hunger for because it helps them solve what they think is the problem" (O'Leary, interview).

Motivation is the product of three factors: value ascribed, degree of coupling, and expectation (Figure D3.1), which Vroom (1995) called valence, instrumentality, and expectancy. The greater the strength of each, the greater the individual's overall motivation. Value ascribed is the relative worth that the individual places on the expected outcome. Other things being equal, the more a person values the outcome, the greater his or her motivation to learn the skills and behavior necessary to achieve it. Degree of coupling refers to the personal estimation of the likelihood that the results desired are actually linked to the recommended behavior: for example, you will be more motivated to modify your diet if you are convinced that diet is instrumental in lowering your cholesterol than if you believe that diet has minimal effect. The third element, expectation, is the extent to which individuals believe that the effort to change will actually be rewarded with the outcomes they value: I will work harder if I expect to be rewarded with promotion than if I am convinced that promotion depends entirely on politics. Maximizing learners' motivation requires addressing outcomes that people value and persuading them that the program is coupled to those outcomes in a way that will reward their efforts.

Figure D3.1. Motivation Is Proportional to the
Individual's Perception of Value, the Coupling Between Action
and Result, and the Expectation of Recognition or Reward.

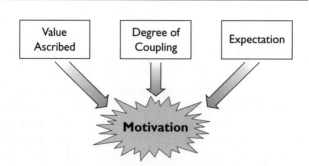

Motivation is especially important in corporate education. Such programs are, in the end, change initiatives. They are intended to help people change the way they work to one that is more productive for themselves and the company. Meaningful change inevitably involves some discomfort and requires effort. Compelling answers to the "What's in it for me?" (WIIFM) question are needed to motivate people to put forth the required effort. WIIFM has been called the "universal radio station" because everyone listens to it. When people understand the WIIFM, they are more receptive to new ideas and more willing to learn and soldier through the discomfort that accompanies any significant change.

Therefore, the first task of delivering for application is to be explicit about the value that participants can expect if they attend the program and apply its teachings. The promised benefits need to be believable and achievable—a task made easier if the objectives have been clearly linked to business priorities. Participants will *want* to attend the program if both its benefit and relevance are clear.

Beverly Kaye, founder of Career Systems International, put it this way (Kaye, 2005):

> To ensure that people get the maximum value from learning and development, we need to engage their hearts as well as their heads. We design and deliver every program so that when participants walk out the door they feel empowered and prepared to take action with a 'can-do' attitude. We intentionally work to get participants' adrenalin going. We engage their hearts so they have a passion to apply what they learn. They leave with an understanding that no one can take charge of their development and job satisfaction but themselves. So learning about taking charge of your own development is more than a cognitive exercise.

MAKE RELEVANCE CLEAR

For adults, relevance and motivation to learn are closely linked. Learners want to know *why* they are being asked to learn something—how the material relates to them, their role, their division, and their business—in order to learn and use it effectively. "Research indicates that the need to know affects motivation to learn, learning outcomes, and post-training motivation to use learning" (Knowles, Holton, & Swanson, 2005, p. 201). It is not surprising, therefore, that perceived lack of relevance is one of the major barriers to the transfer of learning (Newstrom, 1986).

Multivariate analysis of tens of thousands of postprogram evaluations at Hewlett-Packard found strong relationships among the participants' ratings of three global factors that captured the overall reaction to training: (1) the learning experience (techniques used, the instructor, and achievement of program objectives), (2) impact on the learner (content and instruction satisfaction, and the likelihood to recommend to peers), and (3) utility (relevance of skills and concepts; whether the course would lead to improved performance and whether the participants were motivated to apply what they had learned) (Parskey, interview). This triumvirate makes sense; one would hardly be motivated to apply skills or concepts that were deemed irrelevant and therefore not expected to improve performance. In other words, if the course content is not relevant *as perceived by the participants*, then other aspects of the program (instruction, venue, learning exercises) cannot compensate, however brilliantly executed.

It is therefore incumbent upon program designers and facilitators to make the relevance of the overall program and each major topic clear and compelling. If the individual participants have to work out for themselves the links between what is being taught and the needs of the business, some will. But others will not, and the overall effectiveness of the program will be compromised.

How is relevance made clear? First, by being explicit about the business needs that the program is designed to address (D1). Second, by using business-relevant examples to illustrate the connections between the content and the needs of the company. This requires that instructors understand the business needs in depth. What are the key business drivers? How does the company actually generate value? What are the major challenges it faces from competitors, a changing market, regulation, internal inefficiencies, and so forth? What is its vision? What are the expectations of its leaders? A firm grasp of the core business issues greatly enhances an instructor's effectiveness and ability to make the content relevant for participants.

A clear understanding of the big picture—the company's fundamental business and challenges—is essential for an instructor's credibility and relevance. The importance of credibility explains why using senior executives as faculty is one of the fastest growing trends in executive education (Bolt, 2005, p. 11): they have instant credibility and a deep grasp of the issues.

However, it is not always possible or practical to use all internal trainers. External instructors and experts can introduce fresh insights, new perspectives, and new approaches that are important to keep a company from becoming too insular. But it is impossible for instructors from outside the company to be conversant with the details of the multifarious operating divisions and business units in a major corporation. One creative solution to this dilemma is to team-teach by pairing external content experts with internal managers who can provide the business context and examples. This approach achieves the best of both—deep content expertise as well as credible examples of work situations that are immediately recognizable and relevant to the participants (Connolly & Burnett, 2003).

Another rich source of relevant examples are the participants themselves. Effective education of adult learners recognizes and builds on the experience they bring to the program. "It also means that for many kinds of learning, the richest resources for learning reside in the adult learners themselves" (Knowles et al., 2005, p. 66). The key is to draw on the experiences of the group members to generate examples that are immediately relevant to their work environment.

PROVIDE KNOW-HOW

The second prerequisite for learning to produce positive business impact is for learners to *know how* to apply the new information and skills to their work roles. For this prerequisite to be met, the learning activities must stimulate the kind of thinking and actions that will be required during actual application. Thus, if the objective is to improve the ability of the participants to *analyze* business or personnel situations, they must be given the opportunity to practice their analytical skills during the instructional program. It is not sufficient for the instructor to simply *talk about* it.

The program design, therefore, needs to show clear linkage between the ultimate business outcomes desired, the kind of thinking skills required, and how the learning experience will be structured to optimize the results (Exhibit D3.1). The first step is to construct an *impact map* that details the kinds of performance and capabilities that are needed to achieve the desired business outcomes. The capabilities that need to be developed and transferred should be clearly articulated and mapped *before* attention is directed on how best to teach them.

The current interest in action learning reflects the growing recognition of the importance of learning for application. Because action learning takes place in the context of real work, its relevance and utility are

Exhibit D3.1. Examples of Matching Instructional
Methods to the Cognitive and Behavioral Skills
Required to Achieve Performance Objectives.

Ultimate Business Outcome	Cognitive and Behavioral Skills Required	Instructional Methodologies
Improved sales effectiveness	Improved coaching, specifically:	
	Ability to recognize stage of development	Practice using video simulations
	Deeper understanding of the fundamentals of coaching	Lecture and group discussion
	Improved ability to ask rather than tell	Role play with debrief
Increased profitability	Better pricing decisions, specifically:	
	More in-depth understanding of pricing theory	Reading and lecture with examples and discussion
	Better ability to analyze financial impact	Practice using spreadsheets to model effects
	Able to use market research and competitive data to predict market response	Business simulation and debrief

immediately apparent. As a result, it is easier to transfer the lessons of action learning to new problems than to apply theories from traditional classroom instruction.

The downside of action learning is that unless it is carefully managed, it quickly degenerates into simply another task in which action is maximized but learning is minimal. There is concern that "the definition of action learning is getting broader and looser, with anything identified as project-oriented, experiential learning, or related to business problems being defined as action learning" (Bolt, 2005, p. 12). Action learning can be very powerful, provided the learning component is planned with the same level of attention to detail as other forms of instruction. There must be time to reflect on lessons learned and make connections between actions and learning.

For similar reasons, simulations also can be very powerful learning experiences with clear applicability. The kind of thinking (analysis, synthesis, pattern recognition, and so forth) that is required in a well-designed simulation is very closely linked to what will be required to apply the new knowledge successfully to business processes. Simulations also have the advantage of involving the learners—making learning active as opposed to merely passive listening. Active involvement is one of the most frequently cited factors that make learning memorable.

Akerman, Ekelund, and Parisi (2005) summarized the advantages of business simulations in executive education as follows:

- Simulations increase executive business acumen and financial literacy.
- Simulations build competency, alignment, and commitment around complex corporate strategies, business models, and initiatives.
- Simulations are a powerful, engaging, dynamic, and effective way to reach executive audiences. (p. 28)

The challenge is to find simulations that teach skills applicable to real work and not just "gamesmanship." Overly simplistic simulations may actually reinforce behaviors that are inappropriate in practice. Likewise, overly generic simulations that participants feel are irrelevant to their business challenges also will fail to produce the desired results. For these reasons, many companies are now having custom simulations created to address their specific business challenges and educational objectives.

Regardless of the specific simulation or technology employed, skilled facilitation of the simulation debrief is needed to make its application clear and maximize its value. "The goals are two: to make sure the participants clearly understand the relationships between their simulated decisions and market changes on the business result, and also to clarify the key learning points from the simulation" (Akerman, Ekelund, & Parisi, 2005, p. 35). Finally, as in all learning, an action plan and follow-through management process are needed to ensure learning transfer and maximize business value from simulations.

Case studies can be used to draw out principles and illustrate the impact of decisions in the context of real problems. The same caveats apply to case studies as to simulations. They must be sufficiently realistic and close enough to the participants' actual job needs that participants can see how to apply the lessons to their work. As with simulations, deriving value from a case study requires a skilled facilitator who is able to illustrate application to the specific work of those in attendance and facilitate a robust learning transfer process.

MAXIMIZE RETENTION

New insights and skills must be recalled before they can be adapted and applied. Research on learning and memory indicates that humans are best able to remember new information when it is associated with or linked to existing ideas, patterns, and knowledge already stored in long-term memory (Buzan & Buzan, 1993, p. 34). The more "top of mind" the existing knowledge, the better the ability to recall and use the new knowledge linked to it. Helping participants see the relationship between new topics and what they already know about business and leadership greatly strengthens the value of what they learn.

New information that extends or enriches existing knowledge is much easier to recall—and therefore use—days, weeks, or months later. Knowledge presented in context is *meaningful* and therefore has much greater staying power than information presented in the abstract.

Humans also are better able to remember items that they find particularly interesting personally. Each of us knows someone who has deep interest in some particular subject, sport, or hobby. Such people are able to recall information about their favorite topic—dates, names, statistics, and so forth—at a level of detail unimaginable to those who do not share the same passion. Their interests fuel their learning. The challenge for corporate education is to create the same sort of passion for learning by making the relevance of the subject matter so compelling that it captures participants' interest and, in turn, their ability to absorb and retain new learning.

A proportion of corporate education is necessarily dedicated to preparing people for situations that they may not encounter immediately (personnel issues, strategic trade-offs, leadership challenges, crisis management, and so forth). It is particularly important that such topics be *memorable*—presented in a way that facilitates their recall at the crucial moment.

Making Connections

Because each person's prior experience, knowledge, and interests are unique, participants must define *for themselves* how the material relates to their roles and how it can be used to add value. Such self-generated connections are much more memorable than instructor-provided links. To forge these links, participants must be given sufficient guidance and enough time to reflect on what they have learned. Setting aside time for reflection, however, runs counter to instructors' natural zeal to transmit as much information as possible; the temptation is to fill every waking moment of a program with activity and instruction. This "sausage stuffer" approach to corporate education may not be the most efficient.

Forum Corporation convened a panel of leading corporate educators and executive coaches to formulate principles to guide corporate education. In their report, *Principles of Workplace Learning,* Forum[1] concluded that the best practice was alternating periods of action and reflection. "When we are faced with little time and an urgent need for results, we sacrifice reflection for action. But reflection is the motor that propels the cycle—without it, learning slows or stops completely" (Atkinson & Davis, 2003, p. 25).

Leo Burke, director of executive education for the University of Notre Dame, believes that the emphasis on values and reflection is a key contributor to the success of Notre Dame's innovative Integral Leadership program (see From the Top: Leo Burke).

•
_____

From the Top: Leo Burke, University of Notre Dame, on the Importance of Reflection
The University of Notre Dame's Integral Leadership program is a comprehensive approach to leadership development that incorporates both individual and collective, internal and external points of view. According to Leo Burke, associate dean and director of executive education, its success is a result of "the holistic nature of the program. It looks at multiple facets of development and provides significant feedback to participants. In particular, we have built in a more substantive reflective dimension than one would normally find in leadership programs."

Prior to attending the five-day, intense residential portion of the program, participants submit a strategic business issue, threat, problem, or opportunity and complete a customized 360-degree assessment. During the week-long session at Notre Dame, participants use a structured problem-solving and journaling process called Pathfinder that requires them to explore their values, their organization's

_____

values, and societal or more market-related factors that may be influencing their issues, and then look for areas of alignment and misalignment.

"To really get a grasp of that, participants need time to reflect in this exploration process, so we build that in each day," said Burke. "In addition, there are coaching sessions that also give people pause for reflection as well.

"We start off the first night with an approach to participant introduction that is far more in-depth than what they may have experienced in other programs. We are talking about not only name, rank, and serial number, but what is really important to you in your life right now. What is really most important to *you*. People get a sense that it is okay to talk about what is most important to them. Then concerns start to come out that people do not normally talk about in a business setting or business education setting. And it begins to send a message that we do not want the superficial cocktail chatter. We need some real grist for the mill here.

"An analogy we use is if you go to the seashore and you take a thimble, you can come back with a thimble full of water. If you go with a cup, you can come back with a cup full of water; a bucket, a bucket full of water. So you decide how much water you want to come away with at the end of the program and that is the energy that will be required on your part.

"Fred Kofman closes the program. He is very, very strong in terms of how your behavior is aligned with your values, and what happens when it is not. It is very provocative. So all of that together really gels for people in terms of the opportunity to make some changes and choices on how they want to manage going forward.

"We relate all of this back to their business issue. So let's not talk about changed behavior in the abstract, let's talk about it with relation to the issue that you have selected. What are you going to do differently with regard to this issue that you were not going to do prior to coming into this program? And that becomes the litmus test on whether people are really serious about change. One of the key themes we emphasize is that you have a choice in terms of your response to the situation; it is your responsibility.

"Is it working? In follow-up telephone interviews, 95 percent of the participants were extremely satisfied and many rated it as the best leadership program they had ever attended. Most important, they were able to cite specific examples of how they had used what they had learned to make significant improvements to their businesses and personal lives."

•

The most effective programs, in our experience, are those that stop after each key learning segment and give participants time to answer the questions: "How could you use what we have just covered to improve performance in your own area of responsibility?" and "What specific actions could you take to put this learning to use?" This not only helps participants relate the learning to their specific circumstances, but also reinforces the importance and expectation for practical application. Fred Harburg, senior vice president of leadership and management development at Fidelity Investments, is adamant: "If there is not time for reflection, there is almost no chance for improvement" (2004, p. 21).

We recommend asking people to forge connections by writing down their insights and ideas for application in a learning journal, action planning sheet, or other similar device. An example is shown in Figure D3.2. The act of writing down ideas (rather than just thinking about them) is important; it begins the process of personal ownership and commitment. If time permits, ask a few individuals to share their plans for application. Publicly stating a plan deepens the owner's commitment. It may give

Figure D3.2. An Example of a Guided Reflection Worksheet to Help Participants Link New with Existing Knowledge and Think About How It Applies to Their Work in the Organization.

Connections and Applications Worksheet

A key concept from today:	Supports or reinforces what I already knew:	How I can use it: (Links to business priorities)

Forces me to reconsider or revise:	Related program ideas:	What's in it for me?

Source: *Copyright © 2004 Fort Hill Company.*

other participants additional ideas for their own application and, as a side benefit, it enriches the instructor's reservoir of relevant examples.

Setting Objectives for Transfer and Application

If the program has been successful in motivating employees to *want to learn* and the delivery has taught them *how,* then the third precondition for generating results is that they must have opportunities to practice their new knowledge and skills while they are still fresh. An important first step in that process is to set the expectation for use by having each participant write specific goals for learning transfer and application.

Most programs already include a goal-setting exercise toward the end of Phase II in which participants are asked to set specific objectives to apply what they have learned. Ideally, the process should have begun much earlier. For example, building on Brinkerhoff's concept of "learning intentionality," Cisco's Strategic Leader program includes specific Phase I exercises to encourage participants to think about their current skills compared to key leader competencies, so that they come to the program with clearly targeted areas of improvement. Phase I preparation for Pfizer's Advance Transition program includes having each participant meet with her or his boss to identify three top priorities.

In our experience, however, such programs are exceptions. Goal setting is usually left until the end of Phase II and is frequently the weakest aspect of otherwise superlative programs. Inadequate attention to setting objectives for transfer and application seriously compromises a program's full potential.

Learning transfer objectives need to be treated with the same seriousness as business objectives, because they *are* business objectives. They should be planned, executed, tracked, and rewarded with the same degree of attention as other performance metrics. Unfortunately, this is not yet common practice. In most organizations, learning transfer objectives are still seen as distinct from business objectives and of lesser importance. They are not yet afforded the management attention necessary to maximize the value of the learning and development experience.

The most common problems with writing learning transfer objectives and their cures are presented in Exhibit D3.2 and are discussed below.

PROBLEM 1: NOT ENOUGH TIME   For obvious reasons, final goal setting cannot be done until the main topics have been covered. Accordingly, the goal setting and application planning exercise is usually scheduled at the very end of the course. The first cause of poor transfer and appli-

Exhibit D3.2. Problems with
Goal Setting and Recommended Solutions.

Problem	Solutions
1. Not enough time	1.1 Start earlier. 1.2 Allocate enough time initially. 1.3 Stay on time.
2. Anything goes	2.1 Review the goals. 2.2 Send the goals to the participant's manager.
3. Writing strong goals is not easy	3.1 Provide a structure. 3.2 Provide examples. 3.3 Have participants share their goals.

cation goals is failure to schedule enough time for this segment. It takes time and effort to develop a good set of objectives and an implementation plan. This is as true for learning transfer objectives as it is for other business objectives.

The short time scheduled for goal setting and application planning is often further compromised. Educational programs tend to get behind schedule; instructors are, understandably, reluctant to cut off a particularly fruitful or interesting discussion just to stay on schedule. As a result, however, the time allotted for goal setting and action planning is often used to cover the last few topics. Moreover, some participants inevitably leave early, especially in open enrollment programs. They may miss the planning exercise entirely, and their parting farewells disrupt the group, further consuming the limited time available.

The time constraints imposed on educators are real and likely to intensify; companies are increasingly demanding shorter courses to reduce the time out of the office. Under such pressure, there will be the temptation to eliminate goal setting and action planning as part of the curriculum and expect participants to complete them later. This will be a poor trade-off. The evidence is very clear: if people do not complete their goals and plans during the program, less than half ever do, despite repeated requests. Their day-to-day work simply overwhelms even the best intentions. Participants should not be allowed to leave programs without clear and compelling goals for application. Anything less undermines the value of the entire educational program and increases the amount of "learning scrap."

SOLUTION 1.1: START EARLIER As noted above, thinking about learning transfer objectives is most powerful when it begins in Phase I because it fosters learning intentionality, which has multiple benefits in terms of motivation, commitment, and value derived (Brinkerhoff & Apking, 2001, p. 92). Participants should be encouraged to meet with their managers to discuss what business goals the learning will advance; what behaviors (performance of tasks) need to be strengthened, changed, added, or deleted; and why these are important to both individual performance and business success. Ideally, participants' managers should receive similar encouragement and reminders, as well as guidelines on how they can help maximize the value of the learning experience.

Goal setting should begin earlier in the program itself. Build in short, specific times for reflection after each major topic or segment. Encourage learners to reflect on what they have just learned and write down ideas for how they could apply their new knowledge and skills to improve their performance and that of their unit. The time spent in such short, focused periods of reflection is recaptured by making the final objective-setting process more efficient; participants can review the objectives they set in Phase I and the ideas they captured in real time as the learning progressed, and select the most valuable to define as the specific targets of their follow-through.

Another way to reduce the class time required is to have participants create a first draft of their goals as a homework assignment on the night before the last session. That way, class time can be devoted to discussion and refinement rather than initial conceptualization.

SOLUTION 1.2: ALLOCATE ENOUGH TIME INITIALLY The second part of a solution is to be sure that enough time is allocated for goal setting and action planning to begin with. How much is enough? That depends on the nature, length, and complexity of the course, whether the goals are individual or team-based, and how much preliminary work (reflecting on potential application) has been done. In general, at least an hour is needed to generate high-quality goals and initial action plans, more if they are team-based.

The best test for whether enough time has been allotted is for the designers to try to complete the actual exercise to see how long it takes and the quality of the work they produce. We have reviewed program agendas that called for participants to set goals and complete a very complex action planner in twenty to thirty minutes, a clear impossibility. Providing too little time sends the wrong signal. It undermines the importance of goal setting, since it suggests that even the instructional designers did not take it seriously or really expect it to be done.

SOLUTION 1.3: STAY ON TIME Staying on time is hard, but it is vital. Having enough time set aside in the agenda is of no value unless it is respected. Allowing other sessions to run over so that goal setting and action planning are compromised sends the wrong message: it implies that content is more important than application, when quite the opposite is true. It is only application that provides a return from corporate education. To allow participants to leave Phase II without clear goals and plans for application subverts the entire educational initiative.

If portions of the course chronically run overtime, it suggests a flaw in the fundamental design: too little time was allocated originally for the material or exercises. The solution is to consciously revise the program plan, not to skip goal setting. The design team needs to reexamine and adjust the number of topics and the time allotments as part of a continuous improvement effort. It also may be valuable to appoint an impartial timekeeper to remind the facilitators of approaching stop times.

PROBLEM 2: ANYTHING GOES Even if enough time is allocated to goal setting and action planning, it isn't worth much unless the process generates meaningful objectives that (1) are related to the business needs the course was designed to address, and (2) participants are truly committed to accomplish.

We reviewed over ten thousand objectives from a wide range of corporate education programs. We were surprised by how many were anemic or unrelated to the business or the program. A few real examples will suffice:

- "Lose 10 pounds" (after a three-day, $4,000 leadership program at Gettysburg).
- "Read a book on management" (following a leadership development program for high-potential candidates).
- "Be a better listener."

Such objectives are unlikely to produce meaningful transfer or business impact. If they were to become known to management as representative of the output of a program, the program itself would (rightly) be in jeopardy. Either it failed to help participants understand how to apply the material to the work of the firm or it allowed them to make a mockery of the objective-setting exercise. Either way, it reflects badly on the program, instructors, and participants.

SOLUTION 2.1: REVIEW THE GOALS One of the first and simplest steps in improving the quality of postcourse objectives is for the instructors and designers to actually review them. Surprisingly, this is not common practice.

No business enterprise could succeed if it allowed its managers to set their own business goals and then file them away without ever reviewing them with anyone. But that is precisely what happens with most learning and development objectives. Small wonder most participants do not take the process seriously.

One of the benefits of electronic follow-through management systems (discussed in more detail in D4) is that they allow learning leaders to efficiently review both the quality and the distribution of a very large number of goals (Figure D3.3). Knowing the distribution of participants' objectives allows learning and development professionals to adjust emphasis as necessary to focus objectives on the key business needs. A striking example is one client who had planned and conducted a several-day program on change management. When the learning team reviewed the participants' objectives, however, they discovered that fewer than one in ten were concerned with change management. Clearly there was a disconnect: either the program's message was not getting through, or it did not address the most pressing issues perceived by the participants.

**Figure D3.3. An Advantage of an Electronic
Follow-through Management System Is That It Allows
Program Designers and Management to Rapidly Review the
Distribution and Quality of a Large Number of Goals.**

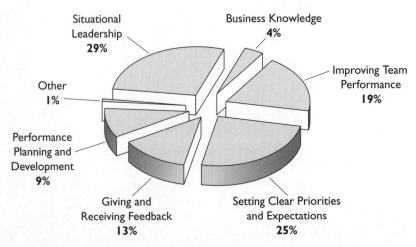

Distribution of 1,455 Participants' Managing@Agilent Goals

Situational Leadership 29%

Business Knowledge 4%

Improving Team Performance 19%

Other 1%

Performance Planning and Development 9%

Giving and Receiving Feedback 13%

Setting Clear Priorities and Expectations 25%

Source: *From Roche, Wick, and Stewart (2005). Used with permission.*

Adjustments were made to the program's focus and presentation. Had learning and development not reviewed the participants' transfer objectives, they might have continued offering the same program, oblivious to the misalignment.

Although an electronic database of goals has many advantages, it is not essential. The participants' learning transfer objectives could be collected, copied, and returned before the end of the program. Instructors could review the copies to determine whether the participants' goals were in synchrony with the business objectives of the program. Such review also presents an opportunity to enhance the program's value through feedback. Instructors, who have unique insight into the material, could provide participants with comments or suggestions related to their goals and plans for implementation (see D5: Deploy Active Support). The process provides high value for the time involved; it is only the "end of class = end of learning" paradigm that prevents learning organizations from doing so.

SOLUTION 2.2: SEND THE GOALS TO MANAGERS The other simple solution to making sure that learning transfer objectives are treated more seriously is to send a copy of each participant's goals to his or her manager. Just as business objectives must be discussed with one's boss and mutually agreed upon, so should learning objectives. Yet discussions of learning objectives between supervisors and their reports happen far less frequently than either management or learning directors suppose, despite clear evidence of the importance and benefit of such discussions.

The extent of the problem was evident in a study we did in collaboration with a leading technology company. We polled managers three months after their direct reports had attended a management training course. The course represented a significant investment for the department and the participants. The sponsoring department was billed $2,500 per participant, each of whom spent a full five days out of the office. Yet when we polled managers, *60 percent admitted that they had no knowledge of what their direct reports' post-program objectives were.*

We instituted an electronic follow-through management system that automatically sent the managers a copy of their direct reports' goals. Thereafter, 100 percent of the managers reported that they were aware of their direct reports' objectives and, most important, the number of discussions between managers and reports about the program more than doubled.

The other salutary effect of sending the manager a copy of the participants' goals is that the quality improves. If participants know that their objectives will be sent to their managers, the amount and quality of thought they put into writing them are very different than if they know the objectives are just going to be put on the shelf. The first time that Hewlett-Packard introduced participants to the idea that their goals would be sent to their managers, there was a stunned silence. The learning director responded, "I guess that changes the way you will write them, doesn't it?"

Managers need to be informed and supportive of their direct reports' Phase III goals because managers can provide (or deny) opportunities to put new knowledge to work. Absent such opportunities, much of the knowledge will be lost and the program will fail to deliver results commensurate with its investment.

Based on our experiences of the past five years, we now recommend to all our clients that they send a copy of each participant's goals to his or her manager. This is most easily accomplished with an electronic follow-through management system, but it could also be accomplished by making an extra copy of paper-based forms. Both the quality of the learning transfer objectives and the effort expended toward their achievement increase when participants know in advance that their manager will receive a copy.

PROBLEM 3: WRITING STRONG GOALS IS NOT EASY A third reason that learning transfer and application goals are often weak is that writing good objectives is more difficult than generally supposed. Instructors assume that because many participants are already accomplished managers, they know how to write good objectives. Our analysis indicates otherwise; indeed, some of the weakest objectives are from the most senior managers.

Going over the SMART (specific, measurable, achievable, relevant, and time-bound—or some variation thereof) acronym in class does not seem to make a great deal of difference. A number of the programs in our database included a discussion or handout on SMART goals. There was no evidence that the goals from these groups were better than those in which SMART was not discussed. It is not clear whether the root cause is that participants have heard about SMART so often that they are inured to the message, or whether not enough time was allocated to assess the goals against the SMART criteria.

Whatever the cause, a high percentage of the goals set following learning and development programs are not specific, quantifiable, business-related, or time-bound. Such goals do not reflect well on the course or the participants and are unlikely to lead to meaningful results. Thus, improving the quality of the transfer objectives set in corporate education programs is essential for improving the business impact and return on investment.

SOLUTION 3.1: PROVIDE A STRUCTURE In our experience, giving participants a template to follow has been much more effective than presenting SMART or other models for goal setting. The template should guide the participants to specify what they will do, by when, why, and how they will know. For example: "In [time period] I will [improve, increase, decrease, or eliminate ____] so that [describe payoff for self and business]. My success will be measured by [describe tangible or observable outcomes]." (See Exhibit D3.3).

Exhibit D3.3. An Example of a Structured Goal-Setting Form.

My Goals   **Leadership Excellence**

Your Name: _____	Your E-mail: _____
Manager's Name: _____	Manager's E-mail: _____

Your manager will receive a copy of your goals and final report. You will be able to send him or her your progress reports for feedback and advice.

Write out your goals below. Check the category that best fits each goal. Your goals will be visible to the other members in this program.

Goal 1

	Indicate Category:
In the next ten weeks, I will: {Describe what you will achieve}	☐ Communication
	☐ Teamwork
So that: {Describe the benefit or pay-off}	☐ Delegation
	☐ Time management
Evidence of my progress will include: {Measurable results or changes observed by others}	☐ Decision making
	☐ Developing others
	☐ Other

Goal 2

	Indicate Category:
In the next ten weeks, I will: {Describe what you will achieve}	☐ Communication
	☐ Teamwork
So that: {Describe the benefit or pay-off}	☐ Delegation
	☐ Time management
Evidence of my progress will include: {Measurable results or changes observed by others}	☐ Decision making
	☐ Developing others
	☐ Other

This is similar to the structured essay concept in academic education. Traditional essay questions present students with a topic to discuss but provide little or no guidance on how to do so. Each student approaches the topic in a different way. As a result, it is difficult for the professor to know whether a student fails to discuss a specific topic because he or she thinks it is not important or because he or she knows nothing about it. The solution is to give students an outline of the topics to discuss, thus *structuring* the essay for them and achieving greater uniformity and completeness. Providing a template for learning transfer goals achieves the same benefit. It gives form to the participants' objectives and ensures that the key elements of strong and actionable objectives are present: specific targets, time frame, rationale, and assessment of success.

SOLUTION 3.2: PROVIDE EXAMPLES Providing well-thought-out examples of goals is a simple but effective means to improve the quality of learning transfer objectives. It is surprising that many programs fail to do so. Perhaps it is simply oversight. Perhaps it is because writing really good examples is difficult. Perhaps it is because too many existing programs skipped the first discipline of defining expected outcomes in business terms. If the sponsors and designers have agreed in advance on the kinds of outcomes that will constitute success of the program, it is much easier to prepare examples of goals that would lead to the desired results. Getting sponsors to agree on exemplary objectives is a good check for agreement on the program's objectives.

There is, of course, danger in presenting samples. Some participants will follow them too slavishly and not "own" the goal in the same way that they own one they generated themselves. We feel, however, that the benefits of providing an exemplar and of being clear about expectations far outweigh this risk. Moreover, if participants know that they will be held accountable for follow-through and results on the objectives they set, they will be less inclined to simply copy the example.

SOLUTION 3.3: HAVE PEOPLE SHARE THEIR GOALS Provide time for participants to work in pairs or learning teams to help one another improve their goals. It is hard to be truly objective about one's own goals. Sharing them with another person who has attended the same program is a good check on whether they are clear and understandable. We encourage learning partners to ask one another to describe what their situation will be like in three months. What will they have accomplished? What will be different and better?

These questions help participants create a vision of a new and better reality. The importance of envisioning improved performance is now widely recognized in sports psychology. Athletes are encouraged to picture themselves making the perfect swing, executing a flawless maneuver, or accepting the gold medal. The ability to envision great performance increases the probability of realizing it. Likewise, having participants envision their own improved performance by applying what they have learned is a first step toward achieving it.

We also encourage learning partners to test each other's commitment to achieving their objectives. Is the objective they have written really something they want to accomplish because they can see the value and payoff, or are they just going through the motions? Little will be achieved without commitment and a vision of a better future. If the program is well-designed and executed, participants should be able to define objectives about which they can honestly say: "This is something I really want to accomplish."

PLAN FOR TRANSFER

The acronym for goals without plans is GWOP. Participants should leave a course with clear and committed objectives, but they need more than GWOP to succeed. Time needs to be spent helping participants think through what they will need to do to accomplish their objectives. Our bias is to keep the action planning high-level and process-oriented rather than excessively detailed.

In part, this is a matter of time. Most programs fail to budget sufficient time for setting goals, let alone for detailed action planning. We would prefer to see participants develop a clear view of the first two or three things they need to do, rather than rush through and superficially fill in a detailed planner.

We also believe that many of the transfer objectives, especially from management and leadership programs, do not lend themselves to overly specific project plans. Since they often involve interpersonal skills, opportunities must be seized when they arise; the plans are more directional than specific. That having been said, we believe that at the very least, participants should leave Phase II of the program with concrete plans for how they will communicate their intentions to their managers and associates (see below).

A fun, efficient, and productive exercise for generating ideas for application is an adaptation of what Marshall Goldsmith calls "feedforward" (Goldsmith, 2002). Have all the participants stand and pair off. One member of the pair should select a capability that they would like to improve and describe it to their fellow participant, then ask for feedforward—one or two suggestions for future actions that might help them achieve a positive change.

The focus should be on the future (feedforward) as opposed to the past (feedback). Even if participants have worked together in the past, they should avoid giving feedback and provide only ideas and suggestions for the future. The people asking for feedforward should listen attentively and take notes; they should not comment on the suggestions in any way, even to make positive judgmental statements. They should simply thank their colleague for the ideas and then ask them what they want to improve. The entire process of giving and receiving feedforward should only take about two minutes. In fifteen minutes, each participant can get five to eight ideas of specific things they can do to apply their learning and improve their performance. Every time we have used this exercise, the energy level in the room has gone up dramatically and participants tell us that they derived real value.

COMMUNICATE THE OBJECTIVES

Participants have an exceptional, but short-lived communication opportunity when they return to work. Their manager, assistants, coworkers, and direct reports are aware that they have participated in a learning and development program. For some it has meant extra work. Some contributed 360-degree feedback. All are interested in what happened. The first question from most will be something like, "So, what did you learn?" or "What happened?" Such an opening provides the participant with an exceptional opportunity to signal his or her intentions, to begin to recruit allies, share a key insight, and thank those who provided feedback or carried on the work of the department.

As in all communication, the message needs to be planned and rehearsed for maximum impact. We strongly encourage giving participants time and help preparing to answer these predictable questions. Well-thought-out answers reinforce the learning, underscore the value of the program, and begin the process of application. Weak, muddled, or otherwise ill-prepared answers will raise questions about the value of attendance.

We encourage course designers to give participants a few minutes to prepare an elevator speech. The concept of elevator speech was developed years ago at the Xerox Corporation. The idea was that if you stepped into an elevator with one of the senior managers and she said to you, "So, tell me about this idea of yours," you needed to be able to articulate the key concepts and benefits between the first and fourth floors. If you could, you greatly improved its chance for success. If you could not, you squandered a golden opportunity and perhaps scuttled your concept.

Have participants write out and practice a one- to two-minute reply to the "What happened?" question. Encourage them to think through the key points they want to make that will help them achieve their goals. Have them practice their elevator speeches in pairs and give each other feedback. Providing a few minutes to craft and practice the message will pay ample rewards for the participants, the program, and the company.

CHECK THE PROCESS

The objective of the third discipline is to deliver new knowledge and skills in a way that promotes their application. Effective practice of D3 motivates participants to learn, makes the relevance and value of the program clear, ensures that participants know how to use their learning, and gives them opportunities to do so. The extent to which the delivery achieves these objectives determines the extent to which business results are achieved.

We recommend building in in-process checks along the way to be sure these objectives are being met, rather than simply waiting for the end product. This is analogous to the in-process checks in manufacturing or business systems that ensure that critical subprocesses are working as expected. In the case of learning and development, the people in the best position to judge whether the program is delivering on its promise are the participants themselves.

At the end of Phase II, they should be asked to rate the degree to which they are motivated to use what they learned, understand how to apply it, and see its relevance. Clearly, if these criteria are not being met, no amount of effort in Phase III will produce effective learning transfer. It does not matter that participants "enjoyed" the program. If they are not motivated or do not understand how or why to apply new capabilities, steps must be taken to identify and address the source of the process failure.

SUMMARY

In this chapter, we have emphasized the importance of D3: Deliver for Application; that is, ensuring that every element of the program supports its ultimate objective: the application of new knowledge and skills to produce better results. The easier it is for participants to see the relevance and application of what they are learning, the better they will be able to remember it and the more likely they will be to use it. Instructors need to help participants answer the WIIFM ("What's in it for me?") question to help motivate them to learn and use the material. Instructional designers need to be certain that how to apply the information and skills from each learning experience is clear. Participants need to set challenging goals for learning transfer that will accelerate their personal improvement and business success.

•

ACTION POINTS

For Learning Leaders

- Ask two fundamental questions about each program component:
  - Will the value be obvious to participants?
  - Will they know how and when to use what they learn?
- The better and more thoroughly these two conditions can be satisfied, the more likely the education will be applied and pay returns to the company.
- Review the objectives that participants set for themselves.
  - Are they well-crafted?
  - Do they reflect the business objectives for which the program was created?
  - If participants' objectives were to be sent to management, would they reflect well on the program and learning organization?
  - If the answer to any of these questions is no, take corrective action.
- Include questions on the end-of-course evaluations to assess the extent to which participants understand the relevance, utility, and value of what they learned and whether they feel confident that they know how to use the course content in their work.
- If any of their responses are suboptimal, do a root cause analysis to determine why.
  - Take corrective action.

For Line Leaders

- Review the learning and development programs that affect your area of responsibility.

- Look for logical links among the business objectives, the kinds of cognitive and behavioral skills required to achieve them, and the learning exercises being used.

- Send programs in which this linkage is not clear back for redesign.

- Ask to see the objectives participants set for Phase III (on-the-job transfer and application).

  - Are these in line with your expectations?

  - Are they relevant to business needs?

  - Are the goals clear and specific with the appropriate amount of stretch?

- Check with the managers who report to you.

  - Are they aware of their direct reports' Phase III objectives? If not, why not?

  - Do they feel an important obligation to provide support and opportunities for putting the learning to work?

  - If they do not, this is a serious management issue that you must address if your investment in learning and development is going to yield results.

- Review end-of-program evaluations.

  - Do they ask participants about the program's utility and whether or not they are motivated and confident to apply their learning? The answers to these latter questions are more important than whether they enjoyed the instructors and venue.

  - If these questions are not currently part of the evaluation, ask that they be added.

  - If they are and the results are suboptimal, ask for an action plan to correct the situation.

- Request reports on the end-of-program utility, motivation, and confidence ratings for each program you pay for.

DRIVE FOLLOW-THROUGH

---

*Organizations should spend ten times more energy
reinforcing the training they have just conducted instead
of looking for the next great learning initiative.*

—Ken Blanchard

VALUE IS CREATED when knowledge is *put to use*. It is in everyone's best interests—the company's, the individual's and the learning organization's—to maximize the transfer and application of learning to the work of the firm. Therefore, the fourth discipline practiced in breakthrough programs is to drive follow-through on learning and development initiatives. The most effective learning organizations implement systems and processes to manage transfer and application, rather than leaving it to chance or individual initiative.

Summarizing "lessons learned" from the Global Supply Management Institute at Johnson & Johnson, Maya Hu-Chan and colleagues concluded: "The key to effective learning is follow-through, not just program delivery" (Hu-Chan, Bergman, & Frugé, 2005, p. 181). Describing the factors that contributed to the success of the course design workshop at the Central Intelligence Agency, Smith-Rutledge notes, "There is no assumption that transfer will happen by magic or osmosis" (1997, p. 118). Rather than relying on "magic and osmosis," these programs created specific plans and processes to execute transfer of capabilities from the workshop to the workplace.

"Without execution, the breakthrough thinking breaks down, *learning adds no value,* people don't meet their stretch goals, and the revolution stops dead in its tracks" (Bossidy and Charan, 2002, p.19) [emphasis added]. For learning and development to deliver against the new finish line of documented results, follow-through must be managed—planned, executed, and evaluated—like any other critical business process.

Topics discussed in this chapter include

- The need for follow-through
- The high cost of doing nothing
- A great learning experience is necessary but insufficient
- Why people don't follow through
- Impediments to transfer and application
- Tipping the balance: Follow-through management
- Time as a lever
- Follow-through breakthrough
- The power of follow-through management
- Increased return on investment
- Implementing follow-through management
- Action points for learning and line leaders

THE NEED FOR FOLLOW-THROUGH

We came to appreciate the true importance of follow-through several years ago in a project we did for a major chemical company. Together with a colleague, Bruce Reed, we were asked to gather insight into a company's flagship development program, which had been presented to approximately six hundred managers over the course of a year. Traditional end-of-course evaluations were excellent and the program had won an award from the American Society for Training and Development. These plaudits notwithstanding, management wanted to know how the program was being applied and the impact it was having. We were engaged to conduct follow-up interviews with participants. We asked three questions:

- What stands out for you about the program?
- What action(s) have you taken?
- What help or support do you need?

What we found was troubling. Only 15 percent (one out of every seven people we interviewed) could give an example of an on-the-job action they had taken as a result of what they had learned. They felt no particular need for help or assistance, because they felt no particular need to apply what they had learned. In their minds, the only requirement had been to attend the class. There was no expectation for anything beyond that. Indeed, for many, our interview was the only follow-up of any kind they had received.

This experience made us realize how much of the potential value that learning and development can deliver is never being realized for want of follow-through. When there is no system to hold people accountable for improvement, they do not practice new skills long enough to master them, they do not discuss their development with their managers, they do not get the support they need to make real progress, and they do not achieve the degree of improvement they could have.

THE HIGH COST OF DOING NOTHING

Other studies suggest that our findings are the rule rather than the exception. A 1997 study by The Conference Board concluded that less than 30 percent of information from training was successfully transferred to the job. A survey of human resource development professionals estimated a transfer rate of 40 percent. Recent meta-analysis by Arthur, Bennett, Edens, and Bell (2003) produced effect size estimates of about 0.6.

Even if the actual rate is nearer to 50 percent than the often cited 10 percent (Georgenson, 1982), it still represents a very low yield for an expensive process. No company could stay in business long if its other processes were as inefficient as most learning and development seems to be. If, for example, its plants produced only one usable part for every two manufactured, the cost of the scrap would soon lead to bankruptcy.

Manufacturing scrap has high direct as well as indirect costs. Direct costs include the raw materials and labor invested in manufacturing unsaleable products; indirect costs include the opportunity cost of tying up resources that could have been put to more productive use, as well as the loss of customers when the product fails to meet expectations. For these reasons, manufacturing companies have worked relentlessly to drive down the scrap rate toward the goal of six sigma quality—roughly one defect per 300,000 opportunities.

It was not always that way. For a surprisingly long time after World War II, American companies believed that they could ignore the quality problem. They were convinced that it was cheaper to produce a certain level of scrap than to try to manage to a higher level of quality. It was only when Japanese firms began to really master quality, and as a direct result to capture market share, that American firms finally realized they could no longer afford to ignore the high cost of scrap and do nothing about it.

"Learning scrap" is training that goes unused. It is the educational equivalent of manufacturing scrap. Like manufacturing scrap, learning scrap has a high cost in terms of the direct costs of trainers, travel, time, materials, and so forth, as well as the lost opportunity costs of having people spend time in programs learning things they cannot or will not use. There is also the very real cost of customer dissatisfaction when departments invest in training but observe no subsequent benefit.

We are not suggesting that developing people will ever be as predictable as manufacturing a product. But there is ample evidence that learning transfer can be improved (Brinkerhoff & Apking, 2001; Phillips & Broad, 1997) so that the cost of learning scrap is reduced. In a competitive economy, no company can afford the high cost of doing nothing.

A GREAT LEARNING EXPERIENCE IS NECESSARY BUT INSUFFICIENT

When Jules Verne wrote his science fiction masterpiece *From the Earth to the Moon* in 1865, he imagined his astronauts reaching their destination by the known technology of his day: he shot them into space from an oversized cannon.

A hundred years later, when NASA did send men to the moon, they did not shoot them out of a cannon. No cannon ever built has been able to put even a small object into space. It is simply not possible to generate sufficient impulse in one big bang to accelerate an object to escape velocity needed to break free of gravity. Even the huge battleships of the Second World War, with their sixteen-inch guns, could not lob a shell much more than twenty-five to thirty miles. Sooner or later, air resistance and gravity take over. The projectile loses momentum and falls back to Earth (Figure D4.1).

It was only the advent of modern rockets, which are capable of providing sustained propulsion over a long period, that made it possible to

Figure D4.1. The Projectiles of the Most Powerful
Cannons Ever Built Always Fall Back to Earth.

finally achieve escape-velocity, tear free of gravity, and put an object into orbit (*Sputnik* in 1957).

The same kinds of issues confront training and development initiatives. No matter how much impetus the program imparts initially, resistance to change and other impediments slow momentum. Unless energy is expended to continue to propel development, the performance of most learners falls back pretty much to the level where it started, following a path like that of the artillery shell (Figure D4.2).

Figure D4.2. Without Sustained Effort and Drive,
Performance Falls Back Toward the Baseline.

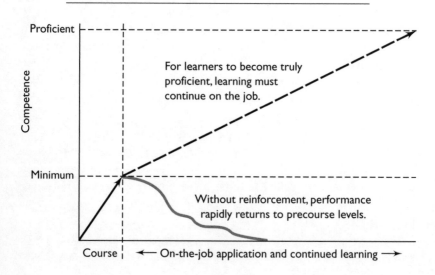

A great learning experience is essential to get the participant started in the right direction with the raw ingredients for success. But great learning alone is insufficient to produce sustained improvement and value.

WHY PEOPLE DON'T FOLLOW THROUGH

We were surprised at how often people attended courses about which they were enthusiastic and rated highly, only to fail to convert their learning into action. So we asked over a hundred trainers and development consultants what they felt prevented people from following through and executing their learning objectives. Their responses fell into three main categories (Exhibit D4.1):

- Environmental factors
- Human factors
- Inadequate follow-through process

Exhibit D4.1. Impediments to Follow-Through Identified by Professional Trainers.

I. The Environment

A. Conflicting Priorities

The single most-often cited barrier to follow-through was the number of other priorities participants face. Typical comments from respondents included

- Too many things to do
- Quantity of work waiting back at the office
- Overcommitting
- Good intentions but other priorities more important
- Top-down pressure and changing priorities
- Lose focus—distracted by incoming work
- Long list of priorities—this new thing falls to the end
- Focus on urgent but not important
- Pressure for short-term results vs. long-term productivity
- Fire-fighting activities

B. Time Pressures

A closely related issue is the overall pace of business and the sense of overwhelming time pressures. A significant proportion of respondents identified time pressure as a key barrier to follow-through. Their comments convey a sense that learners are just out of time; things are already falling off their plates

Exhibit D4.1. Impediments to Follow-Through Identified by Professional Trainers, Cont'd.

at work before adding another opportunity. Typical responses to the question of inhibitors to follow-through:

- Time pressure
- Compressed time
- Tyranny of the urgent

- Lack of time
- False sense of not enough time
- No control of time

C. Lack of Support

A further barrier to follow-through is a perceived lack of support from the organization and management. If participants sense a lack of commitment from their immediate managers or from senior executives, they quickly abandon the follow-through effort—especially in light of the time and priority pressures cited above. A representative sample of respondents' comments includes

- Lack of management commitment to new project
- My boss does not model the things I was taught
- No support or encouragement for follow-through
- No change in environment

- Lack of pull or engagement from the corporation or boss
- Experience that nobody cares about follow-through
- Lack of organization and commitment to deliverables

II. The Human Factor

A second cluster of barriers to follow-through concerns the nature of participants themselves.

A. Lack of Commitment

The item most often cited as a barrier to follow-through and change in the human factor cluster was the lack of commitment among the participants themselves. Weak personal commitment—as a result of poor goal setting or perceived management indifference—leads to inaction, especially in the face of competing priorities and time pressures. Examples of responses:

- Lack of commitment and motivation
- Lack of commitment to the result or risk
- Lack of desire

- Not properly motivated to act
- Lack of real commitment to changing

Exhibit D4.1. Impediments to Follow-Through
Identified by Professional Trainers, Cont'd.

B. Lack of Understanding of Impact

Participants often fail to follow through because they do not appreciate the impact of failing to take action. Examples:

- Lack of understanding impact if change does not occur
- Follow-through does not apply to me
- Not fully understanding or accepting the consequences of the old behavior
- Not fully understanding the urgency and impact of the new behavior
- Don't see the need
- Not seen as a high priority since benefits are not well understood
- Lack of knowledge and understanding, missing skills, competence that needs to be developed

C. Fear

Fear of failure keeps a significant number of people from putting what they learn into action. They do not want to look foolish or attempt to change and not succeed. Without a clear understanding of the benefits of change—or the consequences of inaction—people choose the "safe" route and do nothing. Typical responses:

- Fear of failure
- People don't want to move out of comfort zone
- Politics and fear of risk taking
- Fear of making a mistake
- It's too difficult, too challenging, so do not even try

D. Lack of Initiative

In any group, some individuals are not action-oriented. They fail to follow through as a result of laziness, procrastination, or distraction. Sample responses:

- Lack of initiative
- Procrastination
- Lack of action orientation
- Fall back into comfortable routine

E. Resistance to Change

This category includes a smaller number of responses, but nevertheless captures an important factor that keeps a person from putting learning into action: the inherent human resistance to change. Responses included

Exhibit D4.1. Impediments to Follow-Through Identified by Professional Trainers, Cont'd.

- Human resistance to change
- Lack of individual's desire to change
- Knowing does not equal doing
- We're human—we forget and our emotions get in our way

III. The Follow-Through Process

A. Poor Goals, Poor Plan

Allowing people to leave programs with unclear goals or goals that are not tied to priority work, or to leave without clear plans, creates significant barriers to follow-through. Although it is common practice to ask participants to set goals as part of leadership workshops or feedback sessions, these are rarely examined for quality or importance and less often linked to specific development actions. Poor goals or fuzzy plans are quickly abandoned in the face of the priority conflicts in the time-starved workplace.

- Lack of goals
- Unclear goals
- Too many goals
- Lack of plan
- Not building it into your work
- Lack of clear goals and first steps
- Lack of connectedness to the whole
- Not understanding how links to corporate results and fits with big picture

B. Lack of Accountability, Rewards, and Consequences

Three related themes emerged:

1. There is no accountability whether someone does or does not take action.
2. If a person does take effective follow-through action to change, there is no reward.
3. Similarly, there are no consequences if someone fails to take action.

In most programs, there is no follow-up once the course evaluations are turned in. The lack of reminders, measurement, accountability, and rewards telegraphs a message that no real action is required. As one respondent put it: "People respect what you inspect."

| Accountability | • Lack of accountability
• No pressure to check
• No visibility or accountability
• No measurement in place | • No one keeps them accountable for the change
• Lack of power-based accountability |

**Exhibit D4.1. Impediments to Follow-Through
Identified by Professional Trainers, Cont'd.**

Rewards	• Lack of reward system • No sense of "what's in it for me?" • No reinforcement or reward for making changes	• No reward for follow-through • No skin in the game, i.e., no pressure or reward perceived • Lack of perceived pay-off (confidence that it will really make a difference)
Consequences	• Not big enough carrot or stick • Follow-through is not expected, reinforced, or measured	• No reminders • No consequences for not following through

Environmental Factors

The work environment to which participants return has a profound impact on whether they follow through to apply what they have learned. The impediments to transfer and application most often cited in our research were conflicting priorities, time pressure, and lack of support. The three are closely related. A clear signal from management—in both words *and* actions—is needed to make learning transfer a priority.

Human Factors

The second cluster of factors concerned the learners themselves. The most frequently cited problem was a lack of commitment. For example, participants often go through the motions of writing goals for applications that they are not really committed to executing. In part, this is because they sense their managers' lack of interest. In part, it is because they are not convinced of the value of applying what they learned to their work. Together these produce half-hearted commitments, suboptimal motivation, and failure to execute.

Inadequate Follow-Through Process

The third group of barriers to learning transfer concerned the absence of process in the immediate postlearning period. The most commonly cited issues were weak goals, lack of meaningful planning, and the

absence of reinforcement. These were amplified by the lack of consequences—good *or* bad. Participants perceived that whether they followed through to apply their education made little difference to their
personal success, annual evaluations, promotions, or merit pay.

These findings are in line with what we have observed in our work
and the literature on learning transfer. The most effective programs have
a well-thought-out process for managing the implementation phase of
learning. In such programs, participants are given both the opportunity
and the encouragement to apply what they have learned and to have
their accomplishments recognized.

TIPPING THE BALANCE: FOLLOW-THROUGH MANAGEMENT

Impediments to change exert a powerful force for maintaining the status quo. For learning and development programs to produce meaningful and lasting improvement, line management and the learning and
development organization must work together to create systems and
processes that are sufficiently compelling to tip the balance in favor of
change (Figure D4.3).

**Figure D4.3. For Training and Development to Produce
Meaningful and Lasting Results, Management Must Provide
the Means to Tip the Balance in Favor of Change.**

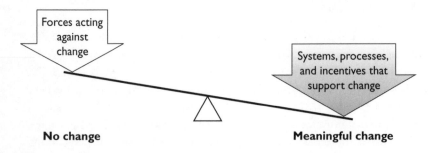

We have coined the term *follow-through management* to describe the
processes, systems, and activities necessary to maximize learning transfer and program impact. In our opinion, the emerging field of follow-
through management is one of the most exciting developments in
organizational and human resource development and one that has
tremendous potential to enhance the value that learning and develop-

ment initiatives create. The goal of follow-through management is to optimize results through the management activities of planning, organizing, directing, and monitoring the transfer and application process.

Like all management processes, follow-through management is, at its most elemental, "paying attention." What management attends to defines what the rest of the organization understands to be important. What management ignores is understood to be unimportant. Therefore, merely paying attention to this hitherto neglected phase of learning and development has a salutary effect. Approaching it with the same rigor and discipline as other business practices will produce a quantum leap in effectiveness.

The key elements of follow-through management as it relates to learning and development initiatives are

- Setting the right expectations
- Gathering and analyzing data
- Providing reminders and mileposts
- Ensuring accountability
- Providing feedback
- Delivering consequences

Setting the Right Expectations

Expectations drive behavior. The expectation of follow-through and application must be set and reinforced in every phase of the program. The goal is to create a culture of execution, a corporate ethos in which every employee feels responsible for following through and executing commitments, without having to be told.

In our work with corporations, we have seen tremendous variability in the degree of postprogram follow-through, which reflects, in part, the culture of the organization. At the top end of the scale, 100 percent of participants in programs at MBNA and MGM Mirage participated in the process and completed more than 90 percent of all possible updates on time. Both are organizations that pride themselves on their ability to execute. In both, line and learning leaders devoted time and energy to making sure that commitments were honored and learning was put to use.

Conversely, the software engineers at a major technology firm (who will remain unnamed) completed less than 20 percent of the requested updates. Many did not participate in the follow-through process at all—reflecting their fiercely independent nature and the unwillingness of management to enforce accountability and standards.

Unfortunately, accountability has not been a feature of learning and development programs in the past. The comments of Peter Gilson, former chairman of Swiss Army Brands, Inc., are typical: "As a young corporate executive, I attended dozens of development programs, but no one ever once followed up with me to see what I had done with what I learned. The most information ever collected was how I rated the instructor."

People like to know what is expected of them, what is required to succeed. The importance of clear expectations is illustrated in work we did with AstraZeneca. As part of the assessment of a program on coaching for sales managers, we asked sales representatives whether they were more or less satisfied with their jobs compared to six months previously (prior to the coaching program for their managers). We also asked independently whether their managers had set clear expectations. The differences were dramatic (Figure D4.4). Forty-seven percent (47 percent) of those who reported that their manager had set clear expectations said they were more satisfied with their jobs; only 7 percent said they were less satisfied. In contrast, of those who said their managers had failed to set clear expectations, 41 percent were less satisfied.

These examples underscore the importance of setting clear expectations. Knowing what counts is prerequisite to peak performance. Participants should never be left in doubt about how they and the program will be assessed. Ken Blanchard related the story that when he was a young assistant professor, he used to give the students a copy of the final examination on the first day of class. Other faculty objected, but Ken persisted, arguing that if the final examination represented what he felt was most important to take away from his course, then students should know that from the onset and energize their learning accordingly.

Gathering and Analyzing Data

Data are the raw stuff of management. To effectively manage the transfer and application process, learning organizations need timely, accurate, and relevant data about the process, just as sales and marketing management needs current, accurate, and relevant information about sales, average selling price, coupon redemption, inventory levels, and so forth.

At present, most learning and development organizations, even those with large-scale learning management systems, have very limited data on what happens once the formal instruction program ends. They are

Figure D4.4. Change in Job Satisfaction Among Sales
Representatives Six Months After a Coaching Program for
Sales Managers. Those Whose Managers Set Clear Expectations
Were Much More Satisfied than Those Whose Managers Did Not.

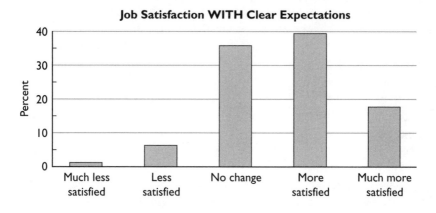

thus unable to analyze the kinds of goals people set, what actions they
take, what success they enjoy, and whether they get the appropriate support from their managers. Absent the data needed to evaluate the effectiveness of the current program, they are unable to improve it.

In addition to gathering the relevant data, effective follow-through
management requires systems to efficiently analyze and display it in ways
that support timely intervention and process improvement. Learning
professionals need the equivalent of a dashboard or instrument panel
that allows them to rapidly assess the status of the learning transfer and
application process.

Providing Reminders and Mileposts

One of the fundamental impediments to learning transfer is the "out of sight, out of mind" problem. Employees are constantly reminded of their other obligations through required reports, balanced scorecards, financial information systems, and conversations with their managers. In contrast, reminders about following through on learning transfer objectives are rare. For the great majority of programs, the participants never hear about learning after the end of class—until they receive a solicitation to sign up for the next course.

In the absence of reminders, commitments to follow through on learning lose "share of mind." With many reminders of other commitments, but nothing to reinforce the importance of following through on learning transfer, the urgency of educational objectives declines. Eventually they are forgotten completely.

Those responsible for marketing a company's products invest heavily to ensure that the brand's message is memorable and encountered with sufficient frequency to stay "top of mind." In their classic book on marketing, *Positioning: The Battle for Your Mind,* Ries and Trout (2001) emphasize that the same message must be repeated many times to get through the clutter of competing ideas. In the clutter of competing priorities that managers face, the message about the importance of transfer and application will be lost if communication stops as soon as the course is over.

Our original insight into the importance of reminders to trigger action came from our own behavior. We realized that one of the few things that was always up-to-date on our computers was the anti-virus software, not because the technology department had impressed us with its importance, but because the software automatically signaled us when it needed to be updated. It was the active reminder that prompted us to take action, not horror stories from colleagues whose computers had been infected. The technology department had also tried to impress upon us of the importance of making regular backups, but in the absence of periodic reminders, few of us did so until *after* we had lost all our data.

As the pace of business has accelerated and schedules have become busier and busier, people have found they need to set automated reminders for important appointments, phone calls, project deadlines, and so forth. Otherwise, it is too easy to get involved in one thing and completely forget some other obligation.

The need for reminders to follow through is not peculiar to business; it extends even to something as important as one's own health: "I had seen this same phenomenon time and time again with the rehabilitation patients I worked with. As long as they were in the hospital, where they were exposed to lots of cues that reminded them of their intention to do whatever it took to recover quickly and fully, they followed through. But soon after leaving the hospital to return home, where there were fewer cues to remind them of what to do and why to do it, these patients often fizzled out" (Levinson & Greider, 1998, p. 169).

If people need reminders to trigger them to take action on something as important as their own health recovery, it is clear that they need reminders to take action to transfer corporate learning. For companies to maximize the value of their investment in educational programs, they need an efficient way to keep transfer and application top-of-mind.

Reminders are the most basic element of follow-through management. Ideally, they should be part of an integrated system of reflection, feedback, and collaboration, but they have value in their own right, as evidenced by comments from participants in programs that included follow-through management:

- "The reminders were very helpful in keeping me focused on my goals and helping me implement them." (Leadership development participant, insurance company)

- "They forced me to think about my goals, even in the middle of what else I was doing. They were a reminder of what I had and hadn't done." (Senior nurse executive)

- "This weekly input has gone a long way to reinforcing the goals I made . . . they are now automatic due to these reminders." (Senior manager, advanced leadership program, international bank)

- "The weekly reporting has helped me continue to focus to make progress." (Manager, international pharmaceutical company)

- "Even though the reminders [were] kind of annoying, they helped me work continually with my goals." (Senior manager, telecommunications company)

Reminders can take any number of forms—mail, e-mail, telephone calls, automated calendar items, or any combination thereof. The most important issue is that there *are reminders* so that the objective is not forgotten. Levinson and Greider (1998) developed a simple device they called the MotivAider®, which was worn like a beeper and did nothing more than vibrate on a set schedule. Nevertheless, it proved remarkably effective in helping people follow-through on a wide variety of goals. Levinson and Greider defined the two key attributes of an effective reminder system as "(1) it must reliably get attention; and (2) it must occur often enough to serve as a useful clue" (1998, p. 173).

Despite the e-mail overload most employees experience, e-mail reminders still work. In a study of over two thousand employees in five workplaces in Canada, Plotnikoff and colleagues tested the efficacy of e-mail reminders for changing behavior related to exercise and nutrition (Plotnikoff, McCargar, Wilson, & Loucaides, 2005). Compared to the control group, the employees who received weekly e-mail reminders for twelve weeks showed improvements in both physical activity and healthy eating.

The optimal timing and number of reminders following a learning or development experience depends on the nature of the program and the kinds of objectives. In our experience, it is important to schedule the first reminder soon—usually the week following the course—before the enthusiasm dissipates entirely under the press of other tasks. "In a series of studies ranging from the introduction of new technologies to managers' approaches to taking on new roles, behavioral scientists have found a consistent 'window of opportunity' effect: We have only a short time to make a real change after any break from routine. After that, things slip quickly into business as usual" (Ibarra, 2004, p. 24).

For most programs, a bi-weekly update schedule works well. Four or five reminders are usually sufficient to help people establish new behaviors and habits, but not so many that they become habituated and begin to ignore the signal. For individual development plans involving mastery of high-level management skills, six to twelve months of monthly follow-through are needed.

Reminders about one's obligations are not necessarily welcome, even if they are helpful. As one participant put it: "It is a little like your mother reminding you to eat your vegetables." So a reminder system will not necessarily be popular—but that is not the point. The question is not whether participants *enjoyed* being reminded or completing updates; the question is whether they got more out of the program as a result, to which the answer is an unqualified yes. Follow-through systems, like other aspects of corporate education, need to be evaluated for effectiveness, not entertainment. Few companies *enjoy* having to file government securities administration reports, but their enjoyment is not what investors want to know or care about. Shareholders want results, well and honestly documented. Investors in corporate education should demand nothing less.

Ensuring Accountability

Reminders are all well and good, but they are much more effective when they are backed by a clear accountability for action. Otherwise, they may simply be ignored. Employees should be held accountable for making effective use of their education, just as they are held accountable for making good use of their time and other company resources.

When you borrow money from a bank, you sign a commitment to repay it. If you fall behind in your payments, the bank does not hesitate to remind you. If you still don't meet your commitment, you receive additional reminders, increasingly strident. Ultimately, you and your credit rating suffer negative consequences; it becomes much more difficult to borrow money in the future.

Participants in corporate-sponsored educational programs likewise incur obligations. A company expects its training investment to be repaid in greater productivity and effectiveness. Employees who are offered the opportunity to participate in such programs should understand that they will be held *accountable* for using what they have learned. If they are unwilling to make the required "payments" in terms of following through (which is in their own best interests, anyway), they are poor candidates for further educational investments.

Being accountable is defined as "subject to the obligation to report or justify something; responsible; answerable" (*Webster's College Dictionary,* 2001). Accountability implies a system of follow-up, a person or agency to answer to, and the means and schedule for reporting.

Participants' first accountability should be to themselves. They have invested their own time in attending a program. Their careers are at stake. They owe it to themselves to make good on the investment by extracting as much value as possible from all three phases of the learning experience.

The second level of accountability should be to their teams—the people who work with them and for them. We strongly encourage participants to "go public" with their goals—to share them with their direct reports and colleagues when they return from an educational program. Making Phase III goals public not only helps raise the level of accountability but also provides a source of ideas and encouragement to follow through. There is a direct correlation between the level of improvement perceived by others and the degree to which participants follow up with their coworkers (Goldsmith, 1996, p. 233).

Finally, program participants must be accountable to their managers. Managers should require their subordinates to develop clear plans for applying what they learned, act on them, and report the progress and results achieved. It is in the manager's best interest to do so, since his or her career depends in part on a proven ability to develop others.

Corporate educators and line leaders have a shared responsibility to put systems in place that ensure accountability. They must work together to make certain that participants understand their obligation for action and are committed to following through. It is important to note that participants are not accountable to the learning organization *per se*. They are accountable to their manager for the wise use of educational resources, the same as for the productive use of any other company resource. Employees understand that their immediate manager has the power to reward accomplishment or reinforce policy, so they will more readily comply with requests from their manager than from the training department.

Recognizing the powerful stimulus that being accountable provides, many progressive companies are building "reporting out" sessions into their programs. In the action learning program at Osram, for example, learning teams had to present their results and recommendations to members of the company's executive committee. Participants needed no prompting to understand the value of being able to demonstrate high-quality work to that audience. At Honeywell, participants in the strategic marketing program are divided into project teams that are expected to report out results to strategic business unit leaders thirty, sixty, and ninety days following the program. (See From the Top: Rod Magee.)

From the Top: Rod Magee, CLO, Honeywell

Rod Magee is the chief learning officer for Honeywell, a leading global technology and manufacturing company with more than 100,000 employees worldwide. When we asked him to speak about some of the ways that Honeywell helps ensure accountability, transfer, and application, he used Honeywell's Strategic Marketing Program (SMP) as an example.

"The Strategic Marketing Program is an internally created program focused on strategic business-to-business marketing. It takes tools and concepts we want people to use and applies them to real-world problems.

"Each of Honeywell's four businesses sends one team to the program. Each team is expected to arrive with a project already defined. It could be around pricing, value proposition, channel strategy, etc. The key is that it is a real business project that is part of their strategic plan, so that the whole SMP program is in support of the business strategy.

"To ensure linkage between the learning teams' projects and the business strategy, the head of corporate strategic business planning and one of the leaders from corporate learning teleconference with the president of each business in advance of the program. The discussion includes: 'What's the project and who are the people you want on it?' to ensure that the right people are in the room. Working with the business presidents, we develop a charter for each team to be sure they have a clear understanding of the expectations before they show up.

"So when the program starts, there are four teams in the room, one from each of the strategic business groups, with clearly defined strategic business projects. We cover core concepts and tools during the five-day program. At least a third to a half of each day is spent in breakout sessions where they apply the theory and the tools we have just talked about to their project.

"We provide one-on-one expert coaching to each group from, for example, former heads of strategic marketing or business consultants with ten to fifteen years of experience in strategic marketing. Because the team members are the ones responsible for business impact, there is immediate relevance to understand the material and apply it. Our goal in this course is to help them do better, because by helping them do better, we will do better as a company and as shareholders. Everybody has a personal interest in their success.

"Every day starts with about an hour of report-out sessions. Each team is accountable for reporting on their project and how they are applying the tools. We have discovered a lot of cross-business opportunities among these teams that only happened because they came to this program and saw that there was huge leverage across their businesses.

"At the end of the program each team has to define deliverables and an action plan for the next ninety days. Rather than letting them go off and assume they will do it, we keep accountability by having scheduled teleconference updates. The teams know when they leave the program that at thirty, sixty, and ninety days, they will have to report to management. So there is clear accountability after the program.

"The first call at thirty days is usually with the head of marketing for their business or the head of business strategy as well as their coach from the program. The goal is to reinforce, validate, or challenge the team's plans and progress. At sixty days, the president of the business usually joins the call. At ninety days, the team has to report its success against their promised deliverables. In each of the calls, the team is joined and supported by the coach they had during the program."

•

Comment: Honeywell's strategic marketing initiative is an outstanding example of all six disciplines working together: the outcomes are tightly linked to strategic business objectives; the process begins well before the formal instruction period and extends three months afterward; the focus is on transfer and application; there is both accountability and support; and the results are documented and reported out to senior management. Proof of the power of such a disciplined approach is that Honeywell's chairman, David Cote, chose to recognize the program in the company's annual report to shareholders: "The focus on functional excellence and introduction of the Strategic Marketing Course is starting to pay off. While the benefits may seem obvious, few industrial companies are truly effective here."

•

Sony Electronics helps drive follow-through after its Leadership Forums by tracking and reporting the participation and progress of the learning teams during the transfer and application period. The goal is to foster "coopetition"—a blend of cooperation and competition designed to maximize results (Grawey, 2005). Ten weeks after the program, participants are asked to estimate the dollar value created by their learning and work, and to present and defend their estimates on a conference call with one of the executives on the talent management council.

The common thread in each of these approaches is that participants know in advance that there is a specific time and forum in which they will be required to account for what they have accomplished. It is impractical and unnecessary to involve the senior-most members of the company in every debrief, but the model of having to report to a group of relevant managers is applicable to all levels of learning and development.

Providing Feedback

It is virtually impossible to improve any skill without feedback. People need to understand what is working and what is not working in order to reinforce positive actions and correct ineffective or negative ones. In the absence of feedback, employees are unable to maximize their strengths or modify counterproductive or downright destructive behaviors. Coaching in the form of insightful, caring, constructive, and honest feedback is invaluable. For these reasons, effective follow-through management includes facilitating coaching and feedback.

The learning organization can accelerate mastery of new skills and behaviors by making sure feedback providers and tools are available and by encouraging their use. Feedback providers can include the person's manager, colleagues who attended the same program, direct reports, peers, and other managers, as well as professional coaches or instructors if these are available. In a multicompany comparative study, Goldsmith and Morgan (2004) concluded that internal coaches can be as effective as external coaches and that the best choice is more a matter of organizational culture and resources than one of absolute efficacy.

A frequently overlooked source of constructive feedback is a person's direct reports and peers, who can not only offer first-hand observations of the extent to which progress is being made but also ideas on how to continue improvement. Participants, especially in management and leadership programs, should be encouraged to share their development objectives with their staffs and ask for feedforward and help in achieving them (Goldsmith, 2002).

Delivering Consequences

Exhortations to follow through, reminders, and even coaching are of limited efficacy unless accountability is backed up by consequences of importance to the participants. If there is no difference between the consequences of doing an exceptional job versus doing nothing, this will soon become general knowledge and will undermine the entire educational effort.

Some of the consequences, such as recognition, can be provided by the learning organization, but most require cooperation and buy-in from line management. The minimum, yet surprisingly powerful, consequence is simply to have one's efforts noticed and affirmed. Ken Blanchard has complained that the only way most people know that they are doing a good job is that "no one's yelled at me lately" (Blanchard, 2004). Simple acknowledgment of the participants' efforts to transfer and apply their learning, especially from their own manager, is a powerful incentive to continue those efforts. Recognizing individuals or teams as exemplars is another low-cost, high-impact strategy.

The most visible and highest impact consequences are, of course, rewarding desired behaviors with merit pay, promotions, and the like. If a company is serious about instilling leadership behaviors and values, then it must be very careful that recognition and promotions are congruent with those values. The acid test is the way in which the company deals with people who achieve results, but do so in a manner that is in conflict with espoused principles and ethics. Promotions and other forms of public recognition are ideal opportunities for management to reinforce the principles and behaviors it promulgates.

It would be lovely if only positive consequences were all that was ever necessary. Unfortunately, this is not the case. There need to be negative consequences for people who fail to follow through or for managers who fail to support learning application. These need not be dire; for many, a mild rebuke—"I noticed you have not reported any progress on your learning objectives"—often suffices. For a company to maximize the return on its training investment, however, it cannot allow participants to ignore their responsibility for making use of their learning. If they are allowed to continue to attend programs or advance in their careers with no regard for application, then the value of the programs themselves will be called into question.

TIME AS A LEVER

Archimedes claimed: "Give me a lever long enough and I can move the world." Follow-through management—by extending the time over which learning takes place—gives learning and development organizations a longer lever arm with which to overcome organizations' and individuals' natural resistance to change.

In business, most educational experiences tend to be intense and of short duration; they have a short "moment arm" (Figure D4.5) with

Figure D4.5. A Training and Development Event
That Lasts Only a Few Days Has Insufficient Leverage
to Overcome Personal and Organizational Inertia.

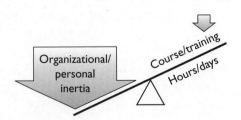

which to overcome inertia. Given the accelerating pace of business, pressure is mounting to shorten Phase II of learning programs even more to minimize time away from ongoing work. This will further reduce the leverage exerted by the formal instruction period itself.

Follow-through management, by acting over a longer period, provides greater leverage to facilitate change (Figure D4.6). As in physics, the longer the lever arm, the less force required. Translated to corporate education, this means that relatively small additional effort during the follow-through period will exert disproportionately large leverage to move the individual and the organization to a new level of performance.

Figure D4.6. A Period of Managed Follow-Through (Phase III) Provides Much Greater Leverage to Raise the Level of Individual and Organizational Performance.

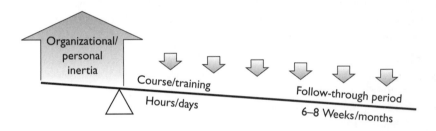

There is a sound neurological basis for the importance of sustaining follow-through, as Daniel Goleman explained in his *Harvard Business Review* article, "Leadership That Gets Results":

> Why does improving an emotional intelligence competence take months rather than days? Because the emotional centers of the brain, not just the neocortex, are involved. The neocortex, the thinking brain that learns technical skills and purely cognitive abilities, gains knowledge very quickly, but the emotional brain does not. To master a new behavior, the emotional centers need repetition and practice. Improving your emotional intelligence, then, is akin to changing your habits. Brain circuits that carry leadership habits have to unlearn the old ones, and replace them with the new. The more often a behavioral sequence is repeated, the stronger the underlying brain circuits become. At some point, the new neural pathways become the brain's default option (Goleman, 2000, p. 89).

Goleman was writing about improving emotional intelligence specifically, but his comments apply to all learning and develop-ment: a change in behavior is necessary to produce a change in results. All behavioral change engages a person's emotions to some degree. Emotion "is born largely in the neurotransmitters of the brain's limbic system, which governs feelings, impulses, and drives. Research indicates that the limbic system learns best through motivation, *extended practice,* and feedback" (Goleman, 1998, p. 97) [emphasis added].

FOLLOW-THROUGH BREAKTHROUGH

Although the importance of extending learning into Phase III—the transfer and application period—has been recognized for at least two decades, efficient methods to manage follow-through emerged only recently. The real breakthrough was the advent of new technology: computer databases, electronic mail, and universal Internet access. In the same way that breakthroughs in rocketry made getting a man to the moon feasible, breakthroughs in computer and communication technology enabled a breakthrough in follow-through management. Newer technologies provide a platform on which to construct an effective and efficient means to drive the transfer and application process.

We introduced the first follow-through management system for learning and development, *Friday5s,* in 1999. Since then we have continued to develop and refine the concept of follow-through management, tempering our ideas and systems in the fire of practice by over 40,000 managers in hundreds of different programs in companies around the world. We have been able to demonstrate that adding follow-through management to learning and development programs increases transfer and application effort, interaction with managers, improvement by participants, and return on investment in the program (see "The Power of Follow-Through Management" on page 127). The discussion that follows summarizes what we have learned over the past six years about the essential elements of an effective follow-through management system and its deployment for maximum effect.

Key Elements

A comprehensive follow-through management system includes seven intercommunicating subsystems linked to a common database: an intelligent reminder system, a flexible update engine, a feedback-coaching loop, an online guidance system, a shared learning capability, an administrative and security subsystem, and a management information system (Figure D4.7).

Figure D4.7. Key Components of an
Effective Follow-Through Management System.

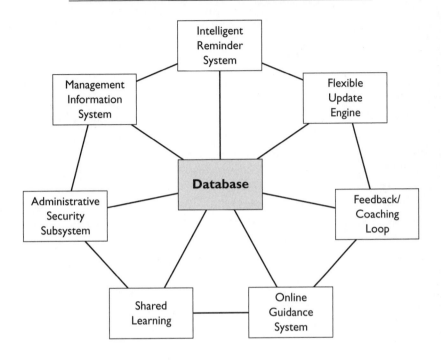

Intelligent Reminder System

The reminder system is the most basic element of a follow-through management system. Sending reminders, however, should not be confused with managing follow-through. Although reminders help encourage action and gather the input needed for management decisions, they are only a small part of the overall process.

The reminder system polls the database to determine when updates have been scheduled for a particular program by the course designers. These can include reminders to participants—as well as to their managers, coaches, or other stakeholders. Participants are reminded to update their progress, reflect to stimulate continued learning, and plan actions to further their progress. Facilitators or program directors can be reminded to check on the group's progress; managers can be sent a copy of their direct reports' objectives as well as their final report if appropriate; program sponsors can be sent links to a dashboard of the group's progress, and so forth. The system needs to be "intelligent" so that it only sends reminders to those who have not completed assignments and generates personalized messages based on the participants' goals, managers, and coaches.

Flexible Update Engine

The update engine provides the motive power. It prompts participants to update their progress by answering a series of questions: to stop, reflect, and record what they have done and learned in their efforts to apply their new capabilities. The act of reflection is itself important to continued learning (Atkinson & Davis, 2003).

The update engine needs to be sufficiently "flexible" to support a wide variety of programs and learning objectives. It should be possible to readily alter the duration of the follow-through period and the timing of updates, as well as the prompting questions and data collected. The system should gather both qualitative and quantitative data and support rating scales, predefined selections (one or many), numerical entry, and free-text responses. It should be possible to ask time-dependent questions at various points during the follow-through process as well as specific questions for different types of objectives (leadership, business, communication, and so on).

Recognizing that time pressures and other priorities are impediments to follow-through on learning, the update engine needs to be fast and simple to use. It should not require any special training to use effectively. The goal of follow-through management is to assist participants in applying what they learned in the program—they should not have to learn a complex program to do so.

Feedback/Coaching Loop

An effective follow-through management system must facilitate feedback and coaching for the reasons discussed previously. Participants should be able to decide from whom they wish to solicit input—their manager, executive coach, peers, or other mentors. Feedback requests should include a link to the participant's objectives, actions, progress, and challenges so that the mentors can review them prior to responding in writing or in person.

The system should make it easy for mentors to provide written feedback while viewing the participant's report. The ability to respond in writing improves the efficiency of coaching, as it obviates the need for both parties to be available at the same time; coaches are able to review the participant's input in advance and to provide input asynchronously. The feedback provided should be added to the participant's private online data so that it is available for later reference.

A frequently-expressed concern is that the ability to provide written feedback would diminish the number of face-to-face meetings. This has not proven to be the case. Quite the contrary. When we compared the number of interactions between managers and direct reports in programs with and without a follow-through management system, we found that the system increased the number of *both* written and personal interactions two- to threefold.

Online Guidance

As we will discuss in greater detail in the next chapter (D5), there is an exceptional "teachable moment" when participants are completing their updates and planning their next steps. A comprehensive follow-through management system should include a just-in-time guidance subsystem that provides context-sensitive advice for continuing development activities.

Shared Learning

Creating and sustaining a "community of learners" can be a powerful contributor to the efficacy of Phase III. The follow-through management system should allow participants to see each other's reflections and updates and encourage ongoing communication and peer coaching. Fellow participants and peers have immediate credibility because they share the same experiences and challenges. As one of the participants in a program for senior executives in nursing wrote: "I learned the most from scrolling through the thoughtful responses of others." Professor Beta Mannix of the Johnson Graduate School of Management said: "It's just amazing to me how much information the peer groups share with each other, from small [tips] on how to handle difficult employees, to strategic initiatives, to tracking down an article" (Wick, 2003, p. 18).

At the same time, the system must be sophisticated enough not to divulge private information, such as personal feedback. It should be possible to turn off sharing for specific kinds of goals or programs. Designated learning and development professionals should be able to review the quantity and quality of online coaching from multiple programs or iterations of the same program.

Administrative and Security Subsystem

A follow-through management system requires an administrative "back-end" that allows designated administrators to set up groups, enroll or delete participants, create teams, manage permission levels, and so forth. Participants should have access to a password-protected site limited to members of their cohort; the security system must be sufficiently robust to prevent "hacking" or other unauthorized access.

Management Information System

The real power of follow-through management systems is the insight that they provide learning and development professionals into Phase III activities and progress—a learning phase that one of our clients characterized as having been historically a "black hole." Effective follow-through management requires robust reporting and data-mining capabilities. Designated program directors, managers, and facilitators should have access to a "dashboard" of the metrics, such as participation rates, goal distribution, and progress indicators, as well as the ability to quickly "drill down" into the details (Figure D4.8).

Analogous to financial management information systems, the follow-through management system dashboard should facilitate "management

**Figure D4.8. The Learning Leader's
Dashboard of a Follow-Through Management System.**

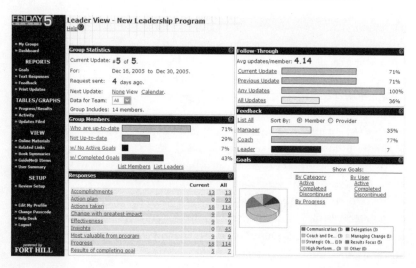

by exception"—recognition for those making real progress and "encouragement" for those who are not following through. It should provide early warning for programs that are "off-track" to permit timely intervention—the essence of management. Learning officers, program directors, instructors, and others should be able to mine the data, generate reports to support continuous improvement, and document the business impact (see D6: Document Results). Program designers should be able to review the quality and distribution of learning transfer goals to gauge the extent to which these match the overall course objectives and monitor the quality and quantity of feedback being provided.

THE POWER OF FOLLOW-THROUGH MANAGEMENT

More and more companies are documenting the positive impact that follow-through management systems can have on learning transfer and program effectiveness. We have now worked with over a hundred companies and business schools to implement follow-through management for courses and individual development plans. The results have been dramatic. As the examples below illustrate, management of the Phase III follow-through process produces greater effort, more rapid progress, improved application, and increased return on investment. Both companies and participants have benefited.

Case-Control Study

To assess the impact of follow-through management, we conducted a controlled trial in cooperation with Sun Microsystems' Sun University (Sun U). We selected the Sun New Manager course because it is an important part of Sun University's effort to create competitive advantage through human capital development. The program introduces newly appointed managers to key concepts of management and leadership and to Sun's expectations for team leaders and managers. Although end-of-course evaluations were excellent, Sun U leadership wanted to test the value of adding follow-through management to this already successful program.

We used a case-control design. Four sessions of the Sun New Manager course were taught to eighty-eight participants (twenty-two per group) with the same materials and curriculum. The *Friday5s* follow-through management system was used to drive learning transfer in Phase III of two groups (*n* = 44). The other two groups were conducted as usual (without specific attention to follow-through). Approximately three months after the class, all the participants and their managers were polled via an anonymous Web-based survey.

Results

Use of the *Friday5s* follow-through management system increased managers' awareness of their direct reports' learning transfer goals. Managers of those in the follow-through management group were significantly more aware of their direct reports' learning transfer objectives than those in the control group. In the absence of the follow-through system, more than half (60 percent) of the managers admitted that they were unaware of their direct reports' goals. In contrast, 100 percent of the managers of the follow-through group reported being aware of their direct reports' goals (Figure D4.9).

Figure D4.9. Use of a Follow-Through Management System Increased Managers' Awareness of Their Direct Reports' Developmental Goals from 40 Percent to 100 Percent.

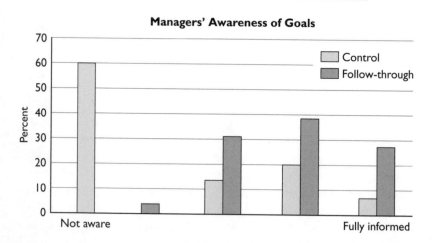

Participants in the sessions that included the follow-through management system were much more likely to discuss the course and their efforts to apply it with their managers. Ninety-four percent of the participants in the group with follow-through reported discussing the program with their managers compared to only 65 percent of the control group (Figure D4.10).

Figure D4.10. Use of a Follow-Through Management System Increased the Number of Discussions Between Managers and Their Direct Reports.

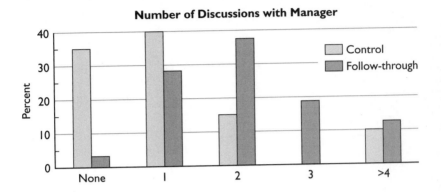

Managers of the follow-through management group reported observing more postcourse effort compared to managers of the group in which follow-through was left to individual initiative (Figure D4.11).

The increased effort, awareness, and discussions were correlated with perceptions of greater effectiveness. Participants *and their managers* in all four groups felt that the program had improved the participants' managerial effectiveness. The effectiveness ratings by both participants and their managers were higher in the follow-through group. Indeed, the only participants that managers rated as "markedly improved" (the highest rating) were in the follow-through group.

Both follow-through and non-follow-through groups had attended sessions with the same program agenda and content, taught by instructors with virtually identical Level 1 evaluations. Yet, three months later, managers rated the change in effectiveness higher for those in the follow-through management group. This supports Baldwin and Ford's (1988) contention that transfer of learning depends on more than the course content and its presentation. It is direct evidence that adding follow-through management, even without other changes to the program, increases the effectiveness of learning and development programs.

Comments from the participants as well as from the instructor and course coordinator also underscored the value of follow-through management.

- "Best thing was the reminder that I had specific goals and needed to work on them every week." (Program participant)

**Figure D4.11. Managers Reported Observing a
Higher Level of Postcourse Effort in Groups That Used the
Follow-Through Management System in Phase III of the Program.**

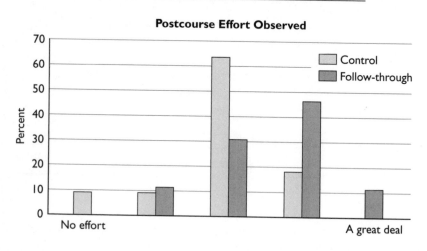

- "I enjoyed the instructor feedback. I truly believe [my] skills were molded by this course." (Program participant)

- "Overall, the best part of *Friday5s* was reading how others were doing. It's good to know others are in the same position you are and are dealing with the same problems you are." (Program participant)

- "Holds people accountable, tracks participant actions, and provides evidence of results. Positive impacts back on the job have been clear across the board with participants who committed to the process. Triggers prompting participants to update are critical." (Instructor)

- "From an instructor's standpoint it's gratifying to know that what's being taught is being applied. From a course effectiveness standpoint, it's critical to loop progress made back to Sun U to gauge what's working and what's not . . . this is critical from an ROI standpoint." (Instructor)

- "The system was most helpful in supporting course participants to take postcourse action. The impact of their actions was easily captured and can really be used as Level 3 evaluation data and evidence. As a course manager, this process really helps in documenting and assessing the real-world effectiveness of the course and its design." (Course coordinator)

By comparing the results of participants in the same program with and without follow-through management, this study clearly demonstrated the value of driving learning transfer. Follow-through management encourages students to apply what they learned in the weeks following a course. The result is greater incorporation of best practices into their personal management style. Participants acknowledged the value of reminders and visible accountability during the postcourse period when they most needed to practice new skills and methods.

Both test and control groups were perceived to have improved their managerial effectiveness, proving the value of well-designed and well-delivered corporate education. However, the degree of change as reported by both the students and their managers was greater when a system of follow-through management was used. In other words, managing the follow-through process allowed the same program to produce greater results.

Reducing Waste at Hewlett-Packard

Connolly and Burnett (2003) reported the results of the *Dynamic Leadership* program at Hewlett-Packard in the *Journal of Organizational Excellence*. The purpose of this global program was to improve the ability of HP managers to accelerate "time-to-value" for customers, shareholders, and employees through conversational leadership. The authors identified six factors that were key to the documented success of the program:

- Strong connection with business imperatives
- Commitment to creating business value
- Use of program tools and concepts by the project team itself
- Fast action and rapid adjustment
- Partnership between content experts and line managers
- Reinforcement and measurement

With respect to the latter, the design team recognized that a two-day event was insufficient to produce the desired change. They decided to extend the learning period for ten weeks by incorporating follow-through as a core component of the program, which "greatly increased its overall value." The follow-through process of the *Dynamic Leadership* program is shown in Figure D4.12.

Figure D4.12. Dynamic Leadership's Follow-Through Process.

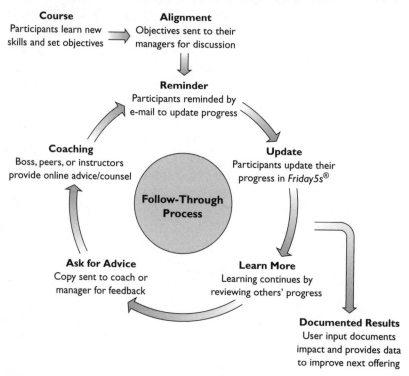

Source: *Connolly & Burnett, 2003. Used with permission.*

Connolly and Burnett (2003) concluded, "The postworkshop support system created a reinforcing cycle of follow-up action, coaching, feedback, and measurement to assure that participants were learning and manifesting the desired new behaviors, and the new behaviors were producing the desired business value."

INCREASED RETURN ON INVESTMENT

Direct evidence of the impact of follow-through management on ROI comes from a study at Pfizer—the world's largest pharmaceutical company and the first firm ever named Best Training Company by *Training Magazine* two years in a row (Schettler, 2003). An important factor in Pfizer's top ranking was their rigorous approach to evaluating training effectiveness. Pfizer's Learning Center maintains a Department of

Measurement, Evaluation, and Strategic Analysis (MESA) specifically for this purpose.

Pfizer was one of the first companies to begin using follow-through management to augment its core leadership development programs. The objective was to improve learning transfer and sustainability. Approximately six months after follow-through management with *Friday5s* was implemented, MESA conducted an in-depth return on investment analysis of the leadership program using methodology recommended by Phillips (2003). Managers who had attended the course were asked to quantify the benefits in financial terms and indicate both their degree of confidence in the estimate and the percentage of the benefit that could be directly ascribed to the program. Over 140 responses were available for analysis. A conservative estimate of the actual benefit was obtained by multiplying

Estimate of financial value × percent
confidence × percent attributed to program

Participants overwhelmingly endorsed the value of the program in helping them improve their managerial and leadership skills. The overall return on investment (ROI) was estimated to be 150 percent. In addition, numerous other benefits were cited that could not be directly dollarized.

Since some of the respondents had attended the program before follow-through management was implemented, it was possible to compare the reported ROI with and without follow-through. The dollarized benefits reported by managers who had attended sessions with follow-through were nearly 50 percent greater than those who had attended sessions without follow-through (Trainor, 2004).

These results further underscore the power of follow-through to increase the return on training investment. They demonstrate that the increased effort, management discussions, and follow-through observed in the Sun study are converted to actual productivity gains in the workplace. According to Van Potter, senior learning consultant at Fidelity Investments, "we want evidence that learning impacts thinking, behavior and results . . . and that it leads to a shift that makes the business more successful. With managed follow-through we have the data to quantify our results and put a dollar figure in the [ROI]" (Wick, 2003, p. 18).

IMPLEMENTING FOLLOW-THROUGH MANAGEMENT

Implementing follow-through management requires making the commitment, selecting a system, putting it in place, and "learning on the fly," that is, improving and perfecting the process over time.

The first step is making the commitment. We hope that by now you are persuaded that follow-through management offers exciting possibilities to enhance the output of already excellent programs. But follow-through management cannot be simply "bolted on" to the end of a program and yield optimal results. It needs to be an integral part of the overall design and execution of the six disciplines.

Questions that need to be addressed include how the concept will be introduced; how support and active engagement of managers will be secured; who in the learning organization will champion the process, check on progress, recommend action; and so forth. A credible supplier of follow-through management systems should be able to provide advice and consulting on these and other implementation matters.

The second step is selecting a system. While some aspects of follow-through management could be implemented using manual systems, achieving a breakthrough in learning transfer requires implementing an electronic follow-through management system. A key decision, as with similar information management systems, is "make or buy." The advantage of designing a custom system is that it can be specifically tailored to the needs, culture, and objectives of the organization. The disadvantages include the time required to design, build, and test the system. Cost savings of "build it yourself" systems often prove illusory when the true cost of design, programming, and ongoing maintenance is taken into account. The advantages of commercial systems are (1) they represent the best practices of accumulated experience from many companies and (2) providers are driven by competition to continually upgrade and improve them.

If the decision is taken to employ a commercial solution, the challenge becomes one of selecting the best system or vendor. The usual questions of track record, experience, and reputation apply. The process should include vetting the provider by consulting with respected current users. In addition, the decision needs to be made between a full-service provider, who will manage many of the administrative functions (such as customizing the application, enrolling participants, providing ongoing support and help desk), versus more of a "do-it-yourself" approach in which these functions are provided by learning and development staff.

Once the system and target program have been selected, it is time to "just do it"—to put follow-through management into place and begin the process of continuously learning and improving this powerful new tool of breakthrough learning.

SUMMARY

Improving the learning transfer and application process has long been recognized as a key to converting more of learning and development into business results. But it has proven to be a daunting challenge. Translating the capabilities acquired through training into enhanced on-the-job performance requires follow-through during Phase III, but historically this phase proved difficult to manage effectively. It is the weakest link in the chain of value created by corporate education and offers the greatest single opportunity for improvement.

No company can leave follow-through on business objectives to chance and still be successful. In well-managed companies, systems are in place to ensure that business objectives are implemented, progress is monitored, and achievement is rewarded. Likewise, no company can afford to leave achievement of learning objectives to chance and individual initiative.

Breakthrough training organizations drive follow-through by actively managing the learning transfer process. They ensure that participants put their learning to use by managing expectations, issuing reminders, ensuring accountability, and providing support. Companies that have embraced follow-through management have experienced significantly higher levels of postcourse effort, achievement, and return on investment for a modest incremental investment. Efficient and effective follow-through management systems represent a true breakthrough in corporate education.

•

ACTION POINTS

For Learning Leaders

- Answer the following questions for each of the key programs that your group delivers:
  - What is your organization doing to drive learning transfer in Phase III?
  - Do you know what the participants' learning transfer objectives are?

- Do you actively remind and support them?
- Are managers actively involved in supporting learning transfer?
- Do you have systems in place to manage follow-through, transfer, and application?
- Based on your answers, develop a plan to take much greater ownership of what happens during Phase III, since you are being held accountable for the results.
  - Explore methods and systems to help support follow-through management.
- Have a candid discussion with senior management about how the participants' manager can enhance or destroy the value of learning.
- Work with management to ensure that follow-through happens. It requires a team effort.
  - Learning and development cannot single-handedly drive follow-through, but neither can it eschew its responsibility because, as Eldridge Cleaver put it: "Either you are part of the solution or you are part of the problem."

For Line Leaders

- Reflect on your own experiences in learning and development programs.
  - Were you expected to follow through and generate a return on the company's investment? Or was the last day of class treated as though it were the finish line?
- Interview employees in your organization who have recently attended programs or who have had direct reports attend programs.
  - Are developmental objectives taken seriously in your unit or not?
  - Is there a culture of execution or a culture of indifference?
- Interview the managers of participants in recent programs.
  - Were they aware of their subordinates' goals for learning transfer and application?
  - Did they hold their subordinates accountable for putting learning to work?

- If you discover that developmental objectives are afforded "second-class citizenship" and are frequently ignored by both participants and their managers, you are wasting time and money on training.
- Work with the learning organization to address the problem.
- Exert leadership to ensure that program participants are held accountable for following-through and transferring their learning to the work of the firm in a way that improves their personal performance and the business's results.

D5

DEPLOY ACTIVE SUPPORT

The problem may not be the programs. In fact,
the personal learning catalyzed by a top-notch program
can be tremendous. The problem, my research suggests,
is what happens when a manager comes back to the
day-to-day routine of the office.

—Herminia Ibarra

IN THE PREVIOUS CHAPTER, we discussed the importance of follow-through management for achieving a breakthrough in Phase III and of holding participants accountable for using what they have learned. In this chapter, we explore the other part of the equation, deploying active support. Optimal results require the right balance between accountability and support (Kirkpatrick & Kirkpatrick, 2005, p. 29). Breakthrough learning and development programs create environments that favor learning transfer by providing both support and accountability. They ensure that participants have the resources they need to maximize the effectiveness and efficiency of their efforts. Topics we discuss include

- The Environment
- Managers
- Instructors and facilitators

- Peers: learning communities
- Critical mass
- Professional coaches
- Feedback sustains follow-through
- Analogy to customer support
- Owner's manuals for corporate education
- Online guides
- Action points for learning and line leaders

In the preface to his book, *The First 90 Days: Critical Success Strategies for New Leaders at All Levels,* Michael Watkins explains what piqued his interest in the topic. "I was struck by how few companies invested in helping their precious leadership assets succeed during transitions—arguably the most critical junctures in their careers. Why did companies leave their people to sink or swim? What would it be worth to companies if managers entering critical new positions could take charge faster?" (Watkins, 2003, p. xii).

The same questions pertain to corporate education. Why do so few companies invest in helping people make the transition from the classroom to the workplace? Having already invested time, effort, and dollars to impart new skills and knowledge, why do companies leave their people to sink or swim when it comes to application?

Our experience suggests that learning and development programs that provide ongoing support for learners—especially during the first few crucial weeks of the transfer phase—enjoy a greater return on their educational investments. Support for transfer and application should include the environment, people, and systems.

THE ENVIRONMENT

The old adage among nurserymen is to "dig a $10 hole for a $5 tree." In other words, how well you prepare the environment is more important than the cost of the tree itself. The same is true for implanting new knowledge and behaviors. The greatest course in the world will fail to produce results if the environment to which the learner returns is barren or hostile.

•

From the Top: David Brennan, CEO, AstraZeneca, on Setting a Vision and Direction

Senior executives exert significant influence by what they choose to focus on. David Brennan, chief executive officer of AstraZeneca International, put it this way: "I can do anything I want, but I can't do everything. You have to pick the things that you think are important and you have to be consistent."

Brennan chose to make training and development a priority, because as he explained: "Our business is based on intellectual capital. The fundamental business model in pharmaceuticals is breakthroughs that we can patent. But the intellectual capital of the people in the organization and what they do with those discoveries is what really makes the difference. And so you have to back that up with a consistent people strategy. We want to attract people into the organization and we want to keep them here. We want them to continue to develop and to gain more knowledge and experience, so that we can build our intellectual capital to make ourselves more competitive. So the learning and development process is key to our success.

"I have it on my agenda. I don't have a lot of things on my agenda, which is why I can pull it through the organization and make sure that things are happening because they know it is a priority."

Brennan made development a priority from the beginning. At the first meeting of six hundred some sales managers following the AstraZeneca merger, Brennan took the podium. "I said that our vision for the organization was to have the best sales management team in the industry and that in order to do that we knew that we had to begin to invest immediately in the development of the people sitting in the room. And I said to them in one year from today you will have all experienced what we are going to do to make you better in your role. If you are a district manager we're going to spend more time on coaching; if you're a regional manager we're going to spend more time on the management of managers; if you're an area sales director we're going to talk about objective setting for broader organizations.

"People were cheering, this is what a sales organization wants to hear. You're going to invest in me. I'm going to be better than I am and you're going to give me the tools to do it, you're going to put more arrows in my quiver so when I shoot I have more choices on how to hit the targets. Wow. People were absolutely taken with the idea.

"And I sat back down and the guy who was running the sales organization said to me, 'But I don't even have a training department yet!' And I said, 'You'll have one very soon because we are going to do this.' And we did.

"It set a course and a direction for our organization that we built on. We took a lot of initiatives. Not everything worked, but we kept experimenting and improving. What we do today is better now because we started investing immediately.

"The single area where we have started to really change our game with newer programs is getting the person's manager engaged in a meaningful way before the person goes to the program, and getting that manager to work with someone from our training group. Why are they recommending their direct report should go do this? What does the manager expect the person to work on and what does the manager need to do when the person comes back to reinforce that?

"So we have really expanded the role of the manager in delivering on our people strategy. That is really where the rubber meets the road. That's exactly the kind of thing that makes the difference."

●

Creating a fertile and receptive environment begins at the top. Senior executives can set the tone that learning and development is a strategic priority, as David Brennan did at AstraZeneca (see From the Top: David Brennan). Senior management support must be manifest in deed as well as in word. It needs to be backed up by systems of accountability to ensure that all managers embrace the importance of their role in learning transfer, since a person's immediate supervisor has profound influence on whether learning is transferred and applied or abandoned.

THE MANAGER

Managers represent the most influential, and most underutilized, resource available to effect application and ensure that education produces results. When Broad and Newstrom (1992) studied the transfer of learning, they found that involving the manager before and after the program ranked, respectively, as the first and third most potent learning transfer strategies. Yet involvement by the manager after the course was the *least frequently used* of the nine role-time combinations they studied. They concluded: "*Managers do not consistently and powerfully support the transfer of training in the work environment.* We believe that this represents a fundamental problem, and also a substantial opportunity for improvement" (p. 53, emphasis in the original).

Since a person's direct manager holds the keys to salary increases, promotions, and advancement, his or her opinion has a profound impact on the participants' attitudes toward learning and its relevance to work.

Given the influence exerted by managers, it is hard to imagine a successful Phase III without support from managers. Managers should be the first line of application support, an integral and crucial part of the overall system for helping employees apply learning and convert it into business results.

Range of Management Support

Kirkpatrick (1998) proposed that a manager's reaction to training falls along a continuum (Exhibit D5.1). At the lowest (and most destructive) end of the range are managers who *prevent* their subordinates from using what they have learned. Such complete contradiction between managers and training suggests a failure to define real business needs and garner management support in the design phase. Nearly as damaging are managers who *discourage* using new methods or approaches. Such a situation squanders resources and leaves employees confused and frustrated. It is a recipe for disaster.

The most telling example in our personal experience comes from a discussion with a major health care firm. We were trying to make the point about the importance of management support. We said: "Managers have a profound influence on the transfer of learning. If people attend a program and come back enthused about using what they learned only to get a negative reaction from their boss when they try, the value of the program is dramatically reduced. In ten minutes, a manager can undo a week's worth of education."

Our client replied: "It is much worse than that. In 15 seconds, a manager can undo a year's worth of work." They explained that in one of their divisions, sales training had worked with sales management for a full year to move the sales force toward more of a consultative selling style. But no one had made sure that the general manager was fully on board and informed. So when he was asked in front of the entire sales force what he thought of the approach, he replied: "Oh, that's just what they teach in training." In one remark, he undermined months of effort.

Kirkpatrick placed "neutral" or "indifferent" in the center of his scale. We disagree. We believe that indifference is negative. If a person attends an educational program and is excited about applying what he or she learned but is told by the boss in so many words, "I really don't care one way or the other," most will understand that to mean, "You have better things to do." Managerial indifference is not neutral; it is destructive and expensive.

Exhibit D5.1. Managers' Reactions to Employees' Using New Capabilities Learned in Development Programs.

Manager's Action ⇨	Prevent Application	Discourage Application	Indifference	Encourage Use	Require Use
Reinforcement	← Negative Reinforcement →			← Positive Reinforcement →	
Effect on Learning	Counteracts benefits of learning and development; reduces return on investment			Enhances benefits of learning and development; increases ROI	
Effect on Employee	Confuses employees; devalues learning and discourages self-development			Encourages employee to continue learning; reinforces value of self-development	

Use Should Be Required

Managers can support programs by *encouraging* their direct reports to apply what they have learned. Ideally, they should *require* that they do so as "the way we do business here." The latter is exceptionally powerful in effecting organizational change.

When Jorge Valls accepted the leadership of SmithKline Animal Health, he identified an urgent need to improve the quality of marketing and marketing plans. He contracted with the Impact Planning Group to conduct an intensive marketing workshop. He included not only the marketing department, but all managers, true to his belief that marketing is everyone's responsibility, because every department contributes positively or negatively to the customer's perception. Most important, at the conclusion of the training he announced a *nonnegotiable requirement:* all future marketing plans had to be prepared in accordance with the principles that had just been taught. He *required* that the training be applied; and he backed up what he said by conducting reviews in accordance with the agreed-upon principles and rejecting any proposal that did not follow the guidelines. The quality of discussions among managers and departments improved immediately because everyone shared common concepts and vocabulary. Within months, the improved quality of planning and marketing were evident in both top-line and bottom-line growth even in the absence of new products.

The point is that learning and development do not take place in a vacuum. To maximize the business impact of learning and development, the environment to which learners return—especially the messages (overt and covert) that they receive from their managers—must support transfer and application.

Motivating Managers to Coach

The challenge for corporate educators, then, is to motivate managers to provide ongoing encouragement and support and to provide them with the required knowledge and tools. Four conditions must be satisfied to motivate managers to support their direct reports in the application of learning and development:

1. They must believe that there is *value* in doing so.
2. They must feel *confident* that they can do so effectively.
3. They must be *aware* of the objectives of both the program and their subordinates.

4. They must themselves be held *accountable*; support must be an expected part of their jobs.

VALUE Managers have to be convinced that investing their time in the short run, coaching their direct reports will be repaid in the long run by greater effectiveness. Adopt a marketing mindset and create a compelling answer to the WIIFM (what's in it for me?) question for managers. Educate the learners' supervisors on their role in maximizing the return on training investments. Show them the evidence about the impact they have. At the same time, you must persuade senior management that a key responsibility of *all* managers is to ensure follow-through on the educational opportunities provided to their direct reports. Demonstrate the value of including the extent to which a manager supports *application* of learning and development in annual reviews and other assessments of managerial effectiveness. The goal is to create a company culture in which both learners *and their managers* accept without question their shared responsibility for maximizing the value of educational programs.

CONFIDENCE To provide effective coaching, managers must feel confident of their ability to do so. No manager wants to be embarrassed by appearing uninformed or unskilled. Managers who are unsure of what was covered in learning and development programs are likely to avoid discussions of the content or its application.

For managers to confidently provide postcourse mentoring, they need to understand the material covered in the program and feel that they have the requisite coaching skills. Ideally, managers should attend the program prior to their direct reports. Unfortunately, this is not always practical; managers are promoted and change, scheduling is difficult. Moreover, courses should continue to evolve in concert with the needs of the company, so that even if the manager previously attended the program, new material may have been introduced.

Thus, there is an ongoing need to keep managers informed of program objectives, content, and expectations. When an employee enrolls in a course, send the manager a short synopsis of the business needs the program is designed to address, the topics covered, and the desired outcomes. Make communications succinct and efficient; managers experience even greater demands on their time than the participants themselves. A brief introductory e-mail with links to more in-depth information and suggestions on the company's intranet is more likely to be read than a lengthy course description.

Help managers enhance their coaching skills. Geoff Rip, CEO of ChangeLever International, a learning transfer consulting firm, feels so strongly about the benefits of managerial support that he holds a course for managers in advance of training their subordinates. The program for managers focuses on general coaching skills as well as how to maximize the benefits of the upcoming training in particular. Companies that have implemented this approach feel that it pays substantial dividends in terms of better results from training (Rip, 2004).

When it is impossible or impractical to provide specific training for managers, provide a guide with advice on how to maximize the benefits of their reports' education. Make the guide concise, practical, and action oriented (for example, "If your report is working to improve X, then you can help him or her most by doing Y"), analogous to the user's guides discussed in detail later in this chapter. Communicate the availability of the guide and make it easily accessible in both print and online versions.

AWARENESS For managers to become actively and meaningfully engaged in the learning transfer process, they have to know what their direct reports are trying to achieve. Encourage managers and their direct reports to meet prior to the program to identify the most important learning opportunities as, for example, Cisco does in its Global Leader Program and Pfizer does in Advance Transition. Prompt a follow-up meeting after Phase II by collecting and sending a copy of each participant's learning transfer objectives to his or her manager. Provide reminders and opportunities for subordinates to seek feedback from managers on their goals, plans, and progress.

In the study we did at Sun Microsystems, we programmed the follow-through management system to automatically send a copy of each participant's goals and final progress report to his or her manager. The results were dramatic: 50 percent more of the participants in the group that used *Friday5s* had discussions with their managers (Figure D4.10) than participants in the group without follow-through management.

We observed a similar phenomenon with respect to individual development plans. We compared two groups of senior managers in a personalized leadership development program at a major pharmaceutical company: one with and one without a formal follow-through process. The follow-through management system significantly increased the amount of interaction between the participants and their managers and coaches (Figure D5.1). All the participants agreed that the follow-through process prompted them to have discussions with their coach or manager and that it helped them stay focused on their development plans.

Figure D5.1. Average Number of Interactions Between Participants in a Six-Month Development Program and Their Managers and Coaches, With and Without Follow-Through Management.

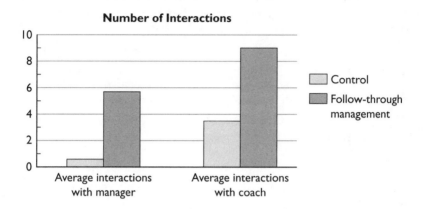

ACCOUNTABILITY Last, managers themselves must be held accountable for providing support. In the best-managed companies, a proven ability to develop direct reports is a prerequisite for further promotion. Breakthrough learning and development initiatives provide a balance of support and accountability for managers, just as they do for program participants.

Programs that have included active oversight and participation by managers' managers in Phase III have been among the most successful. In AstraZeneca's Breakthrough Coaching program, for example, the learning organization used the follow-through management system to help area sales managers identify which regional sales managers were doing a particularly good (or poor) job of supporting their direct reports. Calling attention to these outliers during regional discussions helped recognize and reinforce positive coaching behaviors and strengthen the efforts of less effective coaches. Proactive management of manager involvement contributed to the program's success.

In the Home Depot store management learning initiative, regional vice presidents used the follow-through management system, *Friday5s*, to track participation by store managers and the direction and coaching they were receiving from their district managers. By setting clear expectations for the role of the district managers, by paying attention to the level of support they were providing, and by comparing progress across districts, Home Depot achieved very high levels of participation and accelerated progress, affirming the adage that "people respect what you inspect."

Summary: Manager's Role

Managers are a powerful but underutilized resource to accelerate learning transfer and improve the results delivered by corporate education. To fill their role, however, managers need information about the course, their direct reports' objectives, and how best they can contribute to the process, as well as coaching skills. In breakthrough programs, learning and development helps supply these and senior management makes support for learning transfer a part of every manager's job—one that is monitored, recognized, and rewarded.

INSTRUCTORS AND FACILITATORS

Another important source of support for learning transfer is the learning and development department itself. When we surveyed participants at a leading technology firm about what they valued most about a program and follow-through, they ranked ongoing contact with the instructor very high. Similarly, participants in the University of Notre Dame's innovative Integral Leadership program indicated on follow-up interviews that they would like to have ongoing support from the faculty when they need on-the-job advice.

A Trusted Resource

Writing in *Best Practices in Leading the Global Workforce,* Teresa Roche, vice president, Global Learning and Leadership Development at Agilent Technologies, said: "Facilitators are selected for their superior knowledge and teaching ability. During the program, participants come to value the facilitator's knowledge, opinion and advice. Yet, historically, teaching ended when the class ended; communication was cut off. As a result, there was no support for learning transfer from the facilitators— the very people with the greatest insight into the material and whose opinion the learners value most" (Roche & Wick, 2005, p. 6). There is an untapped opportunity to leverage their knowledge and skills in follow-through management.

Facilitator's New Role

To address this issue, Agilent redefined the role of facilitators so that their responsibilities now extend beyond the last day of class and into the learning transfer period. That is a significant departure from the prevailing paradigm that the role of educators is limited to delivering courses, and it requires a reallocation of resources. The new role definition includes providing "service after the sale." It supports the proposal by Broad and Newstrom (1992) that trainers should redefine their role from "strictly trainers/presenters to *facilitators of behavioral change on the job*" (p. 113) and the Robinsons' (1996) concept of "performance consultants." Roche and Wick (2005) put it this way: "Facilitators must move from the 'sage on the stage' to the 'guide by the side,' from facilitator of learning to facilitator of performance" (p. 13).

Agilent achieved this shift in roles by lightening the teaching schedule of their facilitators to free time for providing Phase III support. You can begin the process of change by asking your instructors to simply contact each participant two to three weeks after the course to ask, "How are things going in your effort to transfer your new skills?"

Recognizing that facilitators' time is valuable and limited, the Phase III support process must be efficient as well as effective. Agilent uses an electronic follow-through management system to streamline and support the process. Facilitators use the "dashboard" to efficiently identify and communicate with individuals in need of encouragement, recognition, or help.

The facilitator's comments can be targeted and personally relevant because they are provided in the context of the participants' goals, progress, and issues. Over time, the process becomes increasingly efficient. Participants tend to encounter the same kinds of challenges and questions. Facilitators can create a personal library of suggestions and responses for the most frequently encountered issues. When one of the issues to which they have already responded recurs, they can quickly personalize a prior response, gaining efficiency with each iteration of the program. An outstanding example of this approach is Richard Jolly at the London Business School, who sent more than six hundred messages to his executive MBA students during their three-month follow-through period. Given that these students represented more than a dozen countries and as many time zones, no other approach would have been practicable.

PEERS: LEARNING COMMUNITIES

A third potent but underutilized resource for ongoing support is the other participants in the program themselves. Linda Sharkey, director of leadership development at General Electric, noted the value of peer-to-peer coaching in GE's renowned leadership development program: "Because all of our leadership teams participated in the 360 survey feedback process, they now work as teams to help each other improve. When the leadership teams share their developmental needs with each other and use the coaching model, they often find three things: 1) they have similar issues, 2) they get great improvement suggestions from each other, and 3) they get support from each other to improve" (2003, p. 198).

Programs should take advantage of the collective knowledge and experience of the participants by encouraging shared learning throughout all three phases. Peer support relationships are especially valuable in the learning transfer (Phase III) period. Etienne Wenger, who studies communities of practice, explained why they are so powerful: "There is something about hearing the word of someone who is a peer that makes the relevance of the knowledge that you get very immediate. So for me that is the fundamental value proposition in a peer-to-peer network" (quoted in Dulworth & Forcillo, 2005, p. 111). Although peer-to-peer support can take many forms, we have found computer-based systems especially valuable in open-enrollment or global programs in which participants disperse to different countries or companies.

Helping participants stay in touch can be as simple as sharing e-mail addresses or as robust as a fully integrated follow-through management system that allows participants to view one another's progress reports and exchange feedback.

Attesting to the value that participants place on maintaining their learning network, participants in one of Cornell's open-enrollment leadership development programs organized a class reunion. Participants in a recent session at the Center for Creative Leadership created their own website to help stay connected, and fellows in one of the Kellogg national leadership programs have meet annually for almost twenty years.

Learning and development can help build and sustain the learning community by reconvening groups, either in person or virtually. Gary Jusela, who has led learning organizations at Boeing, Cisco, and Home Depot, said:

> I am a huge believer in learning events that are designed as multi-stage events. I think multi-stage is always better and more impactful than one-shot. If you can have learning practice and reflection built in, plus coming back for some disciplined collective reflection, it really increases the odds of getting real transferability.
>
> Learning from experience happens by thinking about the experience itself: what worked and what did not. What I love is bringing people back and having them reflect on their experiences in small groups and then also share some of that collectively in the larger room. What people discover is that they are not so alone, or they are

not so weird. Everybody struggles with these things and they can learn from each other and get some tips about how to overcome some of the most perplexing struggles (Jusela, interview).

CRITICAL MASS

Learning transfer is enhanced when a critical mass of employees has received the same training simultaneously. This creates an environment in which learners can provide mutual support and reinforcement for the new language, concepts, and behaviors. Creating critical mass and a supportive environment is especially important if the learning and development is part of a significant change initiative. If possible, train entire teams together, or at least the majority of employees at a particular level and site.

Targeting specific departments, business units, or working groups and training a significant number quickly has greater chance of success than the "shotgun" approach of one here, one there. When only a small number of individuals has been trained, the freshly-minted "evangelists" for the new approach are under tremendous pressure to conform to the old way of doing things when they return to work. If they are "lone voices crying in the wilderness," few will be successful in applying what they learned. A group of disciples has a better chance of keeping the faith. "If you are looking for a substantial uplift in company performance, a lot of people need to be learning similar things, all at the same time" (Bordonaro, 2005, p. 162).

PROFESSIONAL COACHES

Professional coaches are another potential source of active support. Professional mentors can help managers master the art of leadership in the same way that professional coaches help musicians, actors, athletes, and other performers master their arts. According to Mary Jane Knudsen, vice president of human resources at Fidelity Investments, "Nearly every major corporation—and progressive smaller ones as well—identify executive coaching as one of their critical executive and leadership development activities" (2005, p. 40). Professional coaches can be invaluable in helping participants maximize the value of formal training, 360-degree feedback, and on-the-job learning experiences. Having a coach is in itself an incentive to follow through, practice, and reflect.

However, using executive-level coaches is cost prohibitive for most learning and development. In our experience, participants in new manager programs don't need executive coaches, but they do need access to mentors more experienced and knowledgeable than themselves. If outside instructors are used in the program, consider retaining them to provide Phase III coaching. Other sources of coaches include managers, internal development specialists, and HR generalists.

Goldsmith and Morgan (2004) compared the results of development programs in eight different companies. Some used paid external coaches, others used internal coaches. In each case, the most important variable in predicting improved effectiveness was the degree to which the participants followed up with coworkers on their developmental goals. Both internal and external coaches added value. Goldsmith and Morgan concluded: "Coaching can be a great complement to training. Leaders can clearly benefit from coaching, but it does not have to be done by external coaches."

New technologies offer the potential for new forms of ongoing coaching and support that foster interaction and, at the same time, reduce the time commitment for busy providers. The Center for Creative Leadership, for example, has introduced a "blended coaching approach" using a follow-through management system as the vehicle. The goal is to combine the best of "hi-tech with high touch" to provide both immediate and sustained support (Whyman, Santana & Allen, 2005).

Trained psychologist-coaches meet with participants during the Center's Leadership Development Program (LDP)® to help them interpret the results of tests and exercises and the feedback they have received from peers, reports, and managers. Near the end of the residential portion of the program, participants set learning transfer goals for applying what they have learned to their personal development. These are forwarded electronically to the LDP coaches, who respond in writing. Because the coaches and participants have met already in person, subsequent remote coaching is targeted, personal, and credible.

Such a blended approach to coaching—augmenting face-to-face or telephone coaching with written feedback in a follow-through management system—has significant advantages for both the coach and the learner. First, it does not require that both coach and learner be in the same place at the same time, or available by phone simultaneously, for mentoring to take place. The time wasted playing telephone tag is eliminated.

Second, when coaching is part of the follow-through system, the coach can review the participants' most recent activities, successes, issues, and insights before the interchange. This is not only more efficient and accurate than a verbal retelling, but it allows the coach more time to consider the most helpful advice or questions—rather than having to respond off the cuff in real time.

Third, online coaching leaves a record in the database. This is helpful to the learners in that they can refer to it again later. It also is helpful to the coach because over time he or she builds a library of well-thought-through and articulated coaching responses to particular issues. And it is helpful to learning leaders because they are able to monitor both the quantity and quality of the advice being provided. This is especially important when paid coaches are employed. Given the cost of professional coaching, we have been surprised by how many learning organizations invest substantial sums in executive coaching, with no system to monitor the quality or value received.

More and more companies are implementing online coaching as part of the complete learning experience, including British Telecom, Coca-Cola, GlaxoSmithKline, Fidelity Investments, and Cushman and Wakefield, to name a few. They have been able to document thoughtful, constructive input from managers, coaches, and peers (Exhibit D5.2).

Exhibit D5.2. Examples of Online Blended Coaching.

- "Your communication with the staff and your continued efforts to work on your goals have had a positive effect on my relationship with you as my manager, mentor, and team member. . . . I also notice that you now listen to all the team members' opinions on subjects that might normally have been non-discussible at staff meetings before. Even if you don't agree, you have more often listened rather than jumping in and answering quickly."

- "I believe you have made significant progress on the goals you have set for yourself. You have backed away from telling us how to do our jobs to asking us if we need any help with our job tasks and guiding us in the right direction when we get off path."

- "Your progress has been good over the period. I've found that you have been more oriented to driving performance through the what rather than the how. This is important as we take on higher-level activities within the team and we become more experienced."

- "From my own experience I have learned that if you take the time to make the first move and offer to help someone in need and connect on a personal level . . . this goes a long way to build . . . relationships and is very beneficial in helping us become better collaborators (and people!)."

FEEDBACK SUSTAINS FOLLOW-THROUGH

When participants receive feedback on their efforts, it is a powerful incentive to continue those efforts. How important an incentive feedback can be was illustrated by work we did with an international technology company. We reviewed the records from the *Friday5s* follow-through system for over five thousand managers who had participated in a companywide leadership skills program.

We compared the subsequent behavior of those who requested *and received* feedback to those who requested feedback but received none. The difference was dramatic. The group that received written feedback through the *Friday5s* system completed, on average, twice as many Phase III updates as those who did not (Figure D5.2). Since the system did not capture feedback provided in person or by phone, the actual magnitude of the effect is probably even greater.

Figure D5.2. Effect of Feedback. Participants Who Received Written Feedback Completed Twice as Many Phase III Updates as Those Who Did Not Receive Feedback.

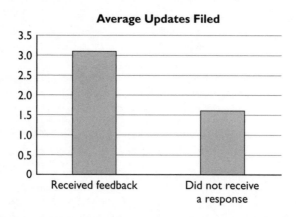

This makes sense. If employees ask their manager for assistance with learning transfer and the manager provides it, that sends a clear signal that what they are doing is important to the manager and worth their time. Conversely, if they ask for feedback and the request is ignored, that sends an equally clear signal (intentional or unintentional) that their manager does not value the effort and that they should spend their time on other things.

The conclusion is that companies need to make sure that *all* the signals employees receive regarding the importance of learning and development are consistent and mutually reinforcing. That means investing in people, systems, and processes to provide, monitor, and continuously improve active support for transfer and application.

ANALOGY TO CUSTOMER SUPPORT

We realized that there were important parallels between postcourse learning support and postpurchase customer support. The most effective programs are those that provide participants with ongoing, active support for the same reasons that the most successful companies are those that provide their customers with ongoing high-quality customer support.

Well-managed companies know that the ability to make future sales depends on the extent to which customers are satisfied with their most recent purchase. Customer satisfaction depends on their "whole product" experience, which includes not only the quality of the product itself, but whether they are able to use it successfully, whether it meets their expectations, and the quality of the postpurchase support (Figure D5.3). Products come with owner's manuals because manufacturers know that even though a feature was demonstrated in the showroom, a consumer may not remember how to use it days or weeks later. If consumers can't figure out how to use something, they won't use it, and they will be dissatisfied with their purchase. They will take their future business to a competitor.

Figure D5.3. Customer Satisfaction Depends
on Variables That Include Service After the Sale.

To prosper in the competition for corporate resources, learning and development must maximize its customers' satisfaction. Learning organizations need to take a page from customer-oriented businesses and think in terms of the "whole product"—which includes service after the sale. In the same way that customers' satisfaction depends on whether they are able to use the product to achieve the purpose for which they bought it, management's satisfaction with a learning and development program depends on whether participants are able to use what they have learned to produce the results that the business leaders need. Therefore, it is in both the company's and the learning organization's best interests to invest resources to provide high-quality equivalents of owner's manuals and after-the-sale support.

Owner's Manuals for Corporate Education

Manufacturers invest significant time and energy putting together and testing product manuals to make sure that they are easy to use and answer the most-frequently asked questions. A well-designed user's manual is not merely a compendium of product information. It anticipates the kind of difficulties a user might encounter and provides practical advice on what to do. If refrigerators, software, quarter-inch drills, and toasters all come with owner's manuals, shouldn't a development program? Doesn't it make sense to provide advice on the kinds of questions and challenges learners will face as they strive to convert capability into performance?

Creating an effective product manual for corporate education requires a new way of thinking about educational content. The challenge is not so much how to make the knowledge available, but how to make it *accessible* in a way that facilitates its application. Typical program binders are designed to support instruction rather than as references for transfer and application. It is difficult to locate specific topics and suggestions for action in course notebooks, which may be why most of the program participants we interviewed said they rarely refer to them once the program is over.

Participants in corporate education programs often struggle to translate their development objectives into concrete actions once they return to work. What seemed clear during the classroom exercise is less so in the context of day-to-day work. They value guidance about how to apply course principles. In other words, they need an owner's manual for their new capabilities that explains how to use them in the same way that a product manual explains how to install a new printer cartridge or reset the VCR's clock.

A number of texts have been published to fulfill this need, such as *FYI: For Your Improvement* (Lombardo & Eichinger, 2000), *Successful Manager's Handbook* (Gebelein et al., 2005), *Essential Manager's Handbook* (Heller & Hindle, 1998), and others. The most useful of these provide specific suggestions on how to improve particular competencies. For example, the *Essential Manager's Manual* provides this advice on running team meetings:

> Making team meetings effective is a major test of leadership skills. The key to holding a productive meeting is to actively involve everybody in the proceedings. Ensure that team members understand the purpose of each meeting and what is expected of them.
>
> Change the chairperson at each meeting to involve everybody.
>
> Try to delegate as much as possible to other members of the team.
>
> Distribute agendas in advance of the meeting to give your team time to prepare. (p. 390)

The popularity of such guides attests to the need they fulfill. The challenge, however, is that more and more companies are electing to define their own leadership models and terms in order to emphasize specific attributes they consider important to their culture and corporate strategy. Examples include Cisco's *Leader Behaviors,* Sun Microsystems's *People Management Standards,* AstraZeneca's *Leadership Capabilities,* Unilever's *Leadership Competencies,* and so forth. Truly embedding these models in a culture requires consistent use of terms and concepts over time.

Although customized assessments and programs reinforce company-specific strategy and leadership concepts, they reduce the utility of more generalized material and "user's manuals." Learners are confused when they are provided materials, instruments, and guides that use different terminology for the same concepts, none of which may exactly match the corporate credo. The welter of conflicting terms and concepts creates suspicion about whether the company is truly committed to the avowed model or whether it is yet another "trend du jour." To maximize reinforcement and utility, all the program materials, including the post-course user's guides, should use a consistent set of terms and concepts.

Online Guides

The Internet is increasingly being used to provide customer support. On-line user's guides can be more comprehensive, more readily updated, more easily expanded, and more quickly searched than printed versions. Online Phase III support for corporate education could provide similar advantages, as well as offer customized content to meet specific learning objectives and reinforce company-specific terms and concepts.

To realize the potential benefits of online systems, however, requires a new approach. Simply offering electronic copies of books and binders fails to take advantage of technology, nor do such compendia meet the information needs of time-pressed managers. To be truly effective in supporting learning transfer, a Phase III guidance system must

- Be an integral part of the follow-through process
- Make information available at the place and moment it is needed
- Provide simple, fast, and specific access
- Offer suggestions that are concrete and actionable
- Supply information in short, digestible segments without being superficial
- Continue to evolve, adding company-specific knowledge and best practices after each iteration of the program

MUST BE AN INTEGRAL PART OF THE FOLLOW-THROUGH PROCESS Even superlative support systems will languish if they are not part of an overall system of follow-through. A core principle of andragogy (adult education) is that adults require a "need to know" before they will seek out information and learn (Knowles, Holton & Swanson, 2005, p. 64). In recent years, many companies have invested substantial sums to buy or build extensive content sites, only to be disappointed by the paucity of "hits." The problem is that today's time pressures preclude "browsing" sites, however rich and interesting, unless there is a specific need, a problem to solve, or task to complete. Online information systems will be used more often when they are embedded in the learning transfer process.

MAKE INFORMATION AVAILABLE AT THE PLACE AND MOMENT IT IS NEEDED Solutions are most valuable and best remembered when they are discovered in the context of an immediate and pressing problem. The ideal moment to reinforce a technique, skill, or principle from corporate learning and development is when a relevant problem is encountered in the conduct of work. Thus the ideal transfer support system needs to offer the learner ideas just in time—at the moment and in the context when he or she needs it.

Income tax preparation software, such as *TurboTax®*, is an excellent example of this principle at work. Each form contains links to the relevant income tax instructions and expert advice. The links are context-sensitive, so they go directly to the pertinent section of the tax code. Links provide practical how-to suggestions, as well as definitions and examples.

The principle of immediate, context-sensitive availability can be applied to any Internet- or intranet-based learning transfer support system. The beauty of hypertext transfer protocol (http) is that it does not require linear progression. Users can follow their unique approach to the topic, and many different paths can link to the same resource (Figure D5.4).

In planning support for Phase III learning, consider where there will be a need to know. Place links there to relevant items in the knowledge system, as these are the times and places where additional information will be most valuable and employed most often.

Figure D5.4. The Beauty of Hypertext and Electronic Databases Is That They Provide Many Different Paths to the Same Information Based on the Needs and Thought Patterns of Different Users.

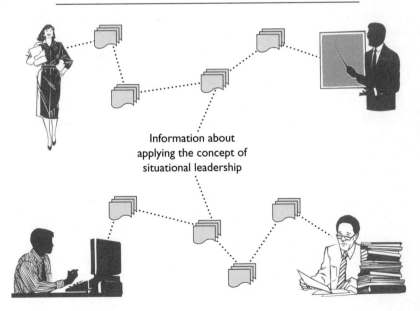

Information about applying the concept of situational leadership

The Phase III support system we developed to support our follow-through management system is an example of integrating the user's guide into the transfer and application process (Wick & Pollock, 2004a). As part of the Phase III process, participants are required to periodically stop, reflect, and plan for their continued progress. We placed a link called GuideMe® immediately adjacent to the question about the participant's plans for next steps (Figure D5.5). This ensures that the information needed to support planning is available when and where it is needed: at the time participants are considering what they should do next.

Figure D5.5. An Example of Making Advice Available at the Time and Place It Is Needed. The Link to the Online Support System (GuideMe®) Is Placed Adjacent to the Question About Action Plans.

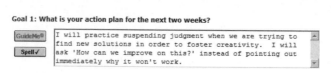

Goal 1: What is your action plan for the next two weeks?

```
GuideMe®    I will practice suspending judgment when we are trying to
            find new solutions in order to foster creativity.  I will
Spell✓      ask 'How can we improve on this?' instead of pointing out
            immediately why it won't work.
```

PROVIDE SIMPLE, FAST, AND SPECIFIC ACCESS Lack of time is the most common reason that participants give for not doing more to transfer and practice new skills after training. E-mail, cell phones, voice mail, faxes, memoranda, and other communications pour in. Time runs out. Speed matters. A system that purports to support ongoing development in Phase III has to be simple, specific, and *fast*. If it takes too long to learn or to glean information, it will fail.

To meet the challenge of simple, fast, and specific, you need to work with the system designers to balance elegance with simplicity. The system must be easy to use and yet provide valuable information to high-potential, discriminating managers. Focus on utility, not glitz or entertainment. Avoid layouts, flashy graphics, or complex navigation; Web developers too often "think the most important part of a Web site is design" (Flanders & Willis, 1996, p. xvii), when in fact the most important part of the design is *functionality*.

Remember that the audience for the system is busy employees and managers who want to use it to quickly locate relevant information. Speed of access and relevance of the information are more important than the size of the database *per se*. The vast store of information available, coupled with fast and powerful search engines, should be an advantage of online information systems. But a search of the Internet for "how to delegate" returned over 37,000 links. "How to delegate effectively" returned 650. (Apparently it is easier to delegate than to do so effectively!) In both cases, some of the links were useful, but many were a waste of time. The sheer number is so overwhelming as to discourage all but the most dedicated searcher. Moreover, some of the advice is poor, or may run counter to your organization's principles and procedures.

When it comes to providing support for learning transfer, less is often more. Just as a user's guide is more useful than a technical reference manual for all but experts in a field, a targeted, relevant, coherent subset of practical advice about each subject will prove more useful for participants than an exhaustive treatment.

OFFER SUGGESTIONS THAT ARE CONCRETE AND ACTIONABLE An effective Phase III support system provides concrete, actionable suggestions—practical steps people can take to change their behavior in ways that will improve performance and deliver results. For a time-challenged executive looking to improve his or her performance, nothing is more frustrating than to invest the time seeking guidance, only to receive vague and general platitudes such as: "Be more strategic."

To ensure that the suggestions in the systems we developed are actionable, we insist that each be written as a positive statement in first-person future: "I will . . . ." This forces our contributors to think about how specific principles can be *applied* or specific skills *practiced,* not merely contemplated. The third discipline (deliver for application) applies as much to the learning transfer support system as it does to the course itself.

SUPPLY INFORMATION IN SHORT, MANAGEABLE SEGMENTS WITHOUT BEING SUPERFICIAL When people look at material on computer screens, only 16 percent read word by word (Nielsen, 1997). Most scan the material to rapidly pick out key concepts. They tend to avoid long, dense passages typical of books and articles. They prefer short, clear writing, frequent paragraph breaks, bullets, and other condensation techniques.

Nielsen (1997) recommends that material for presentation on the Web be rewritten specifically for this purpose by using "scannable" text:

- Highlighted *keywords* (hypertext links serve as one form of highlighting; typeface variations and color are others)
- Meaningful *subheadings* (not "clever" ones)

- Bulleted *lists*
- *One idea* per paragraph (users will skip over any additional ideas if they are not caught by the first few words in the paragraph)
- The *inverted pyramid* style, starting with the conclusion
- *Half the word count* (or less) than conventional writing

Researchers at Sun Microsystems found that they could double the usability of information on the Web when it was rewritten following these guidelines (Nielsen, Schemenaur, & Fox, n.d.). Improvements were seen in all key metrics: reduced task time, fewer errors, greater content retention, and higher user satisfaction.

Brevity, however, carries the attendant risk of superficiality. A savvy manager will be skeptical of unsupported one-liners of "things to do" or guides that reduce the complex tasks of management to superficial sound bites. The solution to the speed-depth paradox is to use the capabilities of electronic media to present "top-line" information succinctly, with hypertext links to more in-depth treatment and references. This allows users to retain control; they can quickly review a large amount of summary information with the option to pursue knowledge in depth in areas of special interest.

We have implemented these concepts in our own work by first filtering the material to be presented by the type of objective the person is pursuing, then providing the first level of suggestions as short action statements. For those who want more explanation or deeper understanding there is a "Tell Me More" link to additional information, background, and references to additional resources (Figure D5.6).

CONTINUE TO IMPROVE AND EVOLVE Companies and individuals must learn and adapt to stay competitive. The Phase III support system must follow suit. The information in the support system should itself evolve and improve over time as conditions change and new best practices emerge.

The most useful suggestions for improving performance are those rooted in the company itself—things that have proven successful for other leaders in its peculiar culture and environment. The challenge is to identify these best practices and capture them in a form that can be fed back into the system and rapidly disseminated to others. Companies that are able to achieve such organizational learning have a decided competitive advantage.

Figure D5.6. An Example of an Online
Support System That Illustrates Action Orientation as
Well as the Ability to (Optionally) View Additional Details.

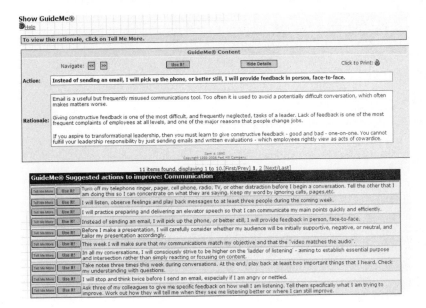

•

Case Study: Home Depot—Store Manager Forums

Home Depot was under increasing pressure to improve its performance. After years of unprecedented growth, the company was facing fierce competition, the founders were retiring, a new management team was in place, and the stock price was off 50 percent from its high.

Recognizing that individual store managers were vital to the company's success, then Chief Learning Officer Gary Jusela worked with the senior-most management to design a bold series of large-scale learning forums, first for district managers and then for store managers. Each of the forums consisted of an intensive one-week residential experience followed by ten weeks of managed follow-through.

The goals included elevating leadership and management skills, building confidence in the company and in themselves, and shifting to a culture of focus, discipline, and process. To make it happen quickly and build critical mass, the roll-out was aggressive; programs were delivered to over 250 district managers and 1,600 store managers in less than six months.

Underscoring senior management's support, the CEO, COO, and CFO participated in every forum. They spoke directly to the need for managers to act on what they were learning and to the concept of shared accountability for running effective stores and delivering results. Their message was clear, powerful, and passionate; it left no doubt in the manager's minds of what was expected.

On the last day of the forums, participants each set two high-priority business goals and one leadership goal. Action and communication plans were developed and practiced, and the *Friday5s* follow-through system was introduced and demonstrated. Over the following ten weeks, participants entered their actions, progress, and best practices into the system. Presidents, regional VPs, and district managers all had access to the system; they were able to easily track and review results and provide input where appropriate.

The results were impressive. The forums were widely seen as pivotal for the company—turning the tide by bringing the managers on board with the CEO both emotionally and intellectually. Thousands of innovations were put in place in areas such as driving sales, motivating associates, reducing inventory loss (shrink), improving profitability, and improving in-stock availability. Strong support was generated to cascade the process further.

When we interviewed Jusela, now an independent learning consultant, about critical success factors, he said: "The number one thing that comes to mind is to really think through the receptor site for the learning in terms of the environment you are sending the person back into; and I will go to the Home Depot case here. I think it was very, very significant that we put all the district managers through the learning experience in short order before jumping in and hitting all of the store managers. That way their immediate bosses had the experience of learning, had the experience of working with the follow-through technology, and were better positioned to be supportive coaches. The receive site is extremely important" (Jusela, interview).

●

An excellent example of the potential of this approach comes from the Home Depot's Store Managers Learning Forums (see Case Study: Home Depot). To help drive the performance of its stores, Home Depot embarked on an ambitious program to educate all of its 1,600-plus store managers. To ensure that the program had impact, each manager was asked to report progress over a three-month period via the *Friday5s* follow-through system. At the end of the period, each manager was asked: "What is the one change you have made that has had the biggest impact on making your store run better?" The results were hundreds of examples of changes that had proven effective in actual practice. The recommendations had immediate credibility, since they were generated and tested by working store managers. Such a system, repeated over time, would produce an invaluable repository of shared company knowledge about best practices in their industry.

Another example is Meridian Resources' GlobeSmart program, which provides tips and insights to help executives be effective in cultures different from their own (Meridian Resources, n.d.). The system continues to get smarter by inviting executives who have experience working in particular cultures to contribute ideas and insights. These are checked, edited, and added to the database so that over time the system becomes increasingly rich, deep, and specific.

SUMMARY

The fifth discipline that characterizes breakthrough educational programs is that they deploy active, ongoing support in Phase III after the traditional "course" is over. By providing both accountability and support, they extend the learning period and accelerate learning transfer to the production of results. The best corporate education programs approach Phase III support with the same rigor and customer focus as the best consumer product companies approach product support. They work with senior leaders to create an environment conducive to learning transfer. They engage managers to provide support throughout the application phase, backed up by learning and coaching professionals. They provide high-quality, practical user's guides that help participants be successful in transferring what they learn to their jobs.

Companies that invest a portion of their learning and development resources in providing Phase III support enjoy a greater return on their investment than companies stuck in the mistaken paradigm that equates learning to courses and classrooms.

•

ACTION POINTS

For Learning Leaders

- Think more holistically about your programs.
  - Where is the most value created? Where is it being allowed to dissipate?

- What are the leverage points, especially in Phase III, where there is potential to accelerate value creation?
- Compare where you are spending resources to where the most value is created. Are they proportional?
- Interview a sample of participants three months after a learning or development program.
  - Find out where they have achieved success and what factors supported their efforts. Maximize these in subsequent iterations.
  - Identify the barriers that impeded their progress or worked against learning transfer and application.
  - Present your findings to management with a plan for how to address them.

For Line Leaders

- Review the plans of proposed and ongoing programs at your company.
  - Are there adequate systems and resources to provide support for learning transfer?
  - If not, leave no doubt about the importance you place on active support for learning transfer by rejecting any proposal in which the learning transfer process is not addressed.
- At the same time, review your own actions and those of your team.
  - Is what you do consistent with what you say about the importance of a return on training and development?
  - Do you and your managers model the behaviors you expect of others?
  - Do you hold your team accountable for maximizing the value of what they and what their subordinates learn?
  - Do you recognize and reward managers who do a superior job of developing their direct reports?
  - If not, put your own house in order. Otherwise, employees will sense the disconnect between your words and actions. Both your credibility and the effectiveness of training initiatives will suffer.

D6

DOCUMENT RESULTS

*You, your leaders, and your investors are
interested in learning only insofar as it improves
performance and gets business results.*

—Michael Dulworth and Frank Bordonaro

THE SIXTH DISCIPLINE is to document results. All of the work by designers, facilitators, participants, coaches, and managers is for naught unless it manifests as demonstrable results of importance to the business. Credible, reliable measures are needed to determine whether the training investment is paying dividends and what refinements are needed to further improve the program's effectiveness.

In this chapter, we discuss

- Why document results
- What to measure
- How to measure
- Obstacles
- Solutions
- Making the most of results
- A caveat
- Action points for learning and line leaders

WHY DOCUMENT RESULTS?

Relevant, reliable, and credible measures of the impact of learning and development are essential to (1) justify continued investment and (2) support continuous improvement.

Justify Continued Investment

When we polled learning leaders who attended our Best Practices Summit, everyone reported increased pressure to document results; more than half rated the pressure as "significant" or "very great" (Wick & Pollock, 2004b). The driving force was summed up by Peggy Parskey, of Hewlett-Packard: "Business sponsors are specifically asking, 'Was this a good investment for me? Because I have to decide whether I am going to do it again; I have to decide whether it is worth continuing to invest.'"

If an intervention is producing the desired results, it makes sense to continue to invest in it; if the desired results are not being achieved, it is time to make a change. Data are needed to justify the decision. But this is not just a one-time decision. Measurement and analysis of educational investments need to be ongoing; annual budget cycles and changing business conditions require revisiting resource allocations periodically.

Because learning and development consumes time and money, it competes with other needs and opportunities for corporate resources. The kinds of trade-offs that management must make include: Are the interests of the shareholders, customers, and employees better served by investing resources in a learning program or new product development? Should education be funded rather than CRM software, a marketing program, manufacturing equipment, or an improvement in net profit?

NO EXEMPTIONS In Idalene Kesner's 2003 *Harvard Business Review* Case "Leadership Development: Perk or Priority?" the fictitious learning director, Karen Barton, complains: "I hate it when people make those kinds of comparisons. First, we are talking about people in my case. That's different from calculating the payback from a machine" (p. 31).

Documenting the results of education *is* different from calculating the payback from a machine in terms of the methodology used and the number of other variables that must be taken into account. But arguing that documenting educational results is different, or difficult, or time-consuming does not change the laws of nature; it does not earn you an exemption. If you consume resources, sooner or later you will be called to account for them.

One of the key problems that Lou Gerstner encountered when he arrived at IBM was a lack of accountability. Management meetings were dominated by superficial overheads. He eliminated such "management by foils" and instead required written proposals. More important, he kept the proposals. At appropriate intervals, he required progress reports based on the promised results of the original proposals. "If you said that investing $20 million could generate $60 million in new revenue within a year, you'd be back in his office a year later if those revenues didn't materialize" (Kirkpatrick, 2002).

BELIEVABLE BENEFITS The decision whether or not to fund an initiative depends on the magnitude and believability of the benefits being promised. Believability, in turn, depends on the quality of the analysis and the presenting department's past track record. If it has consistently delivered on its promises, the likelihood of funding is greatly increased. If the unit has poor credibility, either because it has chronically overpromised benefits or because it is unable to document the results of prior investments, the odds of its gaining additional resources are greatly decreased.

A well-established record of adding value is the best defense for the learning and development budget in times of economic constraint. Establishing the track record of contribution must be done before it is needed. Daniel Tobin (1998) put it this way: "If you wait until the CEO asks for an ROI study to . . . try to demonstrate how your training group adds value to your company, it is too late—the CEO has already decided to greatly reduce your budget, or to eliminate the training group altogether."

Programs that demonstrate sound, thorough, credible, and auditable evidence of results are able to garner additional investment; those that cannot are at risk. Those who are able to illustrate the value they add (in terms persuasive to those who make the allocation decisions) will have a seat at the table; those who cannot may find themselves without a place when the rations get short. As Peter Drucker put it: "If you can't measure it, you can't manage it." The only way to prove that the resources have been well used is to document relevant results.

Support Continuous Improvement

The other reason to assess outcomes is to drive continual improvement in learning and development. Measurement is the engine. Effectiveness and efficiency are increased by rigorously assessing the quality of the current output, implementing ideas for improvement, measuring the impact, and repeating the procedure. These concepts originated in manufacturing, but they apply equally to learning and development and other business processes.

Figure D6.1. Improvement Should Be a Continuous Cycle. There Are Four Key Steps in Each Iteration: Plan–Do–Study–Act.

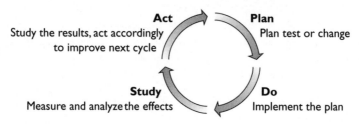

The PDSA Quality Cycle

Act
Study the results, act accordingly
to improve next cycle

Plan
Plan test or change

Study
Measure and analyze the effects

Do
Implement the plan

PDSA CYCLE The Plan–Do–Study–Act (PDSA) cycle (also called the PDCA or Deming cycle) is a core tool of continuous improvement (Figure D6.1). It is a never-ending process of planning improvements, implementing them, measuring the impact, and acting on the results to initiate the next cycle.

The power of a continuous cycle of improvement is enormous. In his best-selling book, *Good to Great,* Jim Collins (2001) likened the process of building a great organization to turning an enormous flywheel: "Good to great comes about by a cumulative process—step by step, action by action, decision by decision, turn by turn of the flywheel—that adds up to sustained and spectacular results" (p. 165).

MODEL FOR IMPROVEMENT Langley and colleagues (1996, p. 3) extended total quality concepts into a model for improvement by adding three questions:

- What are we trying to accomplish?
- How will we know?
- What are our options?

The importance of the first question—What are we trying to accomplish?—is obvious. The surest route to failure is to not define where success lies. As we discussed in D1, programs need to be designed with the end in mind. It follows that they need to be assessed against the objectives for which they were created. Evaluation cannot be simply tacked on as a separate activity after the fact; it needs to be an integral part of the design from the onset. As with the other disciplines that define breakthrough learning and development, documenting results is most effective when it involves partnership between general management and learning leaders.

The second question—How will we know?—is at the heart of D6, documenting results. Without some sort of tracking and evaluation system, it is impossible to know whether a program has been effective and changes have been positive, negative, or superfluous.

The third question—What are our options?—challenges learning leaders to come up with ideas for making good programs even better. The underlying assumption is that no matter how good a current process is, there are always opportunities for improvement. Identifying the most important areas to improve requires data about which objectives are being met or exceeded and which objectives are not. Brinkerhoff and Apking put it this way: "Finally, we see evaluation as the principal tool that learning leaders can use to accomplish this mission: building and strengthening learning capability, so that organizations reap continuously better results from their learning investments" (2001, p. 165).

To achieve Brinkerhoff's vision of "continuously better results from learning investments," learning organizations must:

- Clearly define outcomes (D1)
- Accurately assess *relevant* measures (D6)
- Be willing to make changes, experiment, and evaluate the results (PDSA)

An excellent example of these principles in practice is Humana's leadership development program, with its clear objectives, action plans, documented results, and improvement on subsequent cycles (see From the Top: Ray Vigil).

•
_____

From the Top: Ray Vigil, Chief Learning Officer, Humana, Inc.
Ray Vigil, CLO for Humana, Inc., helped lead a critical transformation of leadership development at Humana. He and his team began with the end in mind—what leaders needed to be able to do differently and better to achieve the organizational vision and transform the organization and industry.

Vigil also understood the need to "close the loop," to put in place systems to measure and rigorously evaluate the outcomes of the program to prove that it was achieving its objectives and support continuous improvement. As he explains: "We targeted the top 150 leaders in the business and proposed to take them through a business simulator that required them to make decisions about investments in the consumer-centric strategy and what they really meant in practice.

"At the end of each session, we asked them to identify an action plan that included the measurable outcomes that would occur if they were to implement the plan. After three or four months, we went back and did a survey to ask them which action plans they had implemented and what results they had been able to identify and value.

"We had savings come in on the order of $7 million. So for a fraction of the cost of the program, we were able to justify the benefits within just a few months. There were also additional savings that were going to take longer to realize; so, in total, we thought that we would achieve at least twice as much once all the returns came in.

"We did some after-action reviews to complete the cycle and used what we had learned to propose a second iteration. We really focus on taking the learning and applying it in action. We expect participants to pick a couple of things that they are accountable for to focus on where they can make changes and measure the results. We let them know that we want to follow up, to check and see how they have done.

"While reaction to the first simulator was very positive, participants feel the second one is even better. Their comments indicate that it is really accomplishing what we wanted: to have them see our business and the challenges we face in a very different way, to know what to do about it and to change behavior."

•

WHAT TO MEASURE

Since the goals of documenting results are to demonstrate that the program is meeting its objectives and identify areas for improvement, what to measure is obvious: what the program promised to deliver. If the ultimate aim of a sales training program is to increase sales, sales results are the "gold standard" for program effectiveness. A leadership development program should improve leadership, six sigma training should result in improved product quality, customer service programs should result in greater customer satisfaction, and so forth.

Yet such direct evidence of the business impact of learning programs is still relatively rare. Why has documenting results proven so challenging in corporate learning and development? There are three traps for the unwary:

- Measuring activity rather than outcomes
- Confusing positive reaction with positive results
- Adopting a learning versus business perspective

Trap 1: Measuring Activity Rather than Outcomes

"Confusing measurable with important" heads Frank Bordonaro's list of measurement traps that learning and development needs to avoid (2005, p. 214). This particular trap is "the practice of paying disproportionate attention to the measurable simply because it is measurable." Many of the aspects of learning and development that are easiest to quantify are not important because they do not measure results; as such, they are potentially misleading.

For example, the amount of training, the cost of training, and the number of programs are all readily quantifiable, but they are only indicators of input, not results. People who buy new cars, for example, don't care how many quality circles the manufacturer has, or how many improvement team meetings were held, or how many hours of quality training were offered. They are interested only in the quality of the product they bought.

In a like manner, businesses are ultimately interested only in the quality of the business-relevant results that learning and development produces. They should not care about the amount of training *per se*. If the results achieve the goal, it is safe to conclude that sufficient time was spent in training. If the results are inadequate, too little training is only one of many possible explanations.

Yet many educational units persist in reporting *activity* (the number of courses held, the number of people trained, and the hours of instruction provided) as opposed to *productivity*, the real measure of interest. In some ways, the advent of computer-based learning management systems (LMS) has made matters worse, since they accelerate the collection and reporting of activity data. The seductiveness of "measures"—such as the number of instructional hours, courses, number of trainees, and expenditures—is hard to resist, although in reality they only quantify the size of the investment, not whether it produced any benefit.

According to Phillips and Stone (2002): "[T]his mentality has contributed to a false expectation for some stakeholders that we can measure the impact of training by cost alone. Because costs can easily be identified, they are communicated in all types of ways, such as the cost of the program, cost per employee, cost per contact hour, and cost compared to industry standard. While these methods may be helpful for efficiency comparisons, they have no relationship to results" (p. 203).

Measuring and reporting only cost may lead to underinvestment; it emphasizes efficiency over effectiveness. The old adage is that "you cannot save your way to success." The least costly solution may not be the best. The "cheapest" approach to training (at least in terms of out-of-pocket expense) is to do nothing—eliminate learning and development altogether. Yet this will prove the most expensive in the long run in terms of competitiveness, innovation, employee retention, and so forth. Likewise, from the myopic point of view of the budget, investing nothing in learning transfer is "free" when in fact it is very costly in terms of diminished return on the overall educational investment.

Trap 2: Confusing Positive Reaction with Positive Results

End-of-course evaluations provide readily available metrics whose importance is frequently over-emphasized. It is unfortunate that participants' immediate reactions to the program are not a better indicator of its value to the business. If they were, then documenting the benefit of learning and development would be as simple as distributing an end-of-course survey. A positive reaction, though desirable, says little about how much actual learning took place, whether the learning was relevant to organizational and personal improvement, and whether it will be usefully applied on the job.

Dixon (1990), for example, found no significant correlation between postcourse test scores and participants' perception of the program's relevance, their estimation of amount learned, enjoyment, or instructor's skill. Studies of instructor evaluation in higher education revealed an inverse correlation between the importance of the instructor's style and the intellectual rigor of the subject. In other words, the instructor's style was much more important in the overall reaction to the course if the material was "lightweight." The more academically demanding the subject matter, the less importance was placed on style per se.

More recently, Ruona and colleagues (2002) studied the relationship between learner reactions and learning transfer by using the Learner Transfer System Inventory. They concluded: "This study supports the position that reaction measures have limited use in evaluating the outcomes of learning and development." That should not be surprising, given the other factors (discussed in D4) that have a powerful influence on the learning transfer process. Thus, the ubiquitous end-of-course evaluations should be viewed as a useful measure of immediate consumer satisfaction, but they should not be confused with, or presented as, proof that value was created.

Trap 3: Adopting a Learning Versus Business Perspective on Results

In 1959, Donald Kirkpatrick wrote a series of articles about evaluating training programs, which he later expanded into a book, *Evaluating Training Programs,* now in its second edition (Kirkpatrick, 1998). He posited four "levels" of evaluation: reaction, learning, behavior, and results. Phillips (2003) subsequently proposed that return on investment (ROI) constitutes a fifth "level" (Exhibit D6.1).

Kirkpatrick's model has had a profound influence on thinking about measurement in learning and development. It is deeply embedded in the training vernacular. Unfortunately, it is not a construct widely shared by business leaders, who are principally concerned with learning's business impact. Thus, when learning leaders write and speak in terms of "levels"

Exhibit D6.1. Levels of Evaluation of Training and Development Programs.

Level 1

The first and most basic level of evaluation in Kirkpatrick's model is reaction. It is essentially a measure of participants' satisfaction with the program, typically collected by end-of-course evaluations.

Level 2

Kirkpatrick defined level 2 as evaluation of the learning that took place, which he defined as changed attitudes, increased knowledge, or improved skill.

Level 3

Level 3 evaluation is an assessment of behavior change on the job, an indicator of the transfer of learning.

Level 4

Kirkpatrick called his fourth level "Results," which he defined as changes in key business metrics such as increased production, improved quality, decreased costs, reduced turnover, and so forth.

Level 5

Phillips has proposed that return on investment should be viewed as a fifth level of evaluation (Phillips, 2003), arguing that the real measure of success is not simply what results were produced, but their value in proportion to the cost of producing them.

of evaluation to their business colleagues, it reflects a learning-centric perspective that tends to confuse rather than clarify issues and contribute to the lack of understanding between the business and learning functions. "History has proven that managers will not learn your language or shift to your focus, so it is you who must adapt" (Sullivan, 2005, p. 283).

What both business leaders and learning leaders are really interested in is the business impact—whether or not the learning and development initiative is contributing to the overall health and prosperity of the enterprise. In this regard, the insistence by some authors that each level must be assessed before the next is attempted (Kirkpatrick, 1998; Phillips & Stone, 2002) is counterproductive, as it directs resources to measuring "levels" of results that are of limited interest or value. We believe that the right approach is to focus first on measuring results that reflect, as closely as possible, the business objectives identified in the impact map. Then, if the results are suboptimal, use assessments of the transfer environment, amount learned, or reaction diagnostically to identify the areas most in need of improvement.

The answer then about what to measure is simple: what the program promised, evaluated from a business perspective. The challenge then becomes how to measure the results in a reliable, efficient, and credible manner.

HOW TO MEASURE

The effort expended to document results should be proportional to the size of the investment (time and dollars) made in the initiative. The greater the cost and strategic value of the program, the more rigorous the evaluation should be. Inevitably, there are more variables than can be collected or analyzed. The key is to pick the "critical few" parameters that yield evidence about whether the program is meeting its objectives and that management will accept as relevant and credible.

Whenever possible, make use of data that the company routinely collects as part of its ongoing business processes, such as sales, expenses, number of complaints, quality index, and so forth. They are credible and "free." Colleagues in finance, quality assurance, or information technology may be able to provide such data and to break out specific subsets to assist in the analysis. For some readily quantifiable output measures, it may be possible to add items to existing data systems at relatively low cost to obtain the needed level of detail. External, third-party data, such as independent customer satisfaction or sales force ratings, may be available. Such measures have the advantage of high credibility because of their independence and objectivity.

If the data needed to judge specific program objectives are not collected routinely, your challenge is to design a reliable and efficient way to obtain them.

Evidence of Behavior Change

Learning and development programs produce business impact through the subsequent actions and behaviors of participants. Although these ultimately can be converted to economic terms as a result of greater customer satisfaction, improved sales efficiency, better employee retention, improved execution, and so forth, behavioral changes are *results* in their own right—evidence that the learning program is having an effect. David Brennan, CEO of AstraZeneca, put it this way:

> Obviously, people want to quantify business results. I think that while that is an important measure, the kinds of things that are much more measurable are the quality of the behavioral outcomes of the programs. If we believe that coaching is an important part of the performance management process, and we put coaching programs in place, then what we want to measure is the quality of the coaching— not as perceived by the coaches, but by the people being coached. If we say that demonstrating behaviors about the team's passion for winning is important to us, then what we have to do is ping the environment to see whether or not those behaviors are being demonstrated by people and that they are being reinforced by management. There are other, harder measures you can put in place . . . but in terms of the operating environment of the organization, evaluation needs to be much more focused on the behavioral outcomes that you're driving for (Brennan, interview).

Evidence of behavior change is based on observation. Credible measures of behavioral changes in leadership skills, strategic thinking, innovation, teamwork, and so forth are ratings from people in a position to observe relevant situations and competent to assess changes (if any) in skills and behaviors. David Campbell put it succinctly: "The opinion of those being led is relevant to the assessment of the leader."

In other words, if you want to evaluate whether there has been a change in leadership ability, you need to ask leaders' direct reports and peers—not simply the leaders themselves. Marshall Goldsmith simply asks peers and subordinates to rate the participant's change in effectiveness on a seven-point scale from –3 to +3 (Goldsmith, 1996, p. 233). Repeated mini-360-degree assessments, DiSC® evaluations, REFLECTIONS®, and similar instruments also can be used to illustrate that the program has produced meaningful and beneficial change "in the eyes of the beholders." Pfizer's learning organization used the improvement between preprogram and postprogram 360-degree assessments to document the impact of its Leading Edge program and justify continued investment (Trainor, 2004).

Coaching comments from online follow-through management systems or surveys provide narrative evidence of change engendered by the program as viewed by those who work with the participant (Exhibit D6.2). They can provide useful examples to amplify the quantitative data, as long as you take care, of course, to protect privacy and personal information.

Exhibit D6.2. Verbatim Examples of Managers' Feedback from a Follow-Through Management System That Provide Independent Confirmation of Behavioral Change and Business Impact.

Dear L.,

I have reviewed the progress for both goals 1 and 2. It is evident that you have benefited from the SLII training and have successfully employed the concepts taught in the class for effectively accomplishing both goals. It will be important for you to continue to use the SLII concepts to promote further positive conversations, goal setting, and delegation.

Dear J.,

On the first objective, you have been doing a great job in keeping the management team up to date on your area and the extra "air time" at the meeting is valuable to all of us.

Dear L.,

Your improvement plans could not be better. You realize the hardest part of managing people in the workplace is to transfer responsibility from the manager to the employee for job completion, realize how the job fits into the whole operation, meet quality and time expectations, and continually improve.

Dear M.,

Your first goal on communication has been acknowledged in several ways, the most significant one being that you have been recognized as a leader.... This is a very positive step in your career and I will be glad to support you in it. You are correct in acknowledging that communication is a continuous, continual (that is, never-ending) task.

Exhibit D6.2. Verbatim Examples of Managers' Feedback from a
Follow-Through Management System That Provide Independent
Confirmation of Behavioral Change and Business Impact, Cont'd.

Dear B.,

I did notice your effort and improvement in your interaction with others and
your customer services. I congratulate you on your progress and encourage
you to continue in this direction.

Dear M.,

I agree that you have accomplished much since your training. I am especially
impressed by the weekly e-mails to colleagues for the exchange of information.
These should, of course, continue. I may even piggy-back on your idea. In summary, you have learned and now are applying one of the most important tools
for your success: communication. Keep up the good work.

Widespread availability of inexpensive online surveys has greatly
streamlined collection and analysis of behavioral observations and ratings. Get assistance from market researchers or others skilled in the art
of designing survey instruments to maximize the reliability and value of
the data. Avoid the temptation to include every possible question of interest; completion rate is inversely proportional to survey length. Ask
only the questions needed to assess the program objectives.

Skeptics may argue that such ratings are "soft" compared to "hard"
data such as economic performance. The argument is specious. Employees act based on their perception of their manager—or as the saying goes: "People quit their boss, they do not quit the company." If, for
example, subordinates consistently rate their managers as more effective
following a development program, then they *are* more effective in that
aspect of their jobs. If customer satisfaction ratings increase following
customer service training, what more immediate and relevant measure
of success is there?

Results in Economic Terms

Nowadays, senior management is increasingly likely to request a financial analysis of the return on learning and development investments.
When this is the case, results need to be converted to currency. As with
all other aspects of the analysis, the conversion must be perceived as

both relevant and credible. Be conservative; claims that are perceived as exaggerated undermine the credibility of the learning organization.

The economic benefits of learning and development include not only new revenue or new business generated, but also cost avoidance, such as the savings that result from reducing employee turnover (see Case Study: Pfizer), accelerating the time to "breakeven," and preventing an accident, regulatory sanction, or lawsuit. Such savings can be substantial but are often overlooked in the analysis. If a true reduction in the cost of such incidents can be documented, it is powerful evidence of the value of learning and development.

•

Case Study: Pfizer—Financial Return on Reduced Turnover

Pfizer recognized that it took a long time and a lot of money to get pharmaceutical sales representatives to the "breakeven point" at which they were contributing as much in gross profit on sales as they cost. Pfizer also noticed that the turnover rate in its sales force was beginning to rise. Given the size of the investment in training for each sales person (about $150,000 all told), not to mention the opportunity cost of lost sales when one had to be replaced, Pfizer developed a special program that helped district managers recognize people at risk and engage them in conversation.

After one year, the turnover had decreased by 2 percent, saving the company in excess of $3 million (Schettler, 2003, p. 40). That kind of problem focus and documented return on investment is one reason that Pfizer was named the top training company two years in a row by *Training Magazine*.

•

The finance department should be asked to supply company-specific data, such as the cost of replacing an experienced sales person or the fully-loaded hourly rate of a manager, and these should be used whenever possible to calculate program costs and benefits. If company-specific data are not available, use industry averages or the results of published studies. Document the source of all estimates and any assumptions made. Be sure to acknowledge the contribution that simultaneous changes, such as new systems, processes, or personnel, may have contributed to the result. Calculate the full cost of the program, including the cost of the time participants spent preparing and attending. Get the finance department to help with the analysis; it will significantly increase the credibility and effectiveness of the final report (Sullivan, 2005).

If the appropriate data are available from company databases, it may be possible to calculate the economic value added directly. Spencer (2001), for example, compared the sales and profitability performance of branch managers who had and had not attended an emotional intelligence training program. The profitability of the units led by those who had attended the training was greater than that of those who had not. The increase was more than seven times the cost of the training, for an ROI of 613 percent.

Unfortunately, relevant measures are not always available. Phillips and Stone (2002) describe a method for obtaining impact estimates directly from participants by asking a series of questions:

- Describe an improvement or achievement following the learning program.
- Estimate its annual value to the company.
- Explain the basis of your estimate.
- What percentage is the result of capabilities gained from the learning and development program?
- Express your confidence in the size of the estimate as a percentage.

A conservative estimate of the value of the program for each participant is obtained by multiplying the estimated annual value by the confidence percentage. The effect of other factors is taken into account by further multiplying the corrected estimate of value by the percentage the participant ascribed to the program. Individuals who fail to respond to the survey are assumed to have created no incremental value.

The American Society for Training and Development published a book of case studies based on this approach (Phillips & Phillips, 2001). KnowledgeAdvisors, Inc., offers an online ROI calculator as part of its Web-based Metrics that Matter™ system. And more recently, Sony and Coca-Cola have automated the process by building it into the final update of their follow-through management process using Fort Hill Company's Follow-Through Tools®.

Although this approach has advantages of being straightforward and efficient, it is credible only if management believes the estimates. You can improve the believability of the estimates by applying the methodology when

- The participants have adequate knowledge of the business and sufficient financial acumen to provide reliable estimates.

(Estimates from experienced business managers will be more credible than those from first-time supervisors.)

- Enough time has elapsed for the claimed achievements or improvements to be real versus only hoped-for.

- Estimates are limited to participants' personal knowledge and experience. For example, if time savings are expected, ask people to report the number of hours saved, rather than dollars; few would know the correct fully-loaded cost to apply.

- The data are reviewed to exclude obvious errors and confirm or eliminate "outliers"—estimates that are so large that they will surely raise questions and potentially discredit the entire analysis.

- Medians rather than averages (means) are used to portray "typical" results in order to reduce the skewing effect of a few unusually large estimates.

Critical Incident

A related technique is the "critical incident" method in which participants are asked to describe a specific instance *from their personal experience,* when they used something they learned from the program to generate a positive result. They are then asked to estimate its impact in variables (such as time saved) that they can reasonably project and to indicate how many similar incidents they have experienced since the end of Phase II. The economic impact of each instance is converted to dollars using independent cost estimates from the finance department and converted to annual savings by conservatively projecting the number of reported incidents to an annual rate.

Hewlett-Packard used this approach to evaluate the return on investment in its Dynamic Leadership Program (Burnett & Wick, 2005). The advantages of this approach are that the incidents reported are detailed and specific and therefore less subject to debate. The disadvantages are that (1) the analysis cannot be automated and (2) there is room for debate about the conversion to annual rates. Because the value of the reported incidents usually far exceeds the cost of the program, the exact annualized rate is moot. In the case of Dynamic Leadership, for example, the median value of *each* reported incident was 50 percent greater than the fully-loaded cost of educating the participant (Burnett & Wick, 2005).

OBSTACLES TO DOCUMENTING RESULTS

Given that most learning and development professionals accept the importance of measuring business-relevant results, why is rigorous analysis of business outcomes so difficult? There are three main reasons:

- The objectives of many programs are not defined clearly enough to measure.

- Business systems are complex and multifactoral so that it is difficult to tease out what proportion of the results should be ascribed to any one factor, such as learning and development, versus another.

- The lag time between the stimulus (in this case training) and a measurable response (business results) is long.

These three realities make it difficult to convincingly isolate the contribution that education made versus confounding factors. Such problems are not unique to corporate education, however. Techniques have been developed in other fields of inquiry—from six sigma quality to epidemiology—to deal with similar problems of multiple causality, long lag times, and so forth. Corporate learning and development organizations should tap the analytical expertise that exists in research, manufacturing, quality assurance, finance, and other departments or outside experts to help them design and execute program evaluations (Sullivan, 2005). Not only is this an opportunity to increase the credibility and impact of their analyses, but also for them to learn and enhance their own capabilities.

Lack of Clear, Quantifiable Objectives

Despite the attention paid to needs analysis, impact mapping, and performance consulting in recent years, we still encountered program leaders during our interviews who were unable to articulate the objectives of their programs in quantifiable business terms. Part of the explanation for the paucity of documented results may be failure to define what results are expected in the first place.

The solution is better practice of the first discipline. Participants in learning and development programs are urged to meet with their managers beforehand to reach mutual agreement on objectives. As learning leaders, we need to be sure to follow our own advice. We need to meet with key customers (those who fund our programs) to be sure that there is agreement on what is expected and how success will be measured. Anything less puts the learning enterprise at risk, because the criteria for success or failure become a matter of opinion.

We recommend that corporate educators approach learning and development programs with more of a "contract" mentality, that is, create a learning contract with the program sponsor. Well-written business contracts include a section on deliverables that spells out in detail what the purchaser considers acceptable in terms of quantity, quality, and timing. In "contracting" to deliver a program, you should work with management to define expectations in writing: "What results does the program need to deliver (quantity, quality, and timing) to be considered a success?" The answers dictate what needs to be measured.

In his book, *Flawless Consulting* (2000), Peter Block argues for using the word "contract" rather than "working agreement" to call attention to the need for specific expectations and for setting them down in writing, even for intra-company initiatives. "[T]he real value of a written contract is to clarify the understanding with the line manager before the project begins. It is a good test of whether you have a solid contract. Writing down the agreement forces you to be more explicit about what you are going to do" (p. 59).

Multiple Causality

Even if *what* to measure is clear, *how* to get reliable measures of impact still presents challenges. The greatest of these is that corporate learning and development is conducted in the real (complex, messy) world. The result of any business process—from the outcome of an advertising campaign to the impact of training—is the algebraic sum of many different factors operating simultaneously. Some factors that affect the outcome are intra-company, such as new marketing initiatives, changes in incentive pay, new leadership, new products, and so forth. Many are external: the economy, actions by competitors, fluctuations in exchange rates, and so on.

Learning and development controls only a small number of the plethora of factors that potentially influence the outcome. The more significant the outcome, the more likely it is that many factors played a part (Bordonaro, 2005, p. 217). For example, a learning and development program can hardly be blamed for a sudden drop in sales following a terrorist attack. But neither should it claim too much credit for the upsurge in profitability after a competitor's plant burns down or a new manufacturing system is brought online. The design of the evaluation has to take into account such extraneous factors and isolate, so far as is possible, the effects of the training program and follow-through (Phillips, 2003).

The challenge faced by learning leaders in fairly assessing the impact of their educational programs is similar to that faced by medical professionals in assessing the benefits of a new drug or the dangers of risk factors like smoking. Many other factors, including genetic background, weight, lifestyle, and exposures over many years, interact in complex ways to influence the outcome.

Nevertheless, when a large enough population is studied carefully and other factors are taken into account by statistical analysis, a clear pattern emerges. No one factor, such as smoking, accounts for all lung cancers, yet its influence is undeniable. People who smoke are, on average, much more likely to develop lung cancer. The risk increases with the duration and intensity of smoking. Occasional exceptions are seen to be just that—exceptions—in the same way that some people are highly successful with no formal training and others fail to benefit despite extensive (and expensive) executive education.

Take advantage of methodologies developed in epidemiology, statistical process control, and related disciplines to enhance the credibility of evaluations. Educate line leaders that the correlation will never be perfect—not everyone who attends a program will improve, not everyone who does not attend will fail, in the same way that not everyone who smokes will die of cancer.

MANAGING MULTIPLE CAUSALITY One of the best ways to minimize the confounding effect of external factors is to conduct a controlled trial—to compare the performance of a group that received training to the performance of a group that did not. The idea is that although many other factors besides the training influence the outcome, these should be more or less randomly distributed between the trained and untrained (control) groups. If the groups are large enough, the effects of these other factors should be about equal and thus cancel out when the two groups are compared, allowing the effect of the training to shine through. Differences in relevant measures of performance observed between the trained and control groups are most likely the result of the application of the educational program.

Since the goal of the case-control design is to have extraneous factors (those that are not being tested) equally distributed between the two groups, the ideal is to randomly assign subjects to one group or another (such as by flipping a coin). This is easy in a laboratory but is difficult or impossible in a corporate setting. When true randomization is not possible, take care to avoid obvious and systematic differences, such as training participants at one location and comparing them to those at another who have not been trained. Significant differences in the environment, leadership, or other factors may exist between the sites that influence performance as much or more than the effect of the program itself.

INCLUDE AS MANY SUBJECTS AS PRACTICABLE Include as many individuals in the study as practicable. In general, the more subjects that can be included in the study, the better. There are two reasons: (1) the larger the size of the groups studied, the more likely they are truly comparable and (2) the larger the group size, the easier it is to confidently detect differences due to the training.

The smaller the number of subjects evaluated, the greater the probability of making *both* type I and type II errors—that is, finding an apparent effect when there is none (type I) or failing to demonstrate a benefit when there really is one (type II). Even when the difference between two groups seems large, it may still not be "significant" statistically. That is, if the groups are small, the difference is just as likely to be due to chance as to some actual effect of the training.

There are statistical methods to determine the number of subjects needed to detect a difference of a particular size. Consult with company statisticians or external consultants *in advance* to determine whether the design of the evaluation is likely to have enough power to detect a difference.

In any event, be forthright about the size of the study when reporting results. Never try to gloss over a small group size; you will destroy your credibility when the actual number comes out in the discussion. Erwin Neter, the late editor-in-chief of *Infection and Immunity,* used to tell a story about receiving a paper that reputedly read: "33 1/3 percent of the mice used in this experiment were cured by the test drug; 33 1/3 percent of the test population were unaffected . . . ; the third mouse got away" (quoted in Day, 1994, p. 43).

HISTORICAL COMPARISONS While contemporaneous test and control groups are a particularly strong way to minimize the impact of extraneous influences, they are not always possible or practicable in a corporate setting. For example, management may want every employee at a particular level or site to attend, with the result that there is no untrained "control" group for comparison. Programs usually roll out over time, however, so it may be possible to compare the performance of those who have completed the program to those who have yet to attend.

A related strategy is to compare performance after the training to performance before training (time 1–time 2 design). Repeating a 360-degree assessment after Phase III is, in essence, using each person as his or her own control. Coworkers or other observers can be asked to make comparisons directly: "How would you rate this person regarding [some parameter or behavior] now compared to [give time before program]?" Such third-party affirmation of positive change is strong and credible evidence that the program is successfully contributing to behavioral change in the organization.

The potential pitfall of comparing measures at two points in time is that the results are much more susceptible to confounding by external factors. If significant changes—such as downsizing, a new IT system, product launch, or change in leadership—occur between the "before" and the "after" evaluation, they can overwhelm the influence of the program itself. Time 1–time 2 comparisons also need to take into account trends that may have already been in place prior to the training (Phillips, 2003, p. 121). For example, if performance had already been improving prior to training (as a result of improved experience, new processes, or other factors), it is not enough to show better results after training; you need to demonstrate that the pace of improvement (slope of the trend line) accelerated following the learning and development initiative.

MINIMIZE BIAS For the results to have credibility, the data gathering and analysis must be seen as fair and unbiased. Preferably, the people doing the scoring and evaluation should have no vested interest in the outcome of the evaluation. Ideally, they would have no knowledge of which data belong to which group. In medical studies, the gold standard is the "double-blind" trial in which neither the patient nor the attending physician know which treatment is the placebo and which is the active drug. In the most rigorous trials, the analysis of results is completed before the identities of the compounds are revealed.

For most purposes, the evaluation of corporate education programs need not approach the level of rigor and detail expected in academic or scientific research. Yet it must be sufficiently well designed and executed to be credible when subjected to scrutiny by senior management. Consult appropriate texts on educational evaluation, consultants, or internal assessment experts for guidance.

Long Lag Time Between Training and Final Results

The third impediment to rigorous assessment of educational impact is that there is usually a considerable lag time before the final results are realized. Even the most successful sales training may not show up as increased revenue for months, depending on the length of the sales cycle. Customer or employee satisfaction may take even longer to change because it requires many new and more positive experiences to recalibrate opinions.

Managing Lag Time

You can rarely postpone evaluation until the full effect is evident. By the time the results are in, they may no longer be relevant. Moreover, the longer you wait to assess impact, the more the effect of the education becomes attenuated by intervening factors. What to do?

IN-PROCESS CHECKS The solution is to measure intermediate stages in the performance improvement process. Similar lag time issues are encountered in efforts to improve product quality. For some changes, it may be months before the final results are evident. If the analysis phase of each PDSA cycle waited for final (global) results, the pace of improvement would be unacceptably slow. The solution is to measure more immediate, intermediate steps (Langley et al., 1996, p. 56). If a change does not produce improvement in the intermediate results of the process, it is highly unlikely that there will be improvement in the final result; the intervention was not effective. If, however, the intermediate results improve, the intervention clearly had a positive effect, which *most likely* will carry through into the final desired result. Certainly it indicates progress in the right direction.

END-OF-COURSE EVALUATIONS End-of-course evaluations can be a source of in-process data to monitor participants' reactions to the program. While these level 1 data do not predict final results, they are nevertheless important because participants' reactions determine how they speak about the program when they return to work. What they say influences the opinions of those who pay for the education, as well as the perception of future participants. If participants' reaction is negative (for example, "the program was a big waste of time, impractical") those comments will reach management. Human nature is such that individual negative comments often carry more weight than they should: we worked with a Fortune 100 company in which we were able to rigorously document widespread application leading to an exceptional return on investment. When the results were presented to senior management, however, one of the leaders responded, "Yes, but I heard from one of my people that the program was not very good."

No program will please everyone, nor should it try. Nevertheless, you need to pay attention to participants' immediate reactions and stay attuned to the "word on the street." Respond promptly and effectively to legitimate criticisms. At the same time, "manage the news" to make sure a balanced view is presented. An unhappy customer will talk to ten people where a satisfied customer might tell three. Document and publicize legitimate positive results so that management has the whole story; it would be criminal for an otherwise excellent program to be derailed by a few unhappy participants.

Well-designed end-of-course evaluations can be an important in-process gauge of whether participants see the utility of the content and thus whether they are likely to apply it. Peggy Parskey, global learning process manager for Hewlett-Packard, working closely with Michael Ross of Performance Challenges Corporation, used several multivariate techniques (including multiple regression and cluster analysis) to analyze tens of thousands of sets of evaluation data to build a model that captures higher-order reaction constructs, predicts overall assessment from three specific metrics, and presents the data in a powerful and easily interpreted way (Figure D6.2). The strongest predictor of a program's overall perceived quality was one facet of each of the following factors: achieved objectives (learning experience), recommend to peers (learner impact), and enhance job performance (utility).

Three ratings contributed to the utility score:

- The relevance of the skills and concepts
- The extent to which learners expected the program to enhance performance
- Whether the learners were motivated to apply what they had learned

By tracking the utility scores of programs in real time, the learning and development group is able to quickly identify and target programs with low utility scores for improvement, without waiting weeks to months for a full impact analysis. The rationale is that if participants leave a program with a poor opinion of its applicability, the probability that they will transfer the learning to produce results on the job is very low. Thus, adding questions about perceived utility to end-of-course evaluations provides an early warning system for programs that need attention.

Figure D6.2. In Hewlett-Packard's Model, Three Metrics—Utility, Learning Experience, and Learner Impact— Predict the Overall Assessment of Value.

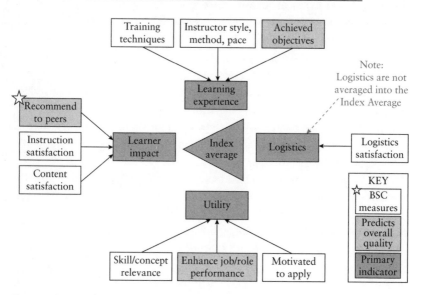

Source: *Copyright © 2003 Hewlett-Packard. Used with permission.*

SUCCESS CASE METHOD To learn what is and is not working as soon as possible in educational programs, Brinkerhoff (2003) recommends "the success case method." The first step is to identify—through a survey, analysis of follow-through system input, or other means—individuals or teams that seem to be the most successful. The second step is to interview these cases to confirm and document the nature of the successes being achieved, as well as a number of unsuccessful cases. The objective is to identify quickly, but with reasonable rigor, what can be changed (increased, decreased, improved, or eliminated) to increase the proportion and magnitude of success cases.

MAKING THE MOST OF RESULTS

Once you have the results, what do you do with them? A thorough evaluation that rigorously documents superb results is of no value if no one knows about it. Our experience suggests that learning and development organizations will benefit greatly by becoming more adept at communicating their value to key audiences; in other words, at marketing their product. Kevin Wilde (CLO, General Mills) put it this way: "You have to market what you are doing, demonstrate value, and know what matters." John Sullivan was even blunter: "You can't be subtle or naïve if you want managers to pay attention to your metrics. Most reports from development are too long, too dull, and just plain uninteresting" (Sullivan, 2005, p. 282).

Having invested time and energy to collect, compile, and analyze reams of data, everyone's natural impulse is to put together a detailed report, print and bind it, and circulate it to senior managers. That is a big mistake. Few will read it and fewer still remember the key messages.

Follow Wilde's advice. Market learning's value by using the same approaches and techniques that the company uses to market its key brands. Adopt a much more customer-focused approach. Ask for help from marketing colleagues; you can't be subtle and be successful.

Segment and Target

As discussed in D1, the first step in strategic marketing is to segment and target customers, dividing them into groups with similar wants and needs and then focusing efforts on the most important. With respect to reporting results, ask yourself

- Who are learning and development's most important customers?
- Which messages need to be communicated to whom?

Clearly, those who make the decisions to fund corporate education constitute one of the key customer segments. The messages that need to be delivered to this group are that the money for training was well spent (it yielded a good return); future investment is likely to yield similar returns; the learning and development organization is competent; and it is serious about continually improving its output.

A second key customer segment is those who participated in the evaluation. They need to know that their efforts were appreciated, that the information is being used constructively, and that they made an important contribution to the success of the company.

A third target is employees who have not yet participated in the program. They are potential customers; communication to this group should make them want to attend. Other targets for communication may include shareholders to illustrate how the company invests in building future capabilities, and the corporate education community to attract the best candidates to your team and foster interchange of best practices.

After you have identified the key audience segments and their pro-
clivities, you need to tailor the messages and select communication
vehicles that are most effective for each. This is no different from product marketing. A children's breakfast cereal needs to appeal to kids, to
whom the message is "fun, tasty, and cool," but it must also appeal to
the parents (who make the buying decision). The message to the parents
stresses the nutritional value, importance of a good breakfast, and so
forth. Same product, different emphasis for different audiences. Apply
the same principles in communicating your results; tailor the message
for different audiences to address their specific interests, needs, and communication preferences.

Repetition, Repetition, Repetition

Advertisers understand that no matter how compelling the message, one
exposure is insufficient. Effective marketing companies repeat the message
many times in a variety of media (magazines, television, direct mail, and
so forth) to create "share of mind." Effective CEOs use a similar approach.
They emphasize a few core themes over and over until everyone in the
company gets the message. Each communication is tailored to the medium
and audience, but reiterates the same few core messages and themes.

Learning and development organizations need to do likewise. To be
sure that "the message gets through," communicate the results of learning and development initiatives multiple times, in different settings and
formats, each tailored to a specific target audience. Suggestions for doing
so follow.

Senior Leaders and Program Sponsors

Senior leadership and program sponsors are by far your most important
target audience. They are also the most difficult to reach and convince.
As investors, they are looking for a critical analysis of the return being
generated. Provide them with persuasive evidence that the program adds
real value.

KEY ASPECTS OF THE COMMUNICATIONS The primary (but not ex-
clusive) communication to this group will be some sort of formal report.
It should be a concise, fact-filled, no-nonsense analysis written in the *language of business*. Avoid educational jargon, such as speaking about levels of evaluation without defining them. Emphasize business results and
business terms.

Executives at this level are extremely busy; they have no tolerance for long, convoluted messages, educational jargon, and poorly written or badly documented materials. If they cannot get to the meat of the matter in the first paragraph or two, they are likely to set the report aside or discard it.

The executive summary is crucial; it is all that many senior managers will read. Make it the first page of the report; write it in straightforward declarative sentences, and keep it to one page or less. Summarize the business need being addressed, the program's objectives, what was done, how it was assessed, the results, and recommendations for the future.

The executive summary is the most difficult part of the report to write. It must contain all the key facts yet be brief and to the point. As the great French mathematician and philosopher Blaise Pascal wrote: "I have made this letter longer than usual only because I have not the time to make it shorter."

The rest of the report should provide the details that support the summary, including the design of the three phases, the evaluation methodology, data tables, examples, and analyses necessary to support the conclusions. Be sure the report reflects the peculiar culture of your organization and management team; for some, too much data is a "turn off," for others, too little data undermines credibility. Include high-level summaries, tables, and graphs in the body of the report; relegate detailed analyses, tables, and so forth to the appendix.

Although most senior managers want to see the "hard" numbers and data, they are also interested in the voice of the customer, so include selected examples and comments. For example, Sue Sullivan Hays, manager of the Leadership Institute for Federated Department Stores, used the success case method to make the results of Federated's Leadership Choice program real and compelling to management. She reviewed participants' input in the online follow-through management system to identify those who had reported good progress. She then conducted follow-up interviews and prepared case studies that illustrated the program's impact in each of management's business priorities. Because these case studies "told a retailing story," they communicated the kind of results that senior management was looking for in a way that was compelling (Wick & Pollock, 2004b).

If the report has been prepared by or with the help of a consultant, be sure to vet it so that it matches the communication preferences of the intended audience. Acknowledge the contribution of others outside the learning organization and be forthright about any limitations of the evaluation or conclusions. Explain your "lessons learned" and plans to make subsequent programs even more effective.

COMMUNICATION VEHICLES Although a formal report to senior leadership is necessary, it is insufficient. A common and costly error is to equate distributing a report with communicating results. To make sure that your message is heard among all the competing noise, it must be reinforced. If possible, ask to give a short presentation of the results in person. We emphasize *short,* given the time constraints senior managers face. Get to the point quickly; use only as many slides as absolutely necessary; deliver the message succinctly and finish within the allotted time. Try to anticipate the most likely questions and be prepared to answer them (with back-up slides if necessary). If there are no questions, resist the urge to keep talking; heed the advice given to salespeople and "don't buy it back."

Keep in mind that communications to other audiences (see below) will also reach management and help shape their opinions. For example, managers will scan articles about the program or profiles of successful participants in company newsletters and other publications. Write and review them with this in mind.

Participants and Their Managers

The participants in the program are interested in the results of their efforts. They will be curious about the outcome of any surveys or other data-gathering exercises in which they participated, as well as what other members of their cohort achieved. Those who made a concerted effort to use what they learned and, as a result, achieved something of significance, crave recognition. Help ensure they receive it.

Do not forget the critical role played by participants' managers in the transfer and application of learning. Call attention to managers' contributions whenever appropriate to encourage other managers to do likewise.

KEY ASPECTS OF THE COMMUNICATIONS The first objective is to thank those who participated in the evaluation (either as subjects or as controls) for their time. Time is perhaps the most precious asset for any employee these days; any time that participants spent assisting in the evaluation should be regarded as a gift. Thank people for their participation and provide a brief synopsis of the findings. In particular, acknowledge their suggestions for improvement and, if possible, highlight changes that will be made as a result.

The second objective of communications to participants is to reinforce the value of the program's principles by highlighting success stories. You can accomplish these goals through "human interest" stories in company publications that report notable accomplishments of individuals or teams. "The heart of the documentation that I think is really critical is stories, not just metrics or numbers," said Richard Leider, founder and chairman of the Inventure Group. Describing a particularly successful learning organization, he said, "They do a lot of work to build leadership stories and communicate them in all kinds of formats so the story and the language are out there everywhere" (Leider, interview).

Jim O'Hern, director of leadership development at Honeywell, uses success stories to recognize participants who have completed their follow-through and also energize new program entrants (O'Hern, interview). He compiles examples of successful application from the follow-through management system (*ResultsEngine*®), including positive feedback from coaches and managers, and shares them with participants in subsequent programs. In this way, he simultaneously recognizes superior performance of prior participants, illustrates what is possible when program principles are transferred and practiced, and motivates members of the current group by indicating that they could be selected as avatars for subsequent sessions.

COMMUNICATION VEHICLES If participants have access to e-mail, an electronic "thank you" letter and brief synopsis of the results may suffice to meet the first objective. Given the e-mail overload most managers now experience, a paper letter and one- or two-page summary may actually get greater notice.

If the program design includes reconvening the group, use it as an occasion to publicly acknowledge examples of superior performance. Take advantage of as many employee communication vehicles as possible, such as newsletters, internal publications, and the company website. The editors of such communications are always on the lookout for stories that are both interesting and illustrative of company values and goals.

If you have a computer-based follow-through management system, use it to identify individuals and teams who have achieved significant results. Refer them to the communications department to develop a complete story through follow-up interviews. Having such success stories reported in company publications greatly enhances the perceived value of educational programs and contributes to their future success. Employees who are featured in such articles will be motivated to even greater accomplishments; future participants will strive to be among those so recognized.

Nonparticipants

Employees who have not yet attended the program are a third key target for communicating results. There are three key objectives for communicating with nonparticipants:

- Create demand among those who are eligible to attend the program in the future.
- Show how the company is investing in its workforce and the positive value of continuing to learn.
- Motivate others by recognizing superior performance.

KEY ASPECTS OF THE COMMUNICATIONS Articles that describe the program and illustrate the value participants have derived will contribute to these objectives. The human interest stories discussed above will be the most compelling, especially if they include quotes, photos, and examples from individual participants, their managers, and teams. Consider awards or other recognition to motivate participation and learning transfer, but be careful to validate claims of success. Public recognition of accomplishments that later prove to be exaggerated or unsubstantiated can discredit the whole program.

COMMUNICATION VEHICLES The main vehicles are the internal employee publications and electronic communications, and team and company meetings. Do not underestimate the power of public recognition; it is a very powerful motivator. "Over and over, research has told us that money is not the major key to keeping good people. When employees across the country answered the question, What kept you?, few had dollars in their top three reasons. People want recognition for work well done" (Kaye & Jordan-Evans, 2005, p. 172).

Other Stakeholders

Promoting corporate education's success in building new competencies and competitiveness contributes positively to a company's reputation. If the initiative generated real value, be sure to also communicate the results to stakeholders outside the company. External stakeholder awareness not only helps enhance the reputation of the company and contribute to its value, it also helps ensure continued support for effective education.

Four external audiences to consider are customers, prospective employees, shareholders, and the corporate education community.

KEY ASPECTS OF THE COMMUNICATIONS A company's overall reputation is one of the factors that customers consider when they make a buying decision. They are more likely to buy, and to pay a premium, from a company that they perceive as high-quality and progressive with good prospects for the future. Communicating examples of how the company is improving its quality and performance through education helps reinforce a positive perception.

A company's reputation as an employer affects its ability to recruit employees. Companies that are perceived as willing to invest in their employees have an easier time attracting good candidates and a lower cost of recruitment. News stories that illustrate how the company invests and benefits from employee development will enhance its reputation as an employer. If you have a great story to tell, work with the public relations department to get it the placement it deserves.

Shareholders are most concerned about a company's future prospects. Conveying tangible evidence that the company is building capabilities in its workforce helps bolster shareholder confidence in its continued prosperity. Include concrete examples and financial analyses; savvy investors have become inured to "spin" without substance.

Finally, it is important for corporate educators to communicate their successes (and failures) to their peers. Not only does doing so increase the learning unit's reputation—allowing it to attract the best and brightest practitioners in the field—it will also help create a network for the open exchange of ideas and best practices that transcends corporation boundaries. Such networks have real economic benefit and substantial ROI in their own right (Dulworth & Forcillo, 2005, p. 116).

COMMUNICATION VEHICLES Success stories about how educational programs are adding value are great fodder for communications to customers (newsletters, websites, and other publications). They may also be of interest to trade publications that are read by customers and prospective employees. The latter have the added benefit of being "independent" as opposed to house organs. Work with the communications and public relations department to secure placement.

Ask for inclusion in the annual report. Competition for space is intense, but if the program truly enhances shareholder value, it may merit mention. Documented results are key. Be aware that such visibility is a two-edged sword. On the one hand, it increases the probability of continued funding. On the other, it also increases the level of scrutiny the program receives and the expectations for future success.

If the program was truly innovative and broad in scope and delivered exceptional results, the story may be picked up by one of the leading business publications, such as the *Wall Street Journal*. The public relations impact would be huge not only for the learning organization but for the company as a whole. To even aspire to such notoriety, however, requires something that is truly newsworthy and well-documented; participant reaction data will not suffice.

There are numerous venues for sharing the results with others in the learning community: conferences, learning and development periodicals, workshops, and networks. Consider applying for one of the annual awards for learning and development, such as those sponsored by the American Society for Training and Development, *Training* Magazine, Corporate University Xchange, *Chief Learning Officer,* and so forth. Well-designed and thorough evaluations are essential.

Truth in Advertising

Historically, learning and development organizations have not done enough to measure their impact and then "market" the results. As a consequence, their contribution is frequently undervalued. A tremendous opportunity exists to increase "share of mind" about the value that well-designed and well-executed programs create. We strongly encourage you to use the ideas in this chapter to better position and communicate the value of learning and development.

But we want to be absolutely clear: do not do so unless you have credible data to support your claims. Never try to use advertising "spin" to sugarcoat a failure or to make grandiose claims for modest success. Sooner or later, the truth will come out and the learning organization will lose its credibility. That loss is irreparable. Kouzes and Posner, in their classic work on leadership, put it well: "Credibility is one of the hardest attributes to earn. And it is the most fragile of human qualities. It is earned minute by minute, hour by hour, month by month, and year by year. But it can be lost in very short order if not attended to. . . . And when leaders have used up all their credibility, they find it virtually impossible to earn it back" (1990, p. 24).

Building a strong brand requires both superior performance and effective marketing; either alone is insufficient.

A CAVEAT

Throughout this discussion, we have implied that the analysis would be positive. Of course, there is the possibility that the evaluation will show that the program had no demonstrable benefit or that the benefit was too small to justify its cost. Such studies are still valuable, as Kevin Wilde (CLO, General Mills) pointed out: "Some studies did not pan out, some did. But unless I am asking, I do not know exactly where the value is. By doing this kind of work, I am interacting with the CEO in a very business-like way that he expects out of all the other business leaders— getting results, producing insights. Some things work out, some things do not. You have to have the courage to ask and figure it out" (Wilde, interview).

The time to decide what to do with negative findings is *before* the evaluation is begun. Address the question: "Suppose the evaluation is not favorable, what will our response be then?" during the planning stage. Once the data have been collected, they cannot be "buried" or ignored. You have both a moral and management responsibility to report your findings and to make a recommendation consistent with the data— to fix the program or to kill it.

When we were asked to speak about measurement at the Center for Naval Leadership, we suggested that evaluation should be handled like high explosives—*very carefully*. Used properly, evaluation will give tremendous boost to the credibility and effectiveness of your organization; mishandle evaluation and it will explode in your face.

Documenting results should not be undertaken lightly. Evaluation is a sharp and powerful tool, but it cuts both ways. A poorly planned, superficial, or naïve evaluation is like a loose cannon: it can do a tremendous amount of damage. Likewise, evaluating a program for which the other five disciplines (clear business objectives, a complete experience, application-focused delivery, follow-through management, and support) are not in place carries a high risk of failure. Analyses of programs that ignore Phase III (follow-through management and active support) are likely to be disappointing. Make certain that every element of a learning and development initiative is optimized before jumping into evaluation.

Finally, documenting results is not the end, but the beginning. What was learned from one program is the starting point for building the next, even better and more effective.

SUMMARY

The last of the six disciplines, documenting results, is critical to demonstrate the value of all the effort and investment that has gone before. Rigorous assessment of outcomes is essential to justify continued investment in learning and development and to support its continuous improvement. Program evaluation must be carefully planned, thoroughgoing, and credible. It must include means to control for the impact of extra-educational factors, and it must document outcomes of relevance to the key customers—those who allocate resources.

Depending on the nature of the program and the objectives of the sponsors, it may or may not be necessary to convert demonstrated behavior changes into monetary terms. If economic analysis is required, it should be conservative and done in concert with the finance department to maximize credibility.

Finally, the results need to be marketed—communicated broadly and effectively through a variety of media—to all the relevant stakeholders. When these criteria are fulfilled, learning and development achieves its full promise and enjoys a well-deserved reputation for contribution.

•

ACTION POINTS

For Learning Leaders

- Review the evidence you have currently to illustrate that learning and development contributes to business success.
  - Can you make a compelling case for the economic value added that learning and development provides?
  - Can you convincingly demonstrate why reducing the investment will hurt the company's long-term performance?
  - If not, begin at once to rectify the situation.
- Ensure that the plans for evaluation and the definition of success are part of every "contract" (explicit or implicit) that you accept for delivering learning and development programs.
- Be proactive. Begin to build multiple lines of evidence of value. If you wait until you are asked to do an ROI study, it will be too late.
- Market the value.

- Get help from the marketing department.
- If you have a great story to tell about the value you create, you cannot be shy and hope people will notice.
- If you believe it, you have to sell it.

For Line Leaders

- Review the current measures used in your business to assess the value of learning and development initiatives.
  - Are you satisfied?
  - Are they as rigorous as the criteria used to assess other investments of similar magnitude?
- Require that every plan for a learning and development initiative include a section that discusses the criteria for success and the plan for evaluation and communication.
  - Provide learning leaders with access to experts on evaluation and communications or from external consultants as necessary.
  - Finally, save the prior year's budget presentations—particularly the section on promised benefits—and require a report against these as part of each new cycle.

CODA

Unless objectives are converted into action,
they are not objectives; they are dreams.

—Peter Drucker

THROUGHOUT THIS BOOK, we have emphasized four key themes:

- Training and development is a strategic investment that a company makes in its workforce. It is as important to a company's future as the investments it makes in research, new product development, sales and marketing, and acquisitions.
- Training and development can produce significant returns and competitive advantage, *provided* they are managed in a systematic and disciplined way.
- Six disciplines (Figure C.1), when practiced in concert, constitute a breakthrough in training that converts a much higher proportion of learning into business results.
- The third phase of learning, the transfer and application of new capabilities, offers the greatest opportunity for transformational change.

REPRISE: THE SIX DISCIPLINES

D1: Define outcomes in business terms is essential to direct resources to the most important problems, gain clarity about what needs to be delivered, and define how results will ultimately be measured. It requires

Figure C.1. The Six Disciplines That
Deliver Results from Training and Development.

Define
Business Outcomes

- Link program objectives to business needs
- Agree on definition of success
- Define what participants will do differently and better

Design
Complete Experience

- Include what happens before and after the classroom
- Redefine the finish line from the end of class to the generation of results

Deliver
for Application

- Show how the content relates to current business issues
- Give participants time to reflect on how they will apply

Drive
Follow-Through

- Actively manage the process
- Involve managers
- Ensure accountability

Deploy
Active Support

- Provide ongoing support from facilitators, coaches, managers
- Provide practical "how-to" guides to facilitate transfer

Document
Results

- Collect credible data on the outcomes defined in D1
- Report results to management and use to market the program

partnership between line management and learning leaders and depends on an open dialogue and process to create an impact map that clearly articulates business aims, the behaviors and performance needed to achieve them, and the capabilities that must be augmented to support them.

D2: Design the complete experience serves as a reminder that the participant's learning experience is much broader than that which occurs during the formal period of instruction. It begins beforehand and continues afterward. It is influenced by many organizational and environmental factors, most especially the role of each person's manager. The discipline of designing the complete experience requires thinking holistically and systematically about learning and influencing elements traditionally outside the scope of learning and development.

D3: Deliver for application requires constant and disciplined attention to the ultimate goal: improving the performance of individuals and hence the organization as a whole. It requires instructional methods that stimulate the kind of thinking and behavior that will be needed on the job to facilitate the transition between instruction and application. It means providing context and making relevance and utility clear, and helping participants continually come back to the question of how they can use what they are learning to advantage.

D4: Drive follow-through is the discipline of ensuring that what gets learned gets used in a way that achieves business aims. Driving follow-through on learning transfer goals requires close collaboration between line management and the learning organization to ensure that participants are held accountable for using what they have learned and that their supervisors support this effort. It requires a new mindset about the importance of this phase of learning and new tools to manage the process.

D5: Deploy active support is the discipline of ensuring that participants receive the support they need to maximize the benefits of their education. It requires marshaling an array of resources—from the participants' manager to peers to coaches, instructors, and online management systems—in order to provide a strong supportive "surround" for the transfer and application process. It requires willingness to redeploy resources, for example, from instruction to support, and to think about information systems in a new way.

D6: Document results is both the end and the beginning of the cycle. It is the discipline of measuring, in a reliable and credible way, the extent to which the program delivered on the promise defined in D1. Documenting results and communicating them widely and well are essential to justify continued investment and support continuous improvement.

The six disciplines work together to increase the amplitude of the results and lower the cost of achieving them. The chain is as strong as its weakest link. If one is missing or weak, the results are diminished, no matter how well the other disciplines are executed.

The greatest opportunity to achieve a breakthrough in the value of training and development is to strengthen the learning transfer (Phase III) period. A systematic method to ensure follow-through is key. A guide to implementing the six disciplines is given in Exhibit C.1.

Exhibit C.1. A Brief Guide to Implementing the Six Disciplines.

D1: Define outcomes in business terms

Make certain that the objectives of each training and development initiative are defined in terms that describe the benefit they will provide to the business. Work closely with business leaders to agree on the desired outcomes and measures of success.

1. Interview business leaders regarding their needs and expectations for post-program results.
2. Review the business and strategic plans; identify where learning can add the most value.
3. Establish a joint business-learning steering committee to define outcomes, set priorities, and ensure tight linkage between business needs and training initiatives.
4. Agree with business leaders on the definition of success as part of the initial design.
5. Create a map that shows the links between the business needs, the required knowledge and skills, and the proposed learning experiences.

D2: Design the complete experience

Think holistically and systemically about the learning experience. Include all the critical factors that contribute to successful transfer and application, including preparation (Phase I) and post-instructional follow-through management and support (Phase III).

1. Use the 6Ds Learning Transfer and Application Scorecard (see Exhibit I.1) to identify opportunities for improvement.
2. Ensure that the program design includes plans for optimizing all three phases of learning (preparation, instruction, and application).
3. Encourage learner-manager discussions prior to the program.
4. Optimize the post-course environment to support transfer and application. Pay particular attention to the role of, and support from, the participants' managers.
5. Redefine the facilitator's role to include post-workshop responsibilities and results.
6. "Staple yourself to the learner." As a final check, walk through all the planned activities from the learner's point of view to ensure that they are comprehensive and mutually reinforcing.

(Continued)

Exhibit C.1. A Brief Guide to Implementing the Six Disciplines, Cont'd.

D3: Deliver for application

Minimize the learning-doing gap by presenting material in a way that emphasizes and illustrates its application. Set the expectation for transfer and stress the need for application throughout.

1. Be explicit about the business needs the program is designed to address.
2. Make the relevance of each topic clear.
3. Answer the WIIFM ("what's in it for me?") question for participants.
4. Provide time after each major topic or section for the learners to reflect and plan on how they can use what they just learned.
5. Have the learners practice new skills (and behaviors) in simulations that mimic the business environment.
6. Provide time and encouragement for learners to link new insights to their prior experiences, skills, and knowledge.
7. Ensure adequate time, direction, and oversight for setting transfer and application goals.

D4: Drive follow-through

Treat learning and development objectives like business objectives; ensure that they are well crafted, agreed to by management, followed-up on, and rewarded.

1. Underscore importance of execution in all communications before, during, and after the program.
2. Introduce the goal-setting process early in the program and encourage people to think about what will be most valuable to apply throughout.
3. Provide examples of high-quality goals for transfer and application.
4. Communicate with managers the importance of their involvement.
5. Send a copy of each participant's application objectives to his/her manager.
6. Remind participants periodically of their objectives and the need to use what they learned.
7. Set clear timelines for reporting out progress and results.
8. Use a follow-through management system to track participation and progress during the transfer and application period.
9. Identify success cases and recognize superior performance to encourage others.

D5: Deploy active support

Because learning only produces value when it is applied to the work of the company, provide the support that learners need to most effectively transfer and apply their new knowledge and skills.

Exhibit C.1. A Brief Guide to Implementing the Six Disciplines, Cont'd.

1. Engage managers in the process; inform them of their role, provide relevant information about the program and what they can do to maximize payback to their departments.

2. Have instructors check in with the class during the transfer period; budget time for providing ongoing support and hold them accountable for results.

3. Provide coaches; track and monitor quality and quantity of coaching.

4. Promote collaboration through learning buddies, teams, shared accountability, online collaboration, and so forth.

5. Provide online content that reinforces course principles.

6. Create a critical mass of people trained in the new approach; rapidly roll out program to enough people so that they can support one another as they attempt to implement new ideas and processes.

D6: Document results

Companies invest in learning and development with the expectation of improved performance and results. Learning and development departments must document the results of their programs in order to justify continued investment and support continuous improvement.

1. Define the desired results in business terms prior to launching the program; agree with business managers on the definition of workplace "success."

2. Clarify expected behavior changes and business drivers; share these with participants.

3. Collect the most relevant data from the most reliable sources based on program objectives.

4. Analyze the results conservatively; discount the results for factors other than training.

5. Compare actual results to those expected.

6. Identify success cases and use them to illustrate program value in reports and to future participants.

7. Conduct a "lessons learned" session with the design and execution team. What went well and should be augmented? What is not working and needs to be changed? Use the information to improve subsequent cycles.

8. Market the results to past and future participants and management.

For additional information and updates on the Six Disciplines, go to http://www.ifollowthrough.com/6Ds.

BEYOND TRAINING AND DEVELOPMENT

Throughout this book we have focused on learning and development. Our clients have convinced us that the six disciplines—especially those related to follow-through—also apply to other business initiatives. The first, and perhaps most obvious, is to ensure completion of individual development plans. A second is to ensure execution of strategic plans. Leadership teams often invest significant time and energy in strategic planning meetings. The output usually includes action items for implementation, additional data gathering, communications, and so forth. Too often, however, these new initiatives are overwhelmed by day-to-day activities and do not get executed, thus diminishing the return on the entire team's efforts.

There is likewise a pressing need for a disciplined approach to implementation of consultants' recommendations. The Achilles' heel of most consulting engagements is lack of implementation. After spending tens or hundreds of thousands of dollars for analysis and recommendations from top consulting firms, an astonishing number of companies fail to follow through with implementation. The consultant's reputation and the firm's performance both suffer. "Clear, simple goals don't mean much if nobody takes them seriously" (Bossidy & Charan, 2002, p. 71).

We are pleased that our ideas are finding currency in fields beyond learning and development. We have seen how a more rigorous approach to follow-through management increases the return on investment in learning and development; we expect that it should also benefit other business processes.

THE FUTURE

Sir Isaac Newton, one of the greatest scientists of all time, said: "If I have seen further than others, it is by standing on the shoulders of giants," acknowledging the contributions of previous thinkers. The ideas we have presented here also build on the shoulders of giants: other thought leaders in learning and development, professional colleagues, learning leaders, program participants, our clients, and employees.

We invite you to apply and build on the concepts and disciplines we have presented here to create breakthroughs of your own, add your wisdom to the accumulating knowledge, and share your insights with others. We look forward to hearing about them.

THE LAST WORD

Marshall Goldsmith

FOR THE PAST TWENTY-EIGHT YEARS my professional life has been devoted to one activity—helping successful leaders achieve positive, lasting change in behavior. I have had the privilege of coaching dozens of chief executives. My partner, Howard Morgan, and I have studied the impact of leadership development programs that have involved tens of thousands of managers from around the world. All of our experience and all of our research point to the same inescapable conclusion:

Leaders who don't follow up don't improve!

In every program in every company we studied, the degree of follow-up has been directly correlated to the extent of increased leadership effectiveness as judged by subordinates, peers, and managers.

Most leadership development activities are based upon a very naïve assumption: "If they *understand,* they will *do.*" I now believe that this assumption is completely invalid. Many leaders understand what they should be doing. Many thought leaders, like me, have spent lots of time studying the desired characteristics of the leaders of the future. Companies have spent lots of money developing well-thought-out leadership profiles.

The major challenge faced by managers is
not understanding the practice of leadership,
it is practicing their understanding of leadership!

If organizations truly want to help leaders achieve a positive, measurable change in behavior, training, when coupled with ongoing follow-up, can make a huge positive difference.

Cal Wick and his colleagues have done a great job of defining the six disciplines that turn learning into business results. As a last word, I want to underscore two: the importance of driving follow-through and of providing ongoing coaching support as critical for transforming learning into real improvement.

The designs for learning and development programs should be considered incomplete if they do not include plans to encourage participants to follow through, practice what they have learned, and reach out to colleagues for feedforward ideas and coaching. When those elements are in place to support well-designed and well-delivered learning, then we have all the ingredients for a true transformation.

Life is good.

REFERENCES

Akerman, J. R., Ekelund, H., & Parisi, D. A. (2005). Using business simulations for executive development. In J. F. Bolt (Ed.), *The future of executive development* (pp. 25–39). San Francisco: Executive Development Associates, Inc.

Alexander, J. (2005). Interview by Cal Wick, May 2005.

American Educational Research Association, American Psychological Association, National Council on Measurement in Education. (1996). Standards for Educational and Psychological Testing. Washington, DC: American Psychological Association.

Arthur, W. Jr., Bennett, W. Jr., Edens, P. S., & Bell, S. T. (2003). Effectiveness of training in organizations: A meta-analysis of design and evaluation features. *Journal of Applied Psychology, 88*(2), 234–245.

Atkinson, T., & Davis, J. (2003). *Principles of workplace learning: Insights and tools for performance improvement.* Boston: Forum Corp.

Baldwin, T. T., & Ford, J. K. (1988). Transfer of training: A review and directions for future research. *Personnel Psychology, 15,* 63–105.

Blanchard, K. (2004). Foreword in S. Blanchard & M. Homan, *Leverage your best, ditch the rest: The coaching secrets top executives depend on* (pp. ix–xii). New York: HarperCollins.

Blee, B., Bonito, J., & Tucker, R. E. (2005). Pfizer Inc. In L. Carter, M. Sobol, P. Harkins, D. Giber, & M. Tarquino (Eds.), *Best practices in leading the global workforce: How the best companies ensure success throughout their workforce* (pp. 249–288). Burlington, MA: Linkage Press.

Block, P. (2000). *Flawless consulting: A guide to getting your expertise used* (2nd ed.). Hoboken, NJ: Wiley.

Bolt, J. F. (2005). Mapping the future of executive development: Forces, trends, and implications. In J. F. Bolt (Ed.), *The future of executive development* (pp. 3–21). San Francisco: Executive Development Associates, Inc.

Bolt, J. F., & McGrath, M. R. (2005). Increasing speed to market and line ownership for new executive development strategies and programs. In Bolt, J. F. (Ed.), *The future of executive development* (pp. 103–111). San Francisco: Executive Development Associates, Inc.

Bordonaro, F. (2005). What to do. In M. Dulworth & F. Bordonaro (Eds.), *Corporate learning: Proven and practical guides for building a sustainable learning strategy* (pp. 123–232). San Francisco: Pfeiffer.

Bossidy, L., & Charan, R. (2002). *Execution: The discipline of getting things done.* New York: Crown Business.

Brennan, D. (2004). Interview by Cal Wick, May 2004.

Brinkerhoff, R. O. (1987). *Achieving results from training.* San Francisco: Jossey-Bass.

Brinkerhoff, R. O. (2003). *The success case method: Find out quickly what's working and what's not.* San Francisco: Berrett-Koehler.

Brinkerhoff, R. O., & Apking, A. M. (2001). *High impact learning: Strategies for leveraging business results from training.* New York: Basic Books.

Brinkerhoff, R. O., & Gill, S. J. (1994). *The learning alliance: Systems thinking in human resource development.* San Francisco: Jossey-Bass.

Brinkerhoff, R. O., & Montesino, M. (1995). Partnerships for learning transfer: Lessons from a corporate study. *Human Resource Development Quarterly, 6*(3), 263–274.

Broad, M. L. (2005). *Beyond transfer of training: Engaging systems to improve performance.* San Francisco: Pfeiffer.

Broad, M. L., & Newstrom, J. W. (1992). *Transfer of training: Action-packed strategies to ensure high payoff from training investments.* Cambridge, MA: Perseus Books.

Burke, L. (2005). Interview by Cal Wick, Jan. 2005.

Burnett, S. (2004). Interview by Cal Wick, Mar. 2004.

Burnett, S., & Wick, C. (2005.) Hewlett-Packard. In Carter, L., Ulrich, D., & Goldsmith, M. (Eds.), *Best practices in leadership development and organization change: How the best companies ensure meaningful change and sustainable leadership* (pp. 181–194). San Francisco: Pfeiffer.

Buzan, T., & Buzan, B. (1993). *The mind map: Radiant thinking.* London: BBC Books.

Campbell, D. (1974). *If you don't know where you're going, you'll probably end up somewhere else.* Valencia, CA: Tabor.

Carter, L. (2004). Interview by Cal Wick, Feb. 2004.

Carter, L., Ulrich, D., & Goldsmith, M. (Eds.). (2005). *Best practices in leadership development and organization change: How the best companies ensure meaningful change and sustainable leadership.* San Francisco: Pfeiffer.

Charan, R., Drotter, S., & Noel, J. (2001). *The leadership pipeline: How to build the leadership-powered company.* San Francisco: Jossey-Bass.

Christensen, C. M., & Raynor, M. E. (2003). *The innovator's solution: Creating and sustaining successful growth.* Boston: Harvard Business School Press.

Collins, J. (2001). *Good to great: Why some companies make the leap . . . and others don't.* New York: HarperCollins.

Connolly, M., & Burnett, S. (2003). Hewlett-Packard takes the waste out of leadership. *Journal of Organizational Excellence, 22*(4), 49–59.

Connolly, M., & Rianoshek, R. (2002). *The communication catalyst: The fast (but not stupid) track to value for customers, investors, and employees.* Chicago: Dearborn Trade Publishing.

Day, R. A. (1994). *How to write & publish a scientific paper* (4th ed.). Phoenix: Oryx.

de Geus, A. (1988). Planning as learning. *Harvard Business Review, 66*(2), 70–74.

Dixon, N. M. (1990). The relationship between trainee responses on participation reaction forms and posttest scores. *Human Resource Development Quarterly, 1,* 129–137.

Dolezalek, H. (2004). *Training* magazine's 23rd annual comprehensive analysis of employer-sponsored training in the United States. *Training, 41*(10), 20–36.

Dulworth, M., & Bordonaro, F. (Eds.) (2005). *Corporate learning: Proven and practical guides for building a sustainable learning strategy.* San Francisco: Pfeiffer.

Dulworth, M., & Forcillo, J. (2005). Achieving the developmental value of peer-to-peer networks. In M. Dulworth & F. Bordonaro (Eds.), *Corporate learning: Proven and practical guides for building a sustainable learning strategy.* San Francisco: Pfeiffer.

Drucker, P. F. (1974). *Management: Tasks, responsibilities, practices.* New York: Harper & Row.

Drucker, P. F. (1954). *The practice of management.* New York: Harper & Row.

Feldstein, H. D., & Boothman, T. (1997). Success factors in technology training. In J. J. Phillips & M. L. Broad (Eds.), *Transferring learning to the workplace* (pp. 19–33). Alexandria, VA: ASTD.

Flanders, V., & Willis, M. (1996). *Web pages that suck: Learn good design by looking at bad design.* San Francisco: Sybex.

Friedman, T. L. (2005). *The world is flat: A brief history of the twenty-first century.* New York: Farrar, Straus and Giroux.

Gebelein, S. H., Nelson-Neuhaus, K. J., Skube, C. J., Lee, D. G., Stevens, L. A., Hellervik, L. W., et al. (Eds.) (2005). *Successful manager's handbook: Development suggestions for today's managers* (7th ed.). Minneapolis: Personnel Decisions.

Georgenson, D. L. (1982). The problem of transfer calls for partnership. *Training and Development Journal, 36*(10), 75–78.

Goldsmith, M. (1996). Ask, learn, follow up, and grow. In F. Hesselbein, M. Goldsmith, & R. Beckhard (Eds.), *The leader of the future: New visions, strategies, and practices for the next era* (pp. 227–237). San Francisco: Jossey-Bass.

Goldsmith, M. (2002). Try feedforward instead of feedback. *Leader to Leader, 25* (Summer), 11–14.

Goldsmith, M., & Morgan, H. (2004). Leadership is a contact sport: The follow-up factor in management development. *Strategy+Business, Fall 2004.* Available: http://www.strategy-business.com/export/export.php?article_id=4517821 [Last accessed Jan. 2006].

Goleman, D. (1998). What makes a leader? *Harvard Business Review,* 76(6), 93–102.

Goleman, D. (2000). Leadership that gets results. *Harvard Business Review,* 78(2), 78–90.

Grawey, J. (2005). "Sony Electronics Talent and Organizational Development." Paper presented at Fort Hill Company's 2005 Best Practices Summit, Wilmington, DE, May 2005.

Hammonds, K. (2005). Why we hate HR. *Fast Company,* August, 40–47.

Harburg, F. (2004). They're buying holes, not shovels. *Chief Learning Officer,* 3(3), 21.

Heller, R., & Hindle, T. (1998). *Essential manager's manual.* New York: DK Publishing.

Hu-Chan, M., Bergman, C., & Frugé, M. (2005). Johnson & Johnson. In L. Carter, M. Sobol, P. Harkins, D. Giber, & M. Tarquino (Eds.), *Best practices in leading the global workforce: How the best companies ensure success throughout their workforce* (pp. 159–200). Burlington, MA: Linkage Press.

Ibarra, H. (2004). Breakthrough ideas for 2004. *Harvard Business Review,* February, 13–32.

International Society for Performance Improvement. (2002). "Performance Technology Standards." Silver Springs, MD: ISPI.

International Society for Performance Improvement. (n.d.). "What is human performance technology?" Available: http://www.ispi.org/hpt_institute/ [Last accessed Jan. 2006].

Jusela, G. (2004). Interview by Cal Wick, Feb. 2004.

Kaye, B. (2005) Love it and use it. *Learning Alert, 15,* Sept. 2005. Available: http://www.ifollowthrough.com/news/learning_alert/learningalert15.html [Last accessed Jan. 2006].

Kaye, B., & Jordan-Evans, S. (2005). *Love 'em or lose 'em: Getting good people to stay.* San Francisco: Berrett-Koehler.

Kesner, I. F. (2003). Leadership development: Perk or priority? *Harvard Business Review,* May, 29–38.

Kirkpatrick, D. (2002). The future of IBM. *Fortune, 145*(4), 60–68.

Kirkpatrick, D. L. (1998). *Evaluating training programs: The four levels* (2nd ed.). San Francisco: Berrett-Koehler.

Kirkpatrick, D. L., & Kirkpatrick, J. D. (2005). *Transferring learning to behavior: Using the four levels to improve performance.* San Francisco: Berrett-Koehler.

Knowles, M. S., Holton, E. F. III, & Swanson, R. A. (2005). *The adult learner: The definitive classic in adult education and human resource development* (6th ed.). Burlington, MA: Elsevier.

Knudson, M. J. (2005). Executive coaching. In J. F. Bolt (Ed.), *The future of executive development* (pp. 40–53). San Francisco: Executive Development Associates.

Kouzes, J., & Posner, B. (1990). *The leadership challenge.* San Francisco: Jossey-Bass.

Langley, G. J., Nolan, K. M., Nolan, T. W., Norman, C. L., & Provost, L. P. (1996). *The improvement guide: A practical approach to enhancing organizational performance.* San Francisco: Jossey-Bass.

Leider, R. (2004). Interview by Cal Wick, Feb. 2004.

Levinson, S., & Greider, P. (1998). *Following through: A revolutionary new model for finishing whatever you start.* New York: Kensington Books.

Lombardo, M. M., & Eichinger, R. W. (2000). *For your improvement: A development and coaching guide* (3rd ed.). Minneapolis: Lominger.

Magee, R. (2005). Interview by Roy Pollock and Cal Wick, Oct. 2005.

Mankins, M. C., & Steele, R. (2005). Turning strategy into great performance. *Harvard Business Review,* July–Aug., 65–72.

Meridian Resources (n.d.). *Training Media Review* [Online]. Available: http://www.meridianglobal.com/TrainingMediaReview.html [Last accessed Jan. 2006].

Mosel, J. D. (1957). Why training programs fail to carry over. *Personnel, 34*(3), 56–64.

Newstrom, J. W. (1986). Leveraging management development through the management of transfer. *Journal of Management Development,* 5(5), 33–45.

Nielsen, J. (1997). *How users read on the web* [Online]. Available: http://www.useit.com/alertbox/9710a.html [Last accessed Nov. 2005].

Nielsen, J., Schemenaur, P. J., & Fox, J. (n.d.). *Writing for the web* [Online]. Available: http://www.sun.com/980713/webwriting/index.html [Last accessed Jan. 2006].

O'Hern, J. (2005). Interview by Roy Pollock and Cal Wick, Feb. 2005.

O'Leary, R. (2004). Interview by Cal Wick, Feb. 2004.

Paige, N. (2003). Presentation at the UNICOM Conference, Ashridge, England, Apr. 2003.

Parskey, P. (2005). Interview by Cal Wick and Roy Pollock, Jan. 2005.

Phillips, J. J. (2003). *Return on investment in training and performance improvement programs* (2nd ed.). New York: Butterworth Heinemann.

Phillips, J. J., & Broad, M. L. (Eds.) (1997). *Transferring learning to the workplace.* Alexandria, VA: ASTD.

Phillips, J., & Phillips, P. (2001). *Measuring return on investment* (vol. 3). Alexandria, VA: ASTD.

Phillips, J. J., & Phillips, P. P. (2002). 11 reasons why training & development fails . . . and what you can do about it. *Training,* Sept., 78–85.

Phillips, J. J., & Stone, R. D. (2002). *How to measure training results: A practical guide to tracking the six key indicators.* New York: McGraw-Hill.

Plotnikoff, R. C., McCargar, L. J., Wilson, P. M., & Loucaides, C. A. (2005). Efficacy of an e-mail intervention for the promotion of physical activity and nutrition behavior in the workplace context. *American Journal of Health Promotion, 19*(6), 422–429.

Restak, R. (2001). *Mozart's brain and the fighter pilot: Unleashing your brain's potential.* New York: Three Rivers.

Ries, A., & Trout, J. (2001). *Positioning: The battle for your mind.* New York: McGraw-Hill.

Rip, G. (2004). Presentation at the Fort Hill Associates Conference, Mendenhall, PA, Oct. 2004.

Robinson, D., & Robinson, J. (1996). *Performance consulting: Moving beyond training.* San Francisco: Berrett-Koehler.

Roche, T. (2004). Interview by Cal Wick, Apr. 2004.

Roche, T., & Wick, C. (2005). Agilent Technologies. In L. Carter, M. Sobol, P. Harkins, D. Giber, & M. Tarquinio (Eds.), *Best practices in leading the global workforce: How the best global companies ensure success throughout their workforce* (pp. 1–23). Burlington, MA: Linkage Press.

Roche, T., Wick, C., & Stewart, M. (2005). Innovation in learning: Agilent Technologies thinks outside the box. *Journal of Organizational Excellence, 24*(4), 45–53.

Ruona, W.E.A., Leimbach, M., Holton, E. F. III, & Bates, R. (2002). The relationship between learner utility reactions and predicted learning transfer among trainees. *International Journal of Training and Development, 6*(4), 218–228.

Saslow, S. (2005). Executive education best practices. In M. Dulworth & F. Bordonaro (Eds.), *Corporate learning: Proven and practical guidelines for building a sustainable learning strategy.* San Francisco: Pfeiffer.

Schaffer, R. H., & Thomson, H. A. (1992). Successful change programs begin with results. *Harvard Business Review,* Jan.–Feb., 2–11.

Schettler, J. (2003). The 2003 *Training* top 100: Top five profile & ranking: Pfizer. *Training, 40*(3), 40–41.

Senge, P. M. (1990). *The fifth discipline: The art and practice of the learning organization.* New York: Doubleday.

Shapiro, B. P., Rangan, V. K., & Sviokla, J. J. (1992). Staple yourself to an order. *Harvard Business Review, 70*(4), 113–122.

Sharkey, L. (2003). Leveraging HR: How to develop leaders in "real time." In R. Gandossy, M. Goldsmith, & M. Effron (Eds.), *Human resources in the 21st century* (pp. 193–198). Hoboken, NJ: Wiley.

Smith-Rutledge, L. (1997). Building transfer of training into the course design process: Central Intelligence Agency. In J. J. Phillips & M. L. Broad (Eds.), *Transferring learning to the workplace* (pp. 109–119). Alexandria, VA: ASTD.

Spencer, L. M. (2001). The economic value of emotional intelligence competencies and EIC-based HR programs. In C. Cherniss & D. Goleman

(Eds.), *The emotionally intelligent workplace: How to select for, measure, and improve emotional intelligence in individuals, groups and organizations.* San Francisco: Jossey-Bass.

Sullivan, J. (2005). Measuring the impact of executive development. In J. F. Bolt (Ed.), *The future of executive development* (pp. 260–284). New York: Executive Development Associates.

Swanson, D. (2005). Interview by Roy Pollock and Cal Wick, Sept. 2005.

Tobin, D. (1998). *The fallacy of ROI calculations* [Online]. Available: http://www.tobincls.com/fallacy.htm [Last accessed Jan. 2006].

Trainor, D. (2004). "Using Metrics to Deliver Business Impact." Presentation at The Conference Board's 2004 Enterprise Learning Strategies Conference, New York, Feb. 2004.

Vicere, A. (2004). Interview by Cal Wick, Feb. 2004.

Vigil, R. (2005). Interview by Cal Wick, Jan. 2005.

Vroom, V. H. (1995). *Work and motivation (classic reprint).* San Francisco: Jossey-Bass.

Wall, S., & White, E. (1997). Building Saturn's organization-wide transfer support model: Saturn Corporation. In J. J. Phillips & M. L. Broad (Eds.), *Transferring learning to the workplace* (pp. 165–187). Alexandria, VA: ASTD.

Watkins, M. (2003). *The first 90 days: Critical success strategies for new leaders at all levels.* Boston: Harvard Business School Press.

Webster's college dictionary. (2001). New York: Random House.

Whyman, W., Santana, L., & Allen, L. (2005). Online follow-up using technology to enhance learning. *Learning in Action, 25*(4), 14–17.

Wick, C. W. (2003). Going beyond the finish line. *Training and Development, 58*(7), 17–18.

Wick, C. W., & Flanagan, R. D. (2005, Jan.). Developing leaders: Practice six basic disciplines. *Organizational Excellence,* 10–11.

Wick, C. W., & Leon, L. S. (1993). *The learning edge: How smart managers and smart companies stay ahead.* New York: McGraw-Hill.

Wick, C. W., & Pollock, R.V.H. (2004a). Just-in-time guidance. In M. Goldsmith, H. Morgan, & A. J. Ogg (Eds.), *Leading organizational learning: Harnessing the power of knowledge* (pp. 121–132). San Francisco: Jossey-Bass.

Wick, C. W., & Pollock, R.V.H. (2004b). Making results visible. *Training and Development, 58*(6), 46–51.

Wilde, K. (2004). Interview by Cal Wick, Feb. 2004.

Zenger, J., Folkman, J., & Sherwin, R. (2005). The promise of phase 3. *Training and Development, 59*(1), 30–35.

INDEX

A

Accountability: follow-through, 115–118; improving IBM's, 169; of manager's support role, 147
Action learning, 77–79
Action points: for complete experience design, 70–71; for delivery for application, 96–97; for document results, 200–201; for follow-through management, 135–137; for reaching business outcomes, 44–45; on six disciplines, 9, 11–12
Action without analysis, 21–23
Administrative/security subsystem, 126
Advertising document results, 198–199
Agilent Technologies, 49, 148–149
Akerman, J. R., 79
Alexander, J., 46, 47–48
American Educational Research Association, 28, 30
American Psychological, 30
American Society for Training and Development, 99, 181, 198
Apking, A. M., 31, 101, 171
Archimedes, 120
Arthur, W., Jr., 100
AstraZeneca, 77, 110, 140, 141
AstraZeneca's Breakthrough Coaching, 147
AstraZeneca's Leadership Capabilities, 157
Atkinson, T., 81

B

Baldwin, T. T., 129
BBC, 43
Behavior change. *See* Change
Bell, S. T., 100
Bennett, W., Jr., 100
Bergman, C., 98
Best Practice Institute, 55
Best Practices in Leading the Global Workforce (Roche), 148
Best Practices Summit, 168
Bias issue, 187
Blanchard, K., 98, 110, 119
Blee, B., 50, 60
Blended coaching approach, 152–153*e*
Block, P., 184
Bolt, J. F., 76, 78
Bonito, J., 50, 60
Boothman, T., 53
Bordonaro, F., 30, 151, 167, 173, 184
Bossidy, L., 1, 57, 99, 208
Brand development, 54
Breakthrough learning: action points to support, 165–166; critical mass impact on, 151; customer support analogy applied to support of, 155–165; described, 8*fig*–9; environment support of, 139–141; feedback sustaining follow-through and, 154*fig*–155; instructor and facilitator roles in, 148–149; manager role in, 141–148; peer learning

communities and, 149–151; professional coaches and, 151–153e. *See also* Deploy active support; Learning

Brennan, D., 140–141, 177

Brinkerhoff, R. O., 19, 31, 53, 84, 101, 171, 190

British Telecom, 153

Broad, M. L., 48, 49, 50, 53, 101, 141, 149

Burke, L., 72, 81–82

Burnett, S., 21–22, 77, 131, 132, 182

Business needs: discovering highest-value, 34; interview guidelines for discovering, 37e; training as answer to filling, 40–41

Business results: action points for reaching, 44–45; applying marketing principles to, 39–41; avoiding pitfalls, 19–30; begin with the end in mind, 14–17; in business terms, 17–19; cautions against measuring activity instead of, 173–174; confusing positive reaction with positive, 174; corporate education producing, 65–66; D1 principle of, 2–3; defining the right problem to reach, 34–39; described, 17; factors affecting, 29fig; Honeywell's experience with, 18–19; implementing, 205e; as including more than finance, 18; learning results versus, 175e–176; managing expectations, 41–43; mapping the impact, 30fig–34; redefining business, 13–14; reprising the, 202–203fig; Sony Electronics case study, 15–17. *See also* D1 (define outcomes in business terms); Drive follow-through

Business results pitfalls: action without analysis ("we need a pro-

gram"), 21–23; bad example on failure to, 20e; confusion between means and ends, 23–24; five key pitfalls listed, 20; laudable intent, 25; learning to avoid, 19–20; no line leader input, 25–28; "training results cannot be measured" excuse, 28, 30

Buzan, B., 80

Buzan, T., 80

C

Campbell, D., 14, 177

Career Systems International, 75

Carter, L., 55

Case studies: AstraZeneca on setting vision/direction, 140–141; on business links and sponsorship, 26–27; The Gap on defining business outcomes, 21–22; General Mills breakthrough learning experience, 53–54; Home Depot's store manager forums, 163–164; Honeywell's Strategic Marketing Program (SMP), 116–118; Humana, Inc., 38–39, 171–178; on importance of reflection, 81–82; instructional value of, 79–80; on learning as a process, 47–48; Pfizer ROI on reduced turnover, 180; on power of follow-through management, 127–131; Sony Electronics on business results, 15–17; When the Video Doesn't Match the Audio, 56

Center for Creative Leadership (CCL), 47–48, 150, 152

Center for Naval Leadership, 199

Central Intelligence Agency, 98

CEO (chief executive officer): linking business and actions directed by, 21–22; "share of mind" promoted by effective, 192; working with the CLO, 19

Change: deliver for application leading to, 5–6, 72–97; facilitator role in job behavior, 148–149; follow-through management leading to, 108–137; in job satisfaction after coaching program, 111*fig*; measuring evidence of behavior, 177–179*e*

ChangeLever International, 145

Charan, R., 1, 57, 58, 99, 208

Chief Learning Officer magazine, 198

Christensen, C. M., 34

Cisco's *DevelopmentEngine*, 61

Cisco's Emerging Leadership and Global Leadership, 61, 146

Cisco's Leader Behaviors, 157

Cisco's Strategic Leader, 50, 84

Claiming Your Place at the Fire (Leider), 42

CLO (chief learning officer), 19

Coaching: feedback as part of, 118–119; motivating managers to take role of, 144–147*fig*; online blended, 152–153*e*; professional, 151–153; value of, 145

Coca-Cola, 54, 153

Collins, J., 170

Communication: document results, 192–199; elevator speech, 94; regarding objectives, 94–95

Competition, besting the, 42–43

Complete experience: action points for, 70–71; D2 discipline on, 3–5, 4*fig*; designing the, 46–71; ongoing cycle of, 68*fig*; reprising the, 203*fig*; "staple yourself to an order" to understand, 68–69. *See also* D2 (design the complete experience)

Complete experience design: corporate learning phases used in, 50–67; evaluation as part of, 68*fig*; factors influencing outcomes of, 48–49*fig*; focus points of, 47; implementing, 205*e*; reprising the, 203*fig*; transfer matrix paradigm used in, 49–50*fig*

Connolly, M., 23, 77, 131, 132

Consequences, 119–120

Continuous improvement support, 169–172, 170*fig*

"Coopeition," 118

Cornell's leadership programs, 150

Corporate education manuals/online guides, 125, 156–165, 160*fig*

Corporate learning phase I: expectations influence outcomes, 51–52*fig*; influence of the manager during, 53–54; strategies for strengthening, 54–61

Corporate learning phase II: employing adult learning principles, 63; example of strategy tree used during, 62*fig*; linking tactics to strategy, 61–62

Corporate learning phase III: coaching during, 151–153*e*; continuing process of education during, 65*fig*–66; follow-through learning during, 63; guidance systems used during, 158; peer learning communities during, 149–151; planning ongoing support, 66–67; trainer role during, 149; transfer of learning during, 64*e*. *See also* Drive follow-through

Corporate University Xchange, 198

COS (conditions of satisfaction), 42*e*

Crest, 54

Critical incident method, 182

Critical mass participation, 151

"Culture of execution," 57

Cushman and Wakefield, 153

Customer satisfaction factors, 155*fig*

Customers: discovering highest-value needs of, 34; follow-through support parallel with support of, 155–165; interview guidelines for discovering needs of, 37*e*; as marketing segments/markets, 39–40; understanding experience of your, 68–69

D

D1 (define outcomes in business terms). *See* Business results

D2 (design the complete experience). *See* Complete experience

D3 (deliver for application). *See* Deliver for application

D4 (drive follow-through). *See* Drive follow-through

D5 (deploy active support). *See* Deploy active support

D6 (document results). *See* Document results

Dashboard of follow-through management system for, 126*fig*

Data collection/analysis, 110–111. *See also* Information

Davis, J., 81

Define outcomes in business terms. *See* Business results

DeGeus, A., 46

Deliver for application: action points for, 96–97; answering the WIIFM question, 75, 95–96; checking the process, 95; communicating objectives, 94–95; creating desire to learn, 73–75, 74*fig*; D3 discipline on, 5–6; described, 72; implementing, 206*e*; listing of strategies for, 72–73; making relevance clear, 75–77; maximizing retention, 80–93; narrowing learning-doing gap, 73; planning for transfer of learning, 93–94; providing know-how, 77–80; reprising the, 203*fig*–204

Deming (PDSA) quality cycle, 170*fig*, 188

Deploy active support: action points for, 165–166; analogy to customer support of, 155*fig*–165; critical mass and, 151; D6 discipline of, 7; environment role in, 139–141; feedback sustaining follow-through and, 154*fig*–155; implementing, 206*e*–207*e*; instructor and facilitator roles in, 148–149; manager role in, 141–148; owner's manuals/online guides for, 125, 156–165, 160*fig*; of peers and learning communities, 149–151; by professional coaches, 151–153*e*; reprising, 203*fig*, 204. *See also* Breakthrough learning

DiSC evaluations, 178

Dixon, N. M., 174

Document results: action points for, 200–201; advertising, 198–199; benefits of, 168–172; caveat to, 199; communication during, 192–199; D6 discipline of, 7–8; deciding what to measure, 172–176; how to measure, 176–182; implementing, 207*e*; making the most of results through, 190–199; obstacles to, 183–190; reprising, 203*fig*, 204

Document results benefits: justifying continued investment, 168–169; supporting continuous improvement, 169–172

Document results measurement traps: 1: measuring activity rather than outcomes, 173–174; 2: confusing positive reaction with positive results, 174; 3:

adopting learning versus business perspective on results, 175*e*–176

Document results measurements: avoiding three traps of, 173–176, 175*e*; critical incident, 182; evidence of behavior change as, 177–179*e*; results in economic terms, 179–182

Document results obstacles: lack of clear objectives, 183–184; long log time between training and final results, 188; managing lag time, 188–190; multiple causality, 184–187

Drive follow-through: D4 discipline on, 6–7; electronic management system for, 88*fig*–89; high cost of doing nothing instead of, 100–101; impediments to, 103*e*–108; implementing, 206*e*; learning as insufficient without, 101–103; management facilitation of, 108*fig*–120; need for, 99–100; setting expectations for, 57–58; using time as a lever for, 120*fig*–122. *See also* Business results; Corporate learning phase III; Learning

Drive follow-through breakthrough: administrative and security subsystem, 123*fig*, 126; feedback loop, 123*fig*, 124–125; flexible update engine, 123*fig*, 124; intelligent reminder system, 123*fig*–124; key elements of, 122–123*fig*; management information system, 123*fig*, 126–127; online guidance, 123*fig*, 125; shared learning, 123*fig*, 125

Drive follow-through impediments: environmental, 103*e*–104*e*, 107; human factors, 104*e*–106*e*, 107; inadequate follow-through

process, 106*e*, 107–108; rewards/consequences system as, 107*e*

Drive follow-through management: action points for, 135–137; breakthrough factors, 122–127, 123*fig*; case-control study/results on, 127–131; delivering consequences, 119–120; electronic, 88*fig*–89; ensuring accountability, 115–118; examples of feedback from managers, 178*e*–179*e*; as facilitating follow-through, 108*fig*–120; gathering and analyzing data, 110–111*fig*; implementing, 134–135; increasing return on training investment with, 132–133; power of, 127–132*fig*; providing feedback, 118–119, 154–155; providing reminders and mileposts, 112–115; setting right expectations, 109–110; training manuals/online guides, 125, 158–165, 160*fig*. *See also* Management

Drotter, S., 58

Drucker, P. F., 13, 17, 169, 202

Dulworth, M., 150, 167, 197

E

E-mail reminders, 113–114

Edens, P. S., 100

Eichinger, R. W., 157

Ekelund, H., 79

Electronic follow-through management system, 88*fig*–89

Elevator speech, 94

Employees. *See* Participants

End-of-course evaluation, 188–190

Environmental support, 139–141

Essential Manager's Handbook (Heller & Hindle), 157

Evaluating Training Programs (Kirkpatrick), 175

Evaluation: complete experience
design and role of, 68*fig*; end-
of-course, 188–190; levels of
training, 175*e*–176
Executive summaries, 193–194

F

Facilitator role, 148–149
Federated Department Stores'
Leadership Institute, 193
Feedback: examples of man-
ager follow-through, 178*e*–
179*e*; follow-through, 118–119,
154–155; follow-through break-
through and, 123*fig*, 124–125;
Friday5s management system use
of, 154*fig*–155; 360-degree feed-
back, 60, 94, 149–150, 151, 178
Feedforward, 93–94
Feldstein, H. D., 53
Fidelity Investments, 13, 83, 133,
151, 153
The Fifth Discipline (Senge), 40
Financial Times (magazine), 47
*The First 90 Days: Critical Success
Strategies for New Leaders at All
Levels* (Watkins), 139
Flanagan, R. F., 73
Flanders, V., 160
Flawless Consulting (Block), 184
Folkman, J., 6, 51
Food and Drug Administration
(FDA), 28, 42
Forcillo, J., 150, 197
Ford, J. K., 129
Fort Hill Computer's Follow-
Through Tools, 181
Forum Corporation, 81
Fox, J., 162
Friday5s management system: CCL
(Center for Creative Leadership)
use of, 48; feedback as part of,
154*fig*–155; follow-through

breakthrough using, 122; Home
Depot's use of, 147, 164; Sun
Microsystem's use of, 128, 130,
133, 146. *See also* Management
Friedman, T. L., 46
From the Earth to the Moon (Verne),
101
Frugé, M., 98
FYI: For Your Improvement
(Lombardo & Eichinger), 157

G

Gap, Inc., 21–22
Gebelein, S. H., 157
General Electric (GE), 149
General Mills, 53–54
Georgenson, D. L., 100
Gerstner, L., 169
Gill, S. J., 31
Gilson, P., 110
GlaxoSmithKline, 153
Goals. *See* Objectives
Goldsmith, M., 55, 93, 116, 119,
152, 177, 178, 209
Goleman, D., 121, 122
Good to Great (Collins), 170
Gordy, B., 14
Grawey, J., 16, 118
Greider, P., 113, 114
Guided Reflection Worksheet, 83*fig*
GuideMe (online support system),
160*fig*

H

Hammond, K., 23
Harburg, F., 3, 13
Harris, S., 4
Harvard Business Review, 27, 68,
121, 168
"Having a program" pitfall, 21–23
Hays, S. S., 193
Heller, R., 157

Hewlett-Packard, 76, 90, 182
Hewlett-Packard's Dynamic
  Leadership programs, 58,
  131–132*fig*, 182
Hewlett-Packard's evaluation model,
  189*fig*–190
Hindle, T., 157
Holton, E. F., III, 62, 75, 158
Home Depot, 147, 163–164
Home Depot Canada, 66
Home Depot's Store Managers
  Learning Forums, 164
Honeywell, 18–19, 116
Honeywell's Strategic Marketing
  Program (SMP), 116–118
HPT (human performance tech-
  nology), 32–34, 50
Hu-Chan, M., 98
Humana, Inc., 38, 55, 171–172
Hypertext, 159*fig*

I

Ibarra, H., 114, 138
IBM, 169
Impact mapping: two examples of,
  33*fig*; using tool of, 31–32*fig*;
  value of constructing, 77
Income tax preparation software,
  159
Infection and Immunity (magazine),
  186
Information: on applying concept
  of situation leadership, 159*fig*;
  availability of training follow-
  through, 158–160*fig*; creating
  manageable segments of, 161–
  162; follow-through systems
  management of, 126–127; gathering and analyzing follow-
  through, 110–111*fig*; online
  surveys used to gather, 179;
  training manuals/online guides,
  125, 156–158, 160*fig*

Innovator's Solution (Christensen
  and Raynor), 34
Instructors. *See* Trainers
Intelligent reminder system, 123*fig*–
  124
Interview Guidelines for Discovering
  Business Needs, 37*e*
Inventure Group, 195
ISPI (International Society for Per-
  formance Improvement), 32, 50

J

Johnson & Johnson' Global Supply
  Management Institute, 98
Jolly, R., 149
Jordan-Evans, S., 196
*Journal of Organizational
  Excellence,* 49, 131
Jusela, G., 150–151, 163, 164

K

Kaye, B., 75, 196
Kellogg leadership programs, 150
Kesner, I. F., 168
Kirkpatrick, D. L., 138, 142, 169,
  175, 176
Kirkpatrick, J. D., 138
Kirkpatrick's levels of training eval-
  uation, 175*e*–176
Know-how, 77–80, 78*e*
KnowledgeAdvisors, Inc., 181
Knowledge/skills: checking delivery
  of new, 95; making connections
  between past/present, 80–84;
  managers' reactions to employees
  use of new, 143*e*; meaningful, 80;
  value created through applied,
  98. *See also* Learning
Knowles, M. S., 62, 75, 77, 158
Knudsen, M. J., 151
Kofman, F., 82
Kouzes, J., 198

L

Lag time management, 188–190

Langley, G. J., 170, 188

LaserJet, 54

Laudable intent, 25

LDP (Leadership Development Program) [CCL], 152

Leaders as teachers, 19

"Leadership Development: Perk or Priority?" (Kesner), 168

The Leadership Pipeline (Charan, Drotter, and Noel), 58

"Leadership That Gets Results" (Goleman), 121–122

Learner Transfer System Inventory, 174

Learning: action, 77–79; building bridge between doing and, 6*fig*; business goals of, 23–24; business results versus results of, 175*e*–176; creating motivation for, 73–75, 74*fig*; gap between doing the work and, 5*fig*; shared, 125; six disciplines characterizing breakthrough, 8*fig*–9; three phases of corporate, 50–67. *See also* Breakthrough learning; Drive follow-through; Knowledge/skills; Transfer of learning

Learning communities, 149–151

Learning leaders: breakthrough learning action points for, 165–166; business outcomes action points for, 44; complete experience action points for, 70; dashboard of follow-through management system for, 126*fig*; delivery for application action points for, 96; document results action points for, 200–201; follow-through management action points for, 135–136; six discipline

action points for, 9. *See also* Managers

"Learning scrap," 101

Learning Transfer and Application Scorecard, 10*e*–11*e*

Learning-doing gap, 73

The Learning4Results Worksheet, 12*e*

Learning/development programs. *See* Training programs

Leider, R., 42, 195

Leon, L. S., 46

Levinson, S., 113, 114

Lexus, 54

Line leaders: breakthrough learning action points for, 166; business outcomes action points for, 45; complete experience action points for, 70–71; delivery for application action points for, 96–97; document results action points for, 201; failure to get input from, 25–28; follow-through management action points for, 136–137; impact mapping tool used by, 32*fig*; six discipline action points for, 11–12. *See also* Managers

LMS (learning management system), 173

Lombardo, M. M., 157

London Business School, 149

Loucaides, C. A., 114

M

McCargar, L. J., 114

McNerney, J., 26

Magee, R., 116–118

Management: influence during corporate learning process, 53–54; range of deploy active support by, 142; securing effective support for learning by, 55–57. *See also* Drive follow-through management; *Friday5s* management system

Management information system, 126–127

Managers: deploy active support role by, 141–148; document results communication with, 194–196; motivated to coach, 144–147*fig*; reactions to employee use of new learned capabilities, 143*e*; sending learning transfer objectives to, 89–90. *See also* Learning leaders; Line leaders

Managing expectations: agreement on what defines success, 41–42; besting the competition, 42–43; COS (conditions of satisfaction) and, 42*e*

Mankins, M. C., 27

Mannix, B., 125

Mapping business results: diagrams of, 30*fig*–31*fig*; HPT (human performance technology) for, 32–34; impact mapping tool used for, 31–32*fig*

Market segments, 39–40, 191–192

Market targets, 39–40, 191–192

Marketing principles, segment and target, 39–40

Merchant University, 21–22

Meridian Resources' GlobeSmart, 165

Metrics that Matter system, 181

Montesino, M., 53

Morgan, H., 119, 152

Mosel, J. D., 57

MotivAider, 113

Motivation: creating learning, 73–75; for managers to act as coaches, 144–147*fig*; propor-

tional to perception of value, 74*fig*

Motown Records, 14

Multiple causality issue, 184–187

N

NASA, 66, 101

National Council on Measurement in Education, 30

Neter, E., 186

Newstrom, J. W., 49, 50, 53, 64, 75, 141, 149

Nielsen, J., 161, 162

Noel, J., 58

Nonparticipant communication, 196

Notre Dame's Integral Leadership, 81–82, 148

O

Objectives: communicating, 94–95; documenting results and lack of clear, 183–184; electronic follow-through management system to reach, 88*fig*–89; example of structured form for goals and, 91*e*; matching instruction to skills required for, 78*e*; problems/solutions for transfer of learning, 84–93; sharing of goals and, 92–93; SMART acronym for, 90; for transfer/application of learning, 84. *See also* Participants

O'Hern, J., 57, 195

Online blended coaching, 152–153*e*

Online corporate education guides: behavioral observation feedback through, 178*e*–179*e*; characteristics of effective, 158–165; GuideMe example of, 160*fig*;

Home Depot case study on, 163–164; importance of providing, 125

Online LMS (learning management system), 173

Outcomes. *See* Business results

P

Paine, N., 43

Parisi, D. A., 79

Parskey, P., 168, 189

Participants: document results communication with, 194–196; maximizing retention by, 80–93; motivation for learning of, 73–75, 74*fig*; relevant as perceived by, 75–77; WIIFM (What's in it for me?) question by, 75, 95–96. *See also* Objectives; Training programs

PDSA (Plan-Do-Study-Act) cycle, 170*fig*, 188

Peer learning communities, 149–151

Performance Challenges Corporation, 189

Performance Consultant, 26

Performance Consulting (Robinson and Robinson), 25

Performance sustaining, 102*fig*

Pfizer case study, 180

Pfizer's Advance Transition, 60, 84, 146

Pfizer's Department of Measurement, Evaluation, and Strategic Analysis (MESA), 132–133

Pfizer's Leading Edge, 178

Pfizer's Learning Center, 58, 132–133, 178

Phillips, J. J., 64, 101, 133, 173, 175, 181, 185, 187

Phillips, P. P., 64

Picking right problem: discovering highest-value needs, 34; doing

your homework, 36–39; market research for, 35–36; putting price on it, 34–35

Plotnikoff, R. C., 114

Pogo (comic character), 24

Pollock, R.V.H., 168, 193

Positioning: The Battle for Your Mind (Ries and Trout), 112

Posner, B., 198

"Pretense" mode, 23

Principles of Workplace Learning (Forum Corporation), 81

Professional coaches, 151–153

Profitability: learning/developing programs adding to, 31*fig*; training expenses offset by increased, 65*fig*; two ways to increase, 30*fig*

Projectiles falling back to earth, 102*fig*

R

Rangan, V. K., 68

Raynor, M. E., 34

REFLECTIONS, 178

Reinforcement on the job, 64

Relevance, 75–77

Reminder systems, 113–115, 123*fig*–124

Repetition of message, 192

"Reporting out" sessions, 116

ResultsEngine, 195

Retention maximization, 80–84

Rianoshek, R., 23

Ries, A., 112

Rip, G., 145–146

Robinson, D., 25, 149

Robinson, J., 25

Roche, T., 49, 148, 149

ROI (return on investment): document results measuring, 180–182; of follow-through management, 132–133; as level of training evaluation, 175*e*–176

Ross, M., 189
Ruona, W.E.A., 174

S

Saslow, S., 28
Schaffer, R. H., 24
Schemenaur, P. J., 162
Schettler, J., 132
Segments (market), 39–40, 191–192
Senge, P. M., 40
Shapiro, B. P., 68
"Share of mind," 112
Shared learning, 125
Sharkey, L., 149
Sherwin, R., 6, 51
Simulation instruction, 79
Six disciplines: action points for learning leaders on, 9; action points for line leaders on, 11–12; beyond training and development, 208; breakthrough learning characterized by, 8*fig*–9; brief guide to implementing the, 205*e*–207*e*; D1: define outcomes in business terms, 2–3; D2: design the complete experience, 3–5; D3: deliver for application, 5–6*fig*; D4: drive follow-through, 6–7; D5: deploy active support, 7; D6: document results, 7–8; illustrated diagram of, 1*fig*; Learning Transfer and Application Scorecard, 10*e*–11*e*; The Learning4Results Worksheet on, 12*e*; reprising the, 202–204; summary of, 8*fig*; See also specific discipline
Skills. See Knowledge/skills
SMART goals, 90
Smith-Rutledge, L., 98
SmithKline Animal Health, 144
Sony Electronics case study, 15–17

Sony's Integrated Leadership Curriculum, 27, 50, 58, 118
Sony's Talent Management Council, 15, 17, 55
Spencer, L. M., 35
Stakeholder communication, 192–199
"Standards for Educational and Psychological Testing" (1996), 28, 30
"Staple yourself to an order," 68–69
Steele, R., 27
Stewart, M., 49
Stone, R. D., 173, 176, 181
Strategy tree (impact maps into exercises), 62*e*
Success case method, 190
Successful Manger's Handbook (Gebelien et al.), 157
Sullivan, J., 176, 180, 191
Sun Microsystems, 162
Sun Microsystems' People Management Standards, 157
Sun Microsystems' Sun University (Sun U), 127–128, 146
Sviokla, J. J., 68
Swanson, D., 15, 16, 18
Swanson, R. A., 62, 75, 158
Swiss Army Brands, Inc., 110

T

Targets (market), 39–40, 191–192
Thomson, H. A., 24
3M, 26–27, 55
3M Accelerated Leadership Development program, 27
360-degree feedback, 60, 94, 149–150, 151, 178
Tobin, D., 169
"Top of mind," 112
Trainers: impact mapping tool used by, 32*fig*; role as facilitators, 148–149; as trusted resource, 148

Training Magazine, 132
Training Magazine, 198
Training programs: adding to profitability, 31*fig*; business results
   offsetting costs of, 65*fig*; critical
   mass attendance at, 151; delivered for application, 72–97;
   fallacy regarding measuring of
   results of, 28, 30; financial value
   of, 34–35; "learning scrap," 101;
   online guides to, 158; owner's
   manuals/online guides for, 125,
   156–165, 160*fig*; phases of corporate learning during, 50–61;
   solving business problems
   through, 40–41. *See also*
   Participants
Trainor, D., 133, 178
Transfer of learning: complete experience of, 3–4*fig*; during corporate learning phase III, 64;
   factors of, 3; impediments to,
   64*e*; Learner Transfer System
   Inventory for, 174; peer learning communities and, 149–151;
   planning for, 93–94; setting
   objectives for, 84–93. *See also*
   Learning
Transfer of learning problems/solu-
   tions: 1: not enough time, 84–87;
   anything goes, 87–90; summary
   of, 85*e*; writing strong goals is
   not easy, 90–93
Transfer matrix, 49–50*fig*
Trout, J., 112
Tucker, R. E., 50, 60
TurboTax, 159

U

Ulrich, D., 23, 55
Unilever's Leadership Competencies,
   157

Unilever's Leading People for
   Growth, 50, 58
"Universal radio station," 75
University of Notre Dame's Integral
   Leadership, 81–82, 148
Update engine, 124

V

Valls, J., 144
Value: coaching, 145; created
   through applied knowledge, 98;
   motivation as proportional to
   perception of, 74*fig*; WIIFM
   (What's in it for me?) question
   on, 75, 95–96
Verne, J., 101
Vershuren, A., 66
Vicere, A., 26–27
Vicere Associates, Inc., 26
Vigil, R., 38–39, 171–172
Vroom, V. H., 74

W

Wall, S., 18
The Wall Street Journal, 198
Watkins, M., 139
Webster's College Dictionary, 115
Welch, J., 21
Wenger, E., 150
When the Video Doesn't Match the
   Audio case study, 56
Whistle While You Work (Leider),
   42
White, E., 18
Wick, C. W., 46, 49, 73, 125, 148,
   149, 168, 182, 193, 209
WIIFM (What's in it for me?): of
   manager coaching role, 145; of
   training participation, 75, 95–96
Wilde, K., 53–54, 191, 199
Willis, M., 160

Wilson, P. M., 114
"Window of opportunity" effect, 114
Worksheets: Guided Reflection,
    83*fig*; The Learning4Results
    Worksheet, 12*e*
The World Is Flat (Friedman), 46

X

Xerox Corporation, 94

Z

Zenger, J., 6, 51

ABOUT THE AUTHORS

Calhoun W. Wick is nationally recognized for his work on improving the performance of managers and organizations. He is the author of *The Learning Edge: How Smart Managers and Smart Companies Stay Ahead* (McGraw-Hill) and numerous articles on leadership development and organizational learning. Cal earned his master's degree as an Alfred P. Sloan Fellow at MIT's Sloan School of Management. He is founder and chairman of the Fort Hill Company.

Roy V. H. Pollock, DVM, Ph.D., is chief learning officer of the Fort Hill Company. He has extensive experience in both line management and strategy development at SmithKline Beecham, Pfizer, and IDEXX. Roy received his B.A. from Williams College and his Doctor of Veterinary Medicine and Ph.D. degrees from Cornell University. He was a member of the faculty at Cornell for eight years, where he also served as assistant dean for curriculum at the College of Veterinary Medicine. He was named a Fellow of the Kellogg Foundation National Leadership Program in 1987.

Andrew McK. Jefferson, JD, is an accomplished executive in both operational and legal roles. Andy has served as the chief executive officer of Vital Home Services and chief operating officer and general counsel of AmeriStar Technologies, Inc. He is currently president and chief operating officer for the Fort Hill Company. He is a graduate of the University of Delaware and the Widener University School of Law, where he currently serves on the school's board of overseers.

Richard D. Flanagan, Ph.D., is a licensed psychologist whose career has focused on developing ways to help people change behaviors and improve their lives and relationships. Richard founded Epotec, Inc., a privately-owned Internet software and content company that developed interactive behavioral health tools and services. A graduate of the University of North Carolina at Chapel Hill, Richard received his Ph.D. in clinical psychology from the University of Delaware. He serves as the senior vice president for business development at Fort Hill Company.

What will you find on pfeiffer.com?

- The best in workplace performance solutions for training and HR professionals

- Downloadable training tools, exercises, and content

- Web-exclusive offers

- Training tips, articles, and news

- Seamless online ordering

- Author guidelines, information on becoming a Pfeiffer Affiliate, and much more

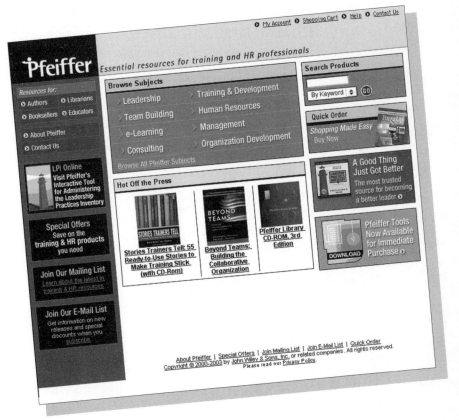

Discover more at www.pfeiffer.com

Customer Care

Have a question, comment, or suggestion? Contact us! We value your feedback and we want to hear from you.

For questions about this or other Pfeiffer products, you may contact us by:

E-mail: **customer@wiley.com**

Mail: **Customer Care Wiley/Pfeiffer**
        10475 Crosspoint Blvd.
        Indianapolis, IN 46256

Phone: **(US) 800-274-4434** (Outside the US: 317-572-3985)

Fax: **(US) 800-569-0443** (Outside the US: 317-572-4002)

To order additional copies of this title or to browse other Pfeiffer products, visit us online at **www.pfeiffer.com**.

For **Technical Support** questions, call **800-274-4434.**

For authors guidelines, log on to www.pfeiffer.com and click on "Resources for Authors."

If you are . . .

A **college bookstore, a professor, an instructor, or work in higher education** and you'd like to place an order or request an exam copy, please contact jbreview@wiley.com.

A **general retail bookseller** and you'd like to establish an account or speak to a local sales representative, contact Melissa Grecco at 201-748-6267 or mgrecco@wiley.com.

An **exclusively online bookseller**, contact Amy Blanchard at 530-756-9456 or ablanchard @wiley.com or Jennifer Johnson at 206-568-3883 or jjohnson@wiley.com, both of our Online Sales department.

A **librarian or library representative**, contact John Chambers in our Library Sales department at 201-748-6291 or jchamber@wiley.com.

A **reseller, training company/consultant, or corporate trainer**, contact Charles Regan in our Special Sales department at 201-748-6553 or cregan@wiley.com.

A **specialty retail distributor** (includes specialty gift stores, museum shops, and corporate bulk sales), contact Kim Hendrickson in our Special Sales department at 201-748-6037 or khendric@wiley.com.

Purchasing for the **Federal government**, contact Ron Cunningham in our Special Sales department at 317-572-3053 or rcunning@wiley.com.

Purchasing for a **State or Local government**, contact Charles Regan in our Special Sales department at 201-748-6553 or cregan@wiley.com.